for
History
Majors

Great Jobs

for

History
Majors

Julie DeGalan & Stephen Lambert

Printed on recyclable paper

 **VGM Career Horizons**
a division of *NTC Publishing Group*
Lincolnwood Illinois USA

Library of Congress Cataloging-in-Publication Data

DeGalan, Julie.
    Great jobs for history majors / Julie DeGalan, Stephen Lambert.
        p.   cm.
    Includes bibliographical references (p.).
    ISBN 0-8442-4353-1
    1. History—Vocational guidance. I. Lambert, Stephen. II. Title.
D16.9.D34   1994
650.14—dc20   94-19533
                                                       CIP

Published by VGM Career Horizons, a division of NTC Publishing Group
4255 West Touhy Avenue
Lincolnwood (Chicago), Illinois 60646-1975, U.S.A.
© 1995 by NTC Publishing Group. All rights reserved.
No part of this book may be reproduced, stored in a retrieval system,
or transmitted in any form or by any means,
electronic, mechanical, photocopying, recording or otherwise,
without the prior permission of NTC Publishing Group.
Manufactured in the United States of America.

4 5 6 7 8 9 0 VP 9 8 7 6 5 4 3 2 1

CONTENTS

Acknowledgments

The authors would like to thank Lucille Brock at the National Audubon Society for information on the educational programs offered through their society, Jane Kenamore at the Society of American Archivists for information on entry-level archival positions, and Teresa Varga Kilday for her fine work on the resume chapter. John Kemp, Director of Colonial Interpretation, Plimoth Plantation, also provided excellent counsel.

Student workers Jen DiDonato, Lauren Fortier, Carla Fortson, Tina Lumia, Brian McLaughlin, and Tricia Swain were as helpful in searching and phoning on this book as they were on the previous three.

Our thanks, too, to Alice Nye, Gary McCool and Joyce Bruce of Lamson Library at Plymouth State College.

The authors have been blessed to have Mr. Fact, Bryon Middlekauff, just a phone call away. Although the authors take full responsibility for the material contained in these volumes, we are grateful for his help. With more than a passing interest in the accuracy and success of the Great Jobs series, he unstintingly took on each information request, from obscure film title to monarchical succession order, with equal seriousness and dispatch. Thank you, Mr. Fact!

To Amy Caroline, Matt III, Cynthia, Michael, Constance and Catherine
with all our love.

"HISTORY: THE MEMORY OF THINGS SAID AND DONE."

arl Becker's definition of history is wonderful because it reminds us that history is the recollection of humanity. It is what particular people have recalled about other people. Those recollections, or memories, are influenced by the rememberers themselves and the influences and biases of their own lives. Just as the word "memory" conjures up an idea of something not quite substantial, not entirely reliable and subject to verification, we need to remember that history is more memory than fact.

For what are facts? Some would say there is no such thing. Each event in life recorded as history is subtly altered by the recorder. That individual, try as they might to be objective, alters the record of the event for all time by filtering it through their own mind, with his or her own impressions, perceptions, biases and judgments. The historian's choice of words, selection of topics and features, emphases, and omissions are what ultimately constitute the "facts."

Most important for the history major to affirm is the emphasis in this quotation on humanity, for humanity is the stuff of history. People and their legacies. Both the participants in the events and the recorders of those events alike are part of the endless stream of humanity which is the essential subject of history. And, as with anything human, including dreams, it is subject to interpretation.

To make sense of this record of humanity is to begin by truly understanding events, analyzing and appreciating what has taken place. Documenting the facts may mean collecting the facts from a number of different observers of the same event. The formal court records of King Henry V, the letters home from a visiting delegation of French ministers, and the diary of a lady-in-waiting may all tell very different versions of the same story. The differences are due to perspective.

For the historian, the history student or the history graduate considering any of the careers in this book, the greatest gift of the study of history may be the development of a sense of perspective. Perspective is the rare ability to place people, events and artifacts in true relation to their setting and to assign to them a sense of their relative importance. Whether it be assessing the stature of Churchill or Madonna, a Ming vase or the early McDonald's roadside architecture, a new business acquisition or a product quality lawsuit, the history major who has learned perspective in his or her academic studies has learned a lifelong and career-valuable skill.

Truly understanding events and the people who populate them, analyzing the facts and appreciating fully what has taken place requires an ability to synthesize large amounts of information and draw conclusions based on that information. For example, a study of court cases at the turn of the century in a small southern town, with a population that is overwhelmingly black, shows that over 90 percent of the court cases involved whites. Obviously this study could make the beginning of a strong argument that blacks were not being afforded due legal process in that town at that time.

The ability to understand events, analyze and appreciate what has taken place, and then synthesize the resulting information to draw conclusions is essential to the historian and a valuable skill learned in the study of history with broad application to other areas of endeavor. These abilities are then combined with a sense of sequence and a natural curiosity to do the necessary detective work. For, when only pieces of evidence appear, extrapolations must be done relying on others' evidence or listening and reading others' accounts and judiciously assessing the information provided.

Hypotheses are drawn, but are only as strong as the care and quality of the information that has led to them. If you were to listen today to the presentation of a skilled historical interpreter at Salem, Massachusetts, discussing the infamous witch trials and compare that to the presentation twenty years ago, you would find today's explanation far more tentative. We know more now about group psychology and "group think," we have a new appreciation, through the work of women historians such as Laurel Ulrich, for the role of women as midwives in colonial America and the enmity that role earned them from men in the community who disapproved of the silent power such life-giving skill gave them. The interpretation of the murders of these women and children has become more psychological, more political and more human.

An appropriate metaphor for the historian might be that of the miner, sifting through the motherlode of human events for the nuggets of significance—

the historic events, people and juxtaposition of conditions that affect human-kind. Sifting through much that is undistinguished, the miner comes to appreciate what is truly worthy of his or her effort.

But the "nugget" of history is not yet ready to be delivered forth to the public. It needs to be assayed for purity, for its value. The miner may then sand or polish this nugget so we can all truly appreciate its worth and importance, giving it a setting that allows us to value its meaning in our lives. Historical facts are like this. They are discovered amidst the detritus of past civilizations and it is the historian's role to appreciate and perceive their importance to history. Before exclaiming "Eureka!", the historian/miner must test the value of the find by assessment. Collaboration, other accounts, and independent verification all help to determine the significance of a historical fact.

To help us appreciate this bit of history, the historian needs to put it in perspective—to set the jewel in a mount, as it were. For any event, personage or discovery, we need to understand the time, the culture, the attitudes and opinions of those involved and their relationship to what is happening to them. Because history is humanity, almost every detail of history needs to be placed in its cultural context to have any impact.

To understand the cultural context of history means the historian must often physically confront evidence, visit sites and simply be impressed by the silent testimony of documents and artifacts that define history. Later in this book, you will read of the controversy surrounding the use of Internet databases for historical research. Much of that controversy involves the reliability and accuracy of the documents that are transcribed.

To become engaged in an understanding of the physical remains of culture and what they express is essential. Imbued with stories of these cultural artifacts, the historian's understanding is deepened. This enriched understanding of history is essential before the historian can begin to make the kinds of generalizations about the past that are the hallmark of the wise. Art, music, literature, sculpture, clothing, decoration and motifs, the performing arts, design, crafts, menu offerings are all indicators of what is important to a culture and help create the context that allows the historian to understand humanity and the memories of that humanity in context.

Laurel Ulrich, the Pulitzer Prize-winning historian from the University of New Hampshire, has moved on in her researches from midwifery to an examination of the "ordinary" fabrics of early American life—dishcloths, table coverings, muslin, plain fabrics—and what they reveal about the role of women in society at that time and the opportunities they had to impact the lives of those around them.

This ability of the historian to make generalizations is the result of years of study, deep reflectivity, and uncompromising loyalty to what is accurate and verifiable. They are the statements of true wisdom, and, as such, are made carefully and respectfully, always fully aware of what remains unknown and undiscovered that can alter the truth as we understand it. But isn't this what history demands of us, whether we practice it in the boardroom or in the recreation of a colonial plantation? History asks the historian to connect one fact to another.

We see a bed and all its coverlets on display in an early American living room and we might incorrectly assume it is located there for the warmth of the great cooking fireplace and the comfort that provides. In point of fact, there was no more sumptuous display of wealth and/or craftsmanship than in the embroidered bed curtains, tatted sheets, and woven coverlets in an early American home than the master's bed. It conveyed status, displayed the needlework skills of his wife, the valuable articles that had come by ship and perhaps some oriental carpets from the east. So, for the historian, this bed is a repository of social systems, commerce, trade, geographical knowledge, design and art, and industry.

The "why" of studying history is clear in Carl Becker's quote. We study history, not to exhume the past and make a religion of what has gone before. We study history, if our intentions are among the best, to appreciate humankind, its wonderful successes and its hideous mistakes, and carry this appreciation and understanding of who we are and what we are capable of forward to yet another generation. Hopefully, among this group will be new historians to whom we can pass the torch and share this memory of things said and done.

The careers outlined in this book and many, many others cry out for the human and far-sighted, analytical perspective of the history major. They may call it something else: archivist, interpreter, manager, dean of institutional research, curator, director of corporate planning and a host of other titles. They all share the skills, the mental discipline, the orientation towards people and their behavior that helps them see events and decisions in perspective. Historians are critical and careful in their judgments and are able to talk and write about these events in ways that help others understand them and learn from them. Could we ask for anything more from a major?

HISTORY AS CAREER PREPARATION

History is at the heart of the liberal arts, but unlike science or business, there is no standard curriculum and a review of history curricula at colleges and universities across the country will display a dizzying variety of programs, including American history, Western Civilization, World History, Peace and War, and Diplomacy Studies.

But this major is more than just any one college's program of courses. It goes beyond the content of these selections. In fact, it cannot be mastered by simply mastering the courses within the curriculum. History is about making connections: across curriculums, nations, and racial, ethnic and economic borders. It is a way of looking at humankind, at events, at whatever task you have in front of you that requires analysis, perceptiveness, accuracy, curiosity and care.

If you engage in your history degree fully, you will read voluminously. You'll learn to sift what you've read and think carefully and critically about it. When you are ready with your own thinking about a topic, good preparation should have you ready to write authoritatively and accurately. This kind of clarity of thought is an excellent preparation for oral presentations. Behind all of this preparation will be solid grounding in research skills emphasizing thoroughness, reliability and ethics.

The relevance of history as an academic preparation for a career is evident in these skills which are found enumerated in countless job postings, some of which are threaded throughout this book and, in fact, throughout all the volumes of the "Great Jobs" series. For history, more thoroughly than any other of the liberal arts degrees, accomplishes two significant learning outcomes: the first is technique: research, reading, analysis, writing, and speaking. The second is in a greater appreciation of yourself and the community of man, its wonderful diversity and expression.

The applicability and vitality of history as a career preparation is assured if you take every advantage of your degree preparation. Most of the skills listed here require *practice* and sheer hard work. One can move passively through four years of a history degree, earning suitable grades and acquiring some knowledge, but in truth learning very little. Or, you can test yourself continually in your powers of research, reading, selectivity, expression and engage your faculty in continual dialogue about the relevance and relationship of history to the present. This second course is the preferred one and essential if you are to graduate with any marketable skills, as a historian or in any other profession.

Knowledge of the past helps you to understand and engage in the present and you will draw upon your history coursework again and again. People have a habit of repeating certain behaviors and the repository of your memory will awaken to similarities and connections between events in the past and the present again and again. History is *not* a set of mathematical formulae that are to be applied in specific incidents for the correct results. History is humanity moving through time and, depending on your vantage point, you see the lessons of humanity from varying perspectives. Your age, your race, your time in life, your country of origin, your employment, your mood, all have an effect on how you view and evaluate the lessons history teaches you.

You learn about yourself in studying history. How you react to events, people, and the choices they make is self-revealing. If you've been an assiduous history student, you may find the next chapter on self-assessment confirming, but not earth-shattering, as you have already faced many of these questions of interest, values, ethics, skills and attributes in your studies. Your reading of history has been like a mirror held before you, reflecting back to you much of whom you truly are as you have grappled with the choices made by those you have studied.

Self-awareness also brings an appreciation for the diversity present in others, not just those of our own cultural background, race or milieu, but those of entirely different surroundings, economics and geography. History identifies and isolates those differences and makes them understandable while at the same time giving a profound sense of the community of humankind. To truly study history is to, in some sense, inhabit the world of another and appreciate and understand the superficial differences that separate us.

Cultural climates come to be understood, but the historian must also be something of a geographer to understand history and the impact of climate, terrain and location. Certainly the self-imposed isolation of the Japanese before the arrival of Admiral Perry had political and geographic underpinnings. The isolation and the resultant dramatic opening of the country have both left strong imprints on the homogeneity of Japanese culture.

Space exploration, the atomic bomb, patent medicines, the automobile, the airplane, penicillin, biological warfare, defoliants, satellite communications all have had historical significance and must be part of the history student's study. History's curriculum is loose because it shares all curriculums, and depending upon the geography, people, events or time you choose to study, you will need to become an art critic, sociologist, ethnomusicologist, gourmet, weapons specialist, or cultural anthropologist. Often, with more lasting effect than any war might have, the scientific and technological advances determine the course of history.

But for all the technological influences, history remains the province of human activity. The incredible response of the British citizenry during World War II, an ethos that remains palpable in British society today among that generation, was fostered in large part by the role of the monarchy as archetypical family. King George VI and Queen Elizabeth (the present Queen Mother) kept their daughters in the country. Buckingham Palace took direct bomb hits on the grounds and the King and Queen toured bombed areas in London, connecting directly with the populace. The Queen donated sixty suites of household goods from royal estates to victims of the bombing. Many of these gestures and more by the royal family were credited with keeping British resolve and spunk high during the dark days of World War II.

The importance of history is not immediately apparent, even to those who are living some of its most memorable moments. History is a term we use in retrospect. Though the present is to become history immediately, we often need the wonderful filter and distance of time to appreciate and understand events, people and their relationship. As you pursue your studies of history and consider some of the wonderful career possibilities it affords you, don't neglect other aspects of your education. If you can travel outside the country, do so. It will forever change your view of your own native land as you begin to see it as others do. Travel, read as much as you can and don't limit your subject matter, for all human activity is grain for the grist mill of history.

Engage your teachers, your classmates and others in good discussion on current events and test your awareness of the forces involved and your appreciation of how others view the same situation. Try to listen carefully and put yourself in someone else's shoes. Try on different opinions. Argue the other side and play the devil's advocate, and never forget that history is not fact, but considered opinion!

THE FUTURE AS HISTORY

The following selected chronology is excerpted from *A Short History of the Future,* by W. Warren Wagar (University of Chicago Press, 1989):

1995　Beginning of severe worldwide depression

1997　American intervention in the Philippines. Soviet-American confrontation in Yugoslavia brings world to the brink of a third world war

1998　Vienna Conference produces East-West detente, signature of comprehensive arms limitations protocol, demilitarization of East and West Germany. Vaccine against AIDS introduced.

1999　Japan acquires nuclear weapons

2001　Sharp economic upturn. Formation of the Arab-Islamic Republic in Cairo

A chronology such as this one is a daring chapter with which to close a book. Written in 1989, we already see Russia (no longer Soviet!) withdrawing its forces from Eastern Europe, there are numerous vaccines for AIDS yielding some results and Germany no longer has a divided East and West. History is volatile and as this brief chronology amply demonstrates, risky to try and predict.

On a lighter note, one of the most public attempts to predict history's future are the World's Fairs. Looking at historical records of these great exhibitions, there are always dramatic dioramas, robotics and miniatures that attempt to suggest the utopia of the future. Cars being propelled along highways automatically and aircraft whizzing in and out of airdromes without the slightest delay. The massive disruption of vehicular traffic caused by the California earthquakes of this decade and the increasingly almost turn-of-the-century delays and slow progress of air travel make these predictions seem laughable.

Former President Richard Nixon's last book, *Beyond Peace,* was published the day after his funeral in April of 1994. In it, he emphasizes that the world now needs another unifying concept beyond peace on which to focus: resources, environment, nurturing humanity. Certainly, peace has not been a reasonable expectation. The Olympic Games of the Winter of 1984 in Sarejevo were intended to be a testament to the ability of countries to put aside conflicts and come together in a spirit of good sportsmanship. Today, as this book goes to press, Sarejevo has been destroyed, shelled to rubble by internecine warfare among the Serbs and Croatians.

Peace is a desirable objective, but may not be realistic in historic terms. Look around at the other frontiers of history. Medicine moves along its curative path, only to be decimated by the mystery of AIDS and Alzheimer's. The situation of the homeless grows exponentially, not just in America, but around the world, and the gap between the haves and the have-nots widens perceptibly. America's devotion to a capitalistic ideal is subtly changed by increased government intervention, a national health plan that would be termed socialized medicine by any other nation and growing numbers of men and women who remain on public assistance.

Technology has brought opportunities and problems. Communications are more rapid than ever before and yet we linger on automated voice mail, hoping to speak to a "real" person. Premature infants can be brought back from the brink of death to be sustained indefinitely on resuscitators at phenomenal cost. Discretionary income allows for protected communities that resemble most closely medieval cities with the drawbridges drawn up against a hostile world.

As a student of history, this may sound pretty gloomy and make you wonder, "What can I do? How can I possibly help or make a difference?" The answers lie in the chapters that follow. Although many pundits do agree that we face serious challenges, both domestic and global, as individuals with an appreciation of the future as history, you can make a difference. Individual differences do count, because they are the beginnings of collective change.

Each of the career paths that this book suggests, for archivists and curators; business, industry and commerce workers and managers; teachers, both in and out of the formal school system; and information specialists, present opportunities to affect our history. With your baccalaureate degree and your appreciation of what makes history, you have the ability to hold up a stop sign at each important decision point in your career and say "consider the implications."

For the archivist and curator, there is the important opportunity of ensuring that the artifacts and records of the past are available and accessible to a public that needs to know the lessons of history. There will be ample opportunity, through exhibitions, catalogs, published articles, talks, and tours to make this information meaningful and real to the public. You'll want to consider the obstacles that have been placed between your collections and the public and the need for these obstacles. You will want to ensure the record you present is comprehensive and accurate. We are still working on historical rewriting of the role of women in history—always half the population but until recently not part of the story.

Those who choose to use their history degree in the world of commerce will have plenty of opportunities to humanize the history of their organization. Making facts and data relevant to the lives of the individuals involved, adding the human dimensions of business strategies and plans, and examining the impact on society for each business decision provides a succession of stop signs where one can consider the history and the consequences for the future.

Teachers in and out of the classroom have the gift of an audience and the techniques and tools to share history with people of all ages. Currently, there is a troop of women traveling New England with an oral history of New England women entitled "It Had To Be Done, So I Did It." In moving recitation, speech and song, using the vivid words of the actual participants, the players bring to life the incomparable ingenuity, industry and labor of American women in New England. For men and women of the present and future, it is an ennobling and inspiring message that continues to reverberate in its audience long after the performance has ended.

Many of our decisions, our plans, our ideas would have this consideration if we were able to retrieve and make use of existing records and documentation. Information specialists can be extraordinarily important in any organization if they position themselves, not as technical librarians whose only job is to store and produce information when requested, but as vital players in how an organization operates and plans for change. We are inundated with information, and the information specialist can be critical in sorting out the vital from the superfluous, directing pertinent data to the correct source and anticipating data needs for good decision (and history) making.

So is this history? Absolutely. Remember Carl Becker's quote at the beginning of this chapter? History is the memory of things said and done. History is individual before it is collective and history is the result of decisions made and not made. Knowing and believing that, what kind of a history do you want to be remembered for in your career and what will your contribution be to that history? Begin your exploration!

PART ONE

THE JOB SEARCH

CHAPTER ONE

THE SELF-ASSESSMENT

Self-assessment is the process by which you begin to acknowledge your own particular blend of education, experiences, values, needs, and goals. It provides the foundation for career planning and the entire job search process. Self-assessment involves looking inward and asking yourself what can sometimes prove to be difficult questions. This self-examination should lead to an intimate understanding of your personal traits, your personal values, your consumption patterns and economic needs, your longer-term goals, your skill base, your preferred skills, and your underdeveloped skills.

You come to the self-assessment process knowing yourself well in some of these areas, but you may still be uncertain about other aspects. You may be well aware of your consumption patterns, but have you spent much time specifically identifying your longer-term goals, or your personal values as they relate to work? No matter what level of self-assessment you have undertaken to date, it is now time to clarify all of these issues and questions as they relate to the job search.

The knowledge you gain in the self-assessment process will guide the rest of your job search. In this book, you will learn about all of the following tasks:

- ❑ Writing resumes

- ❑ Exploring possible job titles

- ❑ Identifying employment sites

- ❑ Networking

- ❑ Interviewing

- ❑ Following up

- ❑ Evaluating job offers

In each of these steps, you will rely on and return often to the understanding gained through your self-assessment. Any individual seeking employment must be able and willing to express to potential recruiters and interviewers throughout the job search these facets of his or her personality. This communication allows you to show the world who you are so that together with employers you can determine whether there will be a workable match with a given job or career path.

HOW TO CONDUCT A SELF-ASSESSMENT

The self-assessment process goes on naturally all the time. People ask you to clarify what you mean, or you make a purchasing decision, or you begin a new relationship. You react to the world and the world reacts to you. How you understand these interactions and any changes you might make because of them are part of the natural process of self-discovery. There is, however, a more comprehensive and efficient way to approach self-assessment with regard to employment.

Because self-assessment can become a complex exercise, we have distilled it into a seven-step process that provides an effective basis for undertaking a job search. The seven steps include the following:

1. Understanding your personal traits

2. Identifying your personal values

3. Calculating your economic needs

4. Exploring your longer-term goals

5. Enumerating your skill base

6. Recognizing your preferred skills

7. Assessing skills needing further development

As you work through your self-assessment, you might want to create a worksheet similar to the one shown in Exhibit 1.1. Or you might want to keep a journal of the thoughts you have as you undergo this process. There will be many opportunities to revise your self-assessment as you start down the path of seeking a career.

STEP 1 Understanding Your Personal Traits

Each person has a unique personality that he or she brings to the job search process. Gaining a better understanding of your personal traits can help you evaluate job and career choices. Identifying these traits, then finding employment that allows you to draw on at least some of them can create a rewarding and fulfilling work experience. If potential employment doesn't allow you to use these preferred traits, it is important to decide whether you can find other ways to express them or

Exhibit 1.1

Self-Assessment Worksheet

STEP 1. Understand Your Personal Traits

The personal traits that describe me are:
(Include all of the words that describe you.)

The ten personal traits that most accurately describe me are:
(List these ten traits.)

STEP 2. Identify Your Personal Values

Working conditions that are important to me include:
(List working conditions that would have to exist for you to accept a position.)

The values that go along with my working conditions are:
(Write down the values that correspond to each working condition.)

Some additional values I've decided to include are:
(List those values you identify as you conduct this job search.)

STEP 3. Calculate Your Economic Needs

My estimated minimum annual salary requirement is:
(Write the salary you have calculated based on your budget.)

Starting salaries for the positions I'm considering are:
(List the name of each job you are considering and the associated starting salary.)

STEP 4. Explore Your Longer-Term Goals

My thoughts on longer-term goals right now are:
(Jot down some of your longer-term goals as you know them right now.)

continued

continued

STEP 5. **Enumerate Your Skill Base**
The general skills I possess are:
(List the skills that underlie tasks you are able to complete.)

The specific skills I possess are:
(List more technical or specific skills that you possess and indicate your level of expertise.)

General and specific skills that I want to promote to employers for the jobs I'm considering are:
(List general and specific skills for each type of job you are considering.)

STEP 6. **Recognize Your Preferred Skills**
Skills that I would like to use on the job include:
(List skills that you hope to use on the job, and indicate how often you'd like to use them.)

STEP 7. **Assess Skills Needing Further Development**
Some skills that I'll need to acquire for the jobs I'm considering include:
(Write down skills listed in job advertisements or job descriptions that you don't currently possess.)

I believe I can build these skills by:
(Describe how you plan to acquire these skills.)

whether you would be better off not considering this type of job. Interests and hobbies pursued outside of work hours can be one way to use personal traits you don't have an opportunity to draw on in your work. For example, if you consider yourself an outgoing person and the kinds of jobs you are examining allow little contact with other people, you may be able to achieve the level of interaction that is comfortable for you outside of your work setting. If such a compromise seems impractical or otherwise unsatisfactory, you probably should explore only jobs that provide the interaction you want and need on the job.

Many young adults who are not very confident about their attractiveness to employers will downplay their need for income. They will say, "Money is not all that important if I love my work." But if you begin to document exactly what you need for housing, transportation, insurance, clothing, food, and utilities, you will begin to understand that some jobs cannot meet your financial needs and it doesn't matter how wonderful the job is. If you have to worry each payday about bills and other financial obligations, you won't be very effective on the job. Begin now to be honest with yourself about your needs.

Inventorying Your Personal Traits.   Begin the self-assessment process by creating an inventory of your personal traits. Using the list in Exhibit 1.2, decide which of these personal traits describe you.

Exhibit 1.2

Personal Traits

Active	Critical	Generous
Accurate	Curious	Gentle
Adaptable	Daring	Good-natured
Adventurous	Decisive	Helpful
Affectionate	Deliberate	Honest
Aggressive	Detail-oriented	Humorous
Ambitious	Determined	Idealistic
Analytical	Discreet	Imaginative
Appreciative	Dominant	Impersonal
Artistic	Eager	Independent
Brave	Easygoing	Individualistic
Businesslike	Efficient	Industrious
Calm	Emotional	Informal
Capable	Empathetic	Innovative
Caring	Energetic	Intellectual
Cautious	Excitable	Intelligent
Cheerful	Expressive	Introverted
Clean	Extroverted	Intuitive
Competent	Fair-minded	Inventive
Confident	Farsighted	Jovial
Conscientious	Feeling	Just
Conservative	Firm	Kind
Considerate	Flexible	Liberal
Cool	Formal	Likable
Cooperative	Friendly	Logical
Courageous	Future-oriented	

continued

continued

Loyal	Precise	Serious
Mature	Principled	Sincere
Methodical	Private	Sociable
Meticulous	Productive	Spontaneous
Mistrustful	Progressive	Strong
Modest	Quick	Strong-minded
Motivated	Quiet	Structured
Objective	Rational	Subjective
Observant	Realistic	Tactful
Open-minded	Receptive	Thorough
Opportunistic	Reflective	Thoughtful
Optimistic	Relaxed	Tolerant
Organized	Reliable	Trusting
Original	Reserved	Trustworthy
Outgoing	Resourceful	Truthful
Patient	Responsible	Understanding
Peaceable	Reverent	Unexcitable
Personable	Sedentary	Uninhibited
Persuasive	Self-confident	Verbal
Pleasant	Self-controlled	Versatile
Poised	Self-disciplined	Wholesome
Polite	Sensible	Wise
Practical	Sensitive	

Focusing on Selected Personal Traits.   Of all the traits you identified from the list in Exhibit 1.2, select the ten you believe most accurately describe you. If you are having a difficult time deciding, think about which words people who know you well would use to describe you. Keep track of these ten traits.

Considering Your Personal Traits in the Job Search Process.   As you begin exploring jobs and careers, watch for matches between your personal traits and the job descriptions you read. Some jobs will require many personal traits you know you possess, and others will not seem to match those traits.

....

A historical interpreter's work, for example, requires public presentation skills and the ability to interact with varying groups of people of different ages and backgrounds. Historical interpreters or guides must be able to build group cohesion and sustain group interest. Their job

> requires strong oral communication skills and the special
> ability to take complex ideas and present them in a simpler,
> easier to understand manner. There may be some time
> pressure, and flexibility is critical as each group has its own
> personality and may require varying responses.
>
> ....

Your ability to respond to changing conditions, decision-making ability, productivity, creativity, and verbal skills all have a bearing on your success in and enjoyment of your work life. To better guarantee success, be sure to take the time needed to understand these traits in yourself.

STEP 2   Identifying Your Personal Values

Your personal values affect every aspect of your life, including employment, and they develop and change as you move through life. Values can be defined as principles that we hold in high regard, qualities that are important and desirable to us. Some values aren't ordinarily connected to work (love, beauty, color, light, marriage, family, or religion), and others are (autonomy, cooperation, effectiveness, achievement, knowledge, and security). Our values determine, in part, the level of satisfaction we feel in a particular job.

Defining Acceptable Working Conditions.   One facet of employment is the set of working conditions that must exist for someone to consider taking a job.

Each of us would probably create a unique list of acceptable working conditions, but items that might be included on many people's lists are the amount of money you would need to be paid, how far you are willing to drive or travel, the amount of freedom you want in determining your own schedule, whether you would be working with people or data or things, and the types of tasks you would be willing to do. Your conditions might include statements of working conditions you will *not* accept; for example, you might not be willing to work at night or on weekends or holidays.

If you were offered a job tomorrow, what conditions would have to exist for you to realistically consider accepting the position? Take some time and make a list of these conditions.

Realizing Associated Values.   Your list of working conditions can be used to create an inventory of your values relating to jobs and careers you are exploring. For example, if one of your conditions stated that you wanted to earn at least $25,000 per year, the associated value would be financial gain. If another condition was that you wanted to work with a friendly group of people, the value that goes along with that might be belonging or interaction with people. Exhibit 1.3 provides a list of

---

Exhibit 1.3

Work Values

Achievement	Development	Physical activity
Advancement	Effectiveness	Power
Adventure	Excitement	Precision
Attainment	Fast pace	Prestige
Authority	Financial gain	Privacy
Autonomy	Helping	Profit
Belonging	Humor	Recognition
Challenge	Improvisation	Risk
Change	Independence	Security
Communication	Influencing others	Self-expression
Community	Intellectual stimulation	Solitude
Competition	Interaction	Stability
Completion	Knowledge	Status
Contribution	Leading	Structure
Control	Mastery	Supervision
Cooperation	Mobility	Surroundings
Creativity	Moral fulfillment	Time freedom
Decision making	Organization	Variety

---

commonly held values that relate to the work environment; use it to create your own list of personal values.

Relating Your Values to the World of Work. As you read the job descriptions in this book and in other suggested resources, think about the values associated with that position.

> For example, the duties of an archivist would include gathering records and providing the mechanisms to do that. Once assembled and catalogued, the archivist must ensure high quality preservation of the documents and provide an efficient retrieval system.

If you were thinking about a career in this field, or any other field you're exploring, at least some of the associated values should match those you extracted from your list of working conditions. Take a second look at any values that don't match up. How important are they to you? What will happen if they are not satisfied on the job? Can you incorporate those personal values elsewhere? Your answers need to be brutally honest. As you continue your exploration, be sure to add to your list any additional values that occur to you.

STEP 3 Calculating Your Economic Needs

Each of us grew up in an environment that provided for certain basic needs, such as food and shelter, and, to varying degrees, other needs that we now consider basic, such as cable TV, reading materials, or an automobile. Needs such as privacy, space, and quiet, which at first glance may not appear to be monetary needs, may add to housing expenses and so should be considered as you examine your economic needs. For example, if you place a high value on a large, open living space for yourself, it would be difficult to satisfy that need without an associated high housing cost, especially in a densely populated city environment.

As you prepare to move into the world of work and become responsible for meeting your own basic needs, it is important to consider the salary you will need to be able to afford a satisfying standard of living. The three-step process outlined here will help you plan a budget, which in turn will allow you to evaluate the various career choices and geographic locations you are considering. The steps include (1) developing a realistic budget, (2) examining starting salaries, and (3) using a cost-of-living index.

Developing a Realistic Budget. Each of us has certain expectations for the kind of life-style we want to maintain. In order to begin the process of defining your economic needs, it will be helpful to determine what you expect to spend on routine monthly expenses. These expenses include housing, food, transportation, entertainment, utilities, loan repayments, and revolving charge accounts. A worksheet that details many of these expenses is shown in Exhibit 1.4. You may not currently spend for certain items, but you probably will have to once you begin supporting yourself. As you develop this budget, be generous in your estimates, but keep in mind any items that could be

---

Exhibit 1.4

Estimated Monthly Expenses Worksheet

		Could Reduce Spending? (Yes/No)
Cable	$ _____	_____
Child care	_____	_____
Clothing	_____	_____

continued

continued

		Could Reduce Spending? (Yes/No)
Educational loan repayment	_____	_____
Entertainment	_____	_____
Food	_____	_____
At home	_____	_____
Meals out	_____	_____
Gifts	_____	_____
Housing		
Rent/mortgage	_____	_____
Insurance	_____	_____
Property taxes	_____	_____
Medical insurance	_____	_____
Reading materials		
Newspapers	_____	_____
Magazines	_____	_____
Books	_____	_____
Revolving loans/charges	_____	_____
Savings	_____	_____
Telephone	_____	_____
Transportation		
Auto payment	_____	_____
Insurance	_____	_____
Parking	_____	_____
—or		
Cab/train/bus fare	_____	_____
Utilities		
Electric	_____	_____
Gas	_____	_____
Water/sewer	_____	_____
Vacations	_____	_____
Miscellaneous expense 1	_____	_____
Expense: _____		
Miscellaneous expense 2	_____	_____
Expense: _____		
Miscellaneous expense 3	_____	_____
Expense: _____		

TOTAL MONTHLY EXPENSES: _____

YEARLY EXPENSES (Monthly expenses x 12): _____

INCREASE TO INCLUDE TAXES (Yearly expenses x 1.35): _____ =
MINIMUM ANNUAL SALARY REQUIREMENT _____

reduced or eliminated. If you are not sure about the cost of a certain item, talk with family or friends who would be able to give you a realistic estimate.

If this is new or difficult for you, start to keep a log of expenses right now. You may be surprised at how much you actually spend each month for food or stamps or magazines. Household expenses and personal grooming items can often loom very large in a budget, as can auto repairs or home maintenance.

Income taxes must also be taken into consideration when examining salary requirements. State and local taxes vary by location, so it is difficult to calculate exactly the effect of taxes on the amount of income you need to generate. To roughly estimate the gross income necessary to generate your minimum annual salary requirement, multiply the minimum salary you have calculated (see Exhibit 1.4) by a factor of 1.35. The resulting figure will be an approximation of what your gross income would need to be, given your estimated expenses.

Examining Starting Salaries. Starting salaries for each of the career tracks are provided throughout this book. These salary figures can be used in conjunction with the cost-of-living index (discussed in the next section) to determine whether you would be able to meet your basic economic needs in a given geographic location.

Using a Cost-of-Living Index. If you are thinking about trying to get a job in a geographic region other than the one where you now live, understanding differences in the cost of living will help you come to a more informed decision about making a move. By using a cost-of-living index, you can compare salaries offered and the cost of living in different locations with what you know about the salaries offered and the cost of living in your present location.

Many variables are used to calculate the cost-of-living index, including housing expenses, groceries, utilities, transportation, health care, clothing, entertainment, local income taxes, and local sales taxes. Cost-of-living indices can be found in many resources, such as *Equal Employment Opportunity Bimonthly, Places Rated Almanac,* or *The Best Towns in America.* They are constantly being recalculated based on changes in costs.

....

If you lived in Cleveland, Ohio, for example, and you were interested in working as a curatorial assistant for an art museum, you would earn, on average, $19,444 annually. But let's say you're also thinking about moving to New York, Los Angeles, or Denver. You know you can live on $19,444 in Cleveland, but you want to be able to equal that salary in the other locations you're considering. How much will you need to earn in those locations to do this? Figuring the cost of living for each city will show you.

Let's walk through this example. In any cost-of-living index, the number 100 represents the national average cost of living, and each city is assigned an index number based on current prices in that city for the items included in the index (housing, food, etc.). In the index we used, New York was assigned the number 213.3, Los Angeles was assigned 124.6, Denver was assigned 100.0, and the index for Cleveland was 114.3. In other words, it costs almost twice as much to live in New York as it does in Cleveland. We can set up a table to determine exactly how much you would have to earn in each of these cities to have the same buying power that you have in Cleveland.

Job: *CURATORIAL ASSISTANT*

CITY	INDEX	EQUIVALENT SALARY

$$\frac{\text{New York}}{\text{Cleveland}} \quad \frac{213.3}{114.3} \text{ x } \$19{,}444 = \$36{,}285 \text{ in New York}$$

$$\frac{\text{Los Angeles}}{\text{Cleveland}} \quad \frac{124.6}{114.3} \text{ x } \$19{,}444 = \$21{,}196 \text{ in Los Angeles}$$

$$\frac{\text{Denver}}{\text{Cleveland}} \quad \frac{100.0}{114.3} \text{ x } \$19{,}444 = \$17{,}011 \text{ in Denver}$$

You would have to earn $36,285 in New York, $21,196 in Los Angeles, and $17,011 in Denver to match the buying power of $19,444 in Cleveland.

If you would like to determine whether it's financially worthwhile to make any of these moves, one more piece of information is needed: the salaries of curatorial assistants in these other cities. The Association of Art Museum Directors reports the following average salary information for curatorial assistants in their 1993 salary survey:

Region	Annual Salary	Salary Equivalent to Ohio	Change In Buying Power
Mid Atlantic (including New York)	$24,072	$36,285	–$12,213
West (including Los Angeles)	$25,001	$21,196	+$ 3,805
Mountain Plains (including Denver)	$21,112	$17,011	+$ 4,101
Midwest (including Cleveland)	$19,444	—	—

If you moved to New York City and secured employment as a curatorial assistant, you would not be able to maintain a lifestyle similar to the one you led in Cleveland; in fact, you would almost have to add an additional two-thirds to your income to maintain a similar life-style in New York. The same would not be true for a move to Los Angeles or Denver. You would increase your buying power given the rate of pay and cost of living in these cities.

You can work through a similar exercise for any type of job you are considering and for many locations when current salary information is available. It will be worth your time to undertake this analysis if you are seriously considering a relocation. By doing so you will be able to make an informed choice.

STEP 4   Exploring Your Longer-Term Goals

There is no question that when we first begin working, our goals are to use our skills and education in a job that will reward us with employment, income, and status relative to the preparation we brought with us to this position. If we are not being paid as much as we feel we should for our level of education, or if job demands don't provide the intellectual stimulation we had hoped for, we experience unhappiness and, as a result, often seek other employment.

Most jobs we consider "good" are those that fulfill our basic "lower-level" needs of security, food, clothing, shelter, income, and productive work. But even when our basic needs are met and our jobs are secure and productive, we as individuals are constantly changing. As we change, the demands and expectations we place on our jobs may change. Fortunately, some jobs grow and change with us, and this explains why some people are happy throughout many years in a job.

But more often people are bigger than the jobs they fill. We have more goals and needs than any job could fulfill. These are "higher-level" needs of self-esteem, companionship, affection, and an increasing desire to feel we are employing ourselves in the most effective way possible. Not all of these higher-level needs can be fulfilled through employment, but for as long as we are employed, we increasingly demand that our jobs play their part in moving us along the path to fulfillment.

Another obvious but important fact is that we change as we mature. Although our jobs also have the potential for change, they may not change as frequently or as markedly as we do. There are increasingly fewer one-job, one-employer careers; we must think about a work future that may involve voluntary or forced moves from employer to employer. Because of that very real possibility, we need to take advantage of the opportunities in each position we hold to acquire skills and competencies that will keep us viable and attractive as employees in a job market that is not only increasingly technology/computer dependent, but also is populated with more and more small, self-transforming organizations rather than the large, seemingly stable organizations of the past.

It may be difficult in the early stages of the job search to determine whether the path you are considering can meet these longer-term goals. Reading about career paths and individual career histories in your field can be very helpful in this regard. Meeting and talking with individuals further along in their careers can be enlightening as well. Older workers can provide valuable guidance on "self-managing" your career, which will become an increasingly valuable skill in the future. Some of these ideas may seem remote as you read this now, but you should be able to appreciate the need to ensure that you are growing, developing valuable new skills, and researching other employers who might be interested in your particular skills package.

··

If you are considering a position in museum work, for example, you would gain a far better perspective of your potential future if you could talk to an entry-level curatorial assistant, a more experienced curator or director, and, finally, a senior museum administrator with a significant work history in museum management. Each will have a different perspective, unique concerns, and an individual set of priorities.

··

STEP 5 Enumerating Your Skill Base

In terms of the job search, skills can be thought of as capabilities that can be developed in school, at work, or by volunteering and then used in specific job settings. Many studies have documented the kinds of skills that employers seek in entry-level applicants. For example, some of the most desired skills for individuals interested in the teaching profession include the ability to interact effectively with students one on one, to manage a classroom, to adapt to varying situations as necessary, and to get involved in school activities. Business employers have also identified important qualities, including enthusiasm for the employer's product or service, a businesslike mind, the ability to follow written or verbal instructions, the ability to demonstrate self-control, the confidence to suggest new ideas, the ability to communicate with all members of a group, awareness of cultural differences, and loyalty, to name just a few. You will find that many of these skills are also in the repertoire of qualities demanded in your college major.

In order to be successful in obtaining any given job, you must be able to demonstrate that you possess a certain mix of skills that will allow you to carry out the duties required by that job. This skill mix will vary a great deal from job to job; to determine the skills necessary for the jobs you are seeking, you can read job advertisements or more generic job descriptions, such as those found later in this book. If you want to be effective in the job search, you must directly show employers that you possess the skills needed to be successful in filling the position. These skills will initially be described on your resume and then discussed again during the interview process.

Skills are either general or specific. General skills are those that are developed throughout the college years by taking classes, being employed, and getting involved in other related activities such as volunteer work or campus organizations. General skills include the ability to read and write, to perform computations, to think critically, and to communicate effectively. Specific skills are also acquired on the job and in the classroom, but they allow you to complete tasks that require specialized knowledge. Computer programming, drafting, language translating, and copy editing are just a few examples of specific skills that may relate to a given job.

In order to develop a list of skills relevant to employers, you must first identify the general skills you possess, then list specific skills you have to offer, and, finally, examine which of these skills employers are seeking.

Identifying Your General Skills.　Because you possess or will possess a college degree, employers will assume that you can read and write, perform certain basic computations, think critically, and communicate effectively. Employers will want to see that you have acquired these skills, and they will want to know which additional general skills you possess.

One way to begin identifying skills is to write an experiential diary. An experiential diary lists all the tasks you were responsible for completing for each job you've held and then outlines the skills required to do those tasks. You may list several skills for any given task. This diary allows you to distinguish between the tasks you performed and the underlying skills required to complete those tasks. Here's an example:

Tasks	Skills
Answering telephone	Effective use of language, clear diction, ability to direct inquiries, ability to solve problems
Waiting on tables	Poise under conditions of time and pressure, speed, accuracy, good memory, simultaneous completion of tasks, sales skills

For each job or experience you have participated in, develop a worksheet based on the example shown here. On a resume, you may want to describe these skills rather than simply listing tasks. Skills are easier for the employer to appreciate, especially when your experience is very different from the employment you are seeking. In addition to helping you identify general skills, this experiential diary will prepare you to speak more effectively in an interview about the qualifications you possess.

Identifying Your Specific Skills.   It may be easier to identify your specific skills, because you can definitely say whether you can speak other languages, program a computer, draft a map or diagram, or edit a document using appropriate symbols and terminology.

Using your experiential diary, identify the points in your history where you learned how to do something very specific, and decide whether you have a beginning, intermediate, or advanced knowledge of how to use that particular skill. Right now, be sure to list *every* specific skill you have, and don't consider whether you like using the skill. Write down a list of specific skills you have acquired and the level of competence you possess—beginning, intermediate, or advanced.

Relating Your Skills to Employers.   You probably have thought about a couple of different jobs you might be interested in obtaining, and one way to begin relating the general and specific skills you possess to potential employer needs is to read actual advertisements for these types of positions (see Part II for resources listing actual job openings).

....

For example, you might be interested in beginning your career as an information specialist in research. A job listing might read, "Initiate/design/produce corporate surveys.

Requires overseas living/working experience, excellent writing skills, communication/presentation skills, word-processing." If you then used any one of a number of general sources of information that describe the job of researcher, you would find additional information. Researchers also analyze data, prepare reports and search sources.

Begin building a comprehensive list of required skills with the first job description you read. Exploring advertisements for and descriptions of several types of related positions will reveal an important core of skills that are necessary for obtaining the type of work you're interested in. In building this list, include both general and specific skills.

Following is a sample list of skills needed to be successful as a researcher. These items were extracted from both general resources and actual job listings:

Job: Researcher

General Skills	Specific Skills
Analyze verbal/ statistical data	Construct data files
Perform interviews	Analyze trend data
Draft correspondence	Travel overseas
Prepare statistical tabulations	Establish department budget
Conduct studies	Work with volunteers
Search sources	Communicate effectively
Obtain data	Install exhibits
Evaluate data for applicability	Use phone extensively
Use calculator/computer	Keep historical records
Write reports	Work under pressure
Present data orally	Track down sources
Answer inquiries	Write articles

On separate sheets of paper, try to generate a comprehensive list of required skills for at least one job that you are considering.

The list of general skills that you develop for a given career path would be valuable for any number of jobs you might apply for. Many of the specific skills would also be transferable to other types of positions. For example, analyzing trend data is a specific skill for some research positions, and it also would be required for many financial analyst jobs.

....

Now review the list of skills you developed and check off those skills that *you know you possess* and that are required for jobs you are considering. You should refer to these specific skills on the resume that you write for this type of job. See Chapter 2 for details on resume writing.

STEP 6 Recognizing Your Preferred Skills

In the previous section, you developed a comprehensive list of skills that relate to particular career paths that are of interest to you. You can now relate these to skills that you prefer to use. We all use a wide range of skills (some researchers say individuals have a repertoire of about 500 skills), but we may not be particularly interested in using all of them in our work. There may be some skills that come to us more naturally or that we use successfully time and time again and that we want to continue to use; these are best described as our preferred skills. For this exercise, use the list of skills that you developed for the previous section and decide which of them you are *most interested in using* in future work and how often you would like to use them. You might be interested in using some skills only occasionally, while others you would like to use more regularly. You probably also have skills that you hope you can use constantly.

As you examine job announcements, look for matches between this list of preferred skills and the qualifications described in the advertisements. These skills should be highlighted on your resume and discussed in job interviews.

STEP 7 Assessing Skills Needing Further Development

Previously you developed a list of general and specific skills required for given positions. You already possess some of these skills; those that remain to be developed are your underdeveloped skills.

If you are just beginning the job search, there may be gaps between the qualifications required for some of the jobs being considered and skills you possess. These are your underdeveloped skills. The thought of having to admit to and talk about these underdeveloped skills, especially in a job interview, is a frightening one. One way to put a healthy perspective on this subject is to target and relate your exploration of underdeveloped skills to the types of positions you are seeking. Recognizing these shortcomings and planning to overcome them with either on-the-job training or additional formal education can be a positive way to address the concept of underdeveloped skills.

On your worksheet or in your journal, make a list of up to five general or specific skills required for the positions you're interested in that you *don't currently possess*. For each item, list an idea you have for specific action you could take to acquire that skill. Do some brainstorming to come up with possible actions. If you have a hard time generating ideas, talk to people currently working in this type of position, professionals in your college career services office, trusted friends, family members, or members of related professional associations.

If, for example, you are interested in a job for which you don't have some specific required experience, you could locate training opportunities such as classes or workshops offered through a local college or university, community college, or club or association that would help you build the level of expertise you need for the job.

You might have noticed in this book that many excellent positions for your major demand computer skills. These computer skills were probably not part of your required academic preparation. While it is easy for the business world to see the direct link between oral and written communication and high technology, some college departments have been markedly reluctant to add this dimension to their curriculums. What can you do now? If you're still in college, take what computer courses you can before you graduate. If you've already graduated, look at evening programs, continuing education courses, or tutorial programs that may be available commercially. Developing a modest level of expertise will encourage you to be more confident in suggesting to potential employers that you can continue to add to your skill base on the job.

In Chapter 5 on interviewing, we will discuss in detail how to effectively address questions about underdeveloped skills. Generally speaking, though, employers want genuine answers to these types of questions. They want you to reveal "the real you," and they also want to see how you answer difficult questions. In taking the positive, targeted approach discussed above, you show the employer that you are willing to continue to learn and that you have a plan for strengthening your job qualifications.

USING YOUR SELF-ASSESSMENT

Exploring entry-level career options can be an exciting experience if you have good resources available and will take the time to use them. Can you effectively complete the following tasks?

1. Understand and relate your personality traits to career choices

2. Define your personal values

3. Determine your economic needs

4. Explore longer-term goals

5. Understand your skill base

6. Recognize your preferred skills

7. Express a willingness to improve on your underdeveloped skills

If so, then you can more meaningfully participate in the job search process by writing a more effective resume, finding job titles that represent work you are interested in doing, locating job sites that will provide the opportunity for you to use your strengths and skills, networking in an informed way, participating in focused interviews, getting the most out of follow-up contacts, and evaluating job offers to find those that create a good match between you and the employer. The remaining chapters guide you through these next steps in the job search process. For many job seekers, this process can take anywhere from three months to a year to implement. The time you will need to put into your job search will depend on the type of job you want and the geographic location where you'd like to work. Think of your effort as a job in itself, requiring you to set aside time each week to complete the needed work. Carefully undertaken efforts may reduce the time you need for your job search.

CHAPTER TWO

THE RESUME AND COVER LETTER

he task of writing a resume may seem overwhelming if you are unfamiliar with this type of document, but there are some easily understood techniques that can and should be used. This section was written to help you understand the purpose of the resume, the different types of resume formats available, and how to write the sections of information traditionally found on a resume. We will present examples and explanations that address questions frequently posed by people writing their first resume or updating an old resume.

Even within the formats and suggestions given below, however, there are infinite variations. True, most resumes follow one of the outlines suggested below, but you should feel free to adjust the resume to suit your needs and make it expressive of your life and experience.

WHY WRITE A RESUME?

The purpose of a resume is to convince an employer that you should be interviewed. You'll want to present enough information to show that you can make an immediate and valuable contribution to an organization. A resume is not an in-depth historical or legal document; later in the job search process you'll be asked to document your entire work history on an application form and attest to its validity. The resume should, instead, highlight relevant information pertaining directly to the organization that will receive the document or the type of position you are seeking.

We will discuss four types of resumes in this chapter: chronological resume, functional resume, targeted resume, and the broadcast letter. The reasons for using one type of resume over another and the typical format for each are addressed in the following sections.

THE CHRONOLOGICAL RESUME

The chronological resume is the most common of the various resume formats and therefore the format that employers are most used to receiving. This type of resume is easy to read and understand because it details the chronological progression of jobs you have held. (See Exhibit 2.1.) It begins with your most recent employment and works back in time. If you have a solid work history, or experience that provided growth and development in your duties and responsibilities, a chronological resume will highlight these achievements. The typical elements of a chronological resume include the heading, a career objective, educational background, employment experience, activities, and references.

The Heading
The heading consists of your name, address, and telephone number. Recently it has come to include fax numbers and electronic mail addresses as well. We suggest that you spell out your full name and type it in all capital letters in bold type. After all, *you* are the focus of the resume! If you have a current as well as a permanent address and you include both in the heading, be sure to indicate until what date your current address will be valid. The two-letter state abbreviation should be the only abbreviation that appears in your heading. Don't forget to include the zip code with your address and the area code with your telephone number.

The Objective
As you formulate the wording for this part of your resume, keep the following points in mind.

The Objective Focuses the Resume.   Without a doubt, this is the most challenging part of the resume for most resume writers. Even for individuals who have quite firmly decided on a career path, it can be difficult to encapsulate all they want to say in one or two brief sentences. For job seekers who are unfocused or unclear about their intentions, trying to write this section can inhibit the entire resume writing process.

Recruiters tell us, time and again, that the objective creates a frame of reference for them. It helps them see how you express your goals and career focus. In

Exhibit 2.1

Chronological Resume

AMY TOWNES

Campus View #801
Indiana University
Bloomington, IN 47401
(812) 555-6666
(until May 1995)

27 Common Man Way
Portsmouth, RI 34877
(401) 555-6666

OBJECTIVE

History Museum Education Coordinator

EDUCATION

Bachelor of Arts in History
Indiana University at Bloomington
Concentration: Early American History
Minor: Communications

HONORS/AWARDS

Dean's List, 1993, 1994
Distinguished Student Orientation Guide Award, 1992
Phi Delta Kappa Honor Society

RELATED COURSES

Interactive Technology Systems
American Art Traditions

Speech
Archaeology

EXPERIENCE

Orientation Leader, Indiana University. 1992–94.
Selected to be part of a special unit of students charged with orienting new students to the history, geography and structure of the college. Large group sessions and smaller interactive program responsibilities. Trained new orientation leaders.

Interpreter/Guide, Strawberry Banke Historic Settlement, Portsmouth, NH. Summers, 1991–94.
Progressively greater responsibilities in a number of different settings as a costumed historic interpreter for this popular year-round historic site. Specific training in Early American gardens, import china and furnishings.

continued

continued

Student Assistant, History Department, Indiana University. Part-time, 1992–94.
A recurring work study position assisting history faculty in test preparation, special event planning, history film series organization, and student library cataloguing and maintenance. Answered inquiries from history students and other staff.

ACTIVITIES

History Club, active member, 1991–present
Medieval Forum participant, 1992–present
Canadian Conference student team assistant, 1994

REFERENCES

Available upon request

addition, the statement may indicate in what ways you can immediately benefit an organization. Given the importance of the objective, every point covered in the resume should relate to it. If information doesn't relate, it should be omitted. With the word processing technology available today, each resume can and should be tailored for individual employers or specific positions that are available.

Choose an Appropriate Length.   Because of the brevity necessary for a resume, you should keep the objective as short as possible. Although objectives of only four or five words often don't show much direction, objectives that take three full lines would be viewed as too wordy and might possibly be ignored.

Consider Which Type of Objective Statement You Will Use.   There are many ways to state an objective, but generally there are four forms this statement can take: (1) a very general statement; (2) a statement focused on a specific position; (3) a statement focused on a specific industry; or (4) a summary of your qualifications. In our contacts with employers, we often hear that many resumes don't exhibit any direction or career goals, so we suggest avoiding general statements when possible.

1. General Objective Statement.   General objective statements look like the following:

- An entry-level educational programming coordinator position

- An entry-level marketing position

This type of objective would be useful if you know what type of job you want but you're not sure which industries interest you.

2. *Position-Focused Objective.* Following are examples of objectives focusing on a specific position:

❑ To obtain the position of Conference Coordinator at State College

❑ To obtain a position as Assistant Editor at *Time* magazine

When a student applies for an advertised job opening, this type of focus can be very effective. The employer knows that the applicant has taken the time to tailor the resume specifically for this position.

3. *Industry-Focused Objective.* Focusing on a particular industry in an objective could be stated as follows:

❑ To begin a career as a sales representative in the cruise line industry

4. *Summary of Qualifications Statement.* The summary of qualifications can be used instead of an objective or in conjunction with an objective. The purpose of this type of statement is to highlight relevant qualifications gained through a variety of experiences. This type of statement is often used by individuals with extensive and diversified work experience. An example of a qualifications statement follows:

....

A degree in history and four years of progressively increasing job responsibility in museums and historical sites have prepared me to begin a career as a preparator or assistant curator with an institution that values hard work and dedication.

....

Support Your Objective. A resume that contains any one of these types of objective statements should then go on to demonstrate why you are qualified to get the position. Listing academic degrees can be one way to indicate qualifications. Another demonstration would be in the way previous experiences, both volunteer and paid, are described. Without this kind of documentation in the body of the resume, the objective looks unsupported. Think of the resume as telling a connected story about you. All the elements should work together to form a coherent picture that ideally should relate to your statement of objective.

Education

This section of your resume should indicate the exact name of the degree you will receive or have received, spelled out completely with no abbreviations.

The degree is generally listed after the objective, followed by the institution name and address, and then the month and year of graduation. This section could also include your academic minor, grade point average (GPA), and appearance on the Dean's List or President's List.

If you have enough space, you might want to include a section listing courses related to the field in which you are seeking work. The best use of a "related courses" section would be to list some course work that is not traditionally associated with the major. Perhaps you took several computer courses outside your degree that will be helpful and related to the job prospects you are entertaining. Several education section examples are shown here:

....

❑ Bachelor of Arts in Interdisciplinary Studies, a self-designed program concentrating in History and Art, State College, Columbus, OH, May 1994

❑ Bachelor of Arts Degree in History
State College, San Antonio, TX, December 1994
Minor: Art

❑ Bachelor of Arts Degree in History
State College, San Francisco, CA, May 1994
Concentration: Modern Western Europe

An example of a format for a related courses section follows:

RELATED COURSES	
Museum Curatorship	Critical Thinking
Technical Writing	Desktop Publishing
Creative Writing	Software Systems

....

Experience

The experience section of your resume should be the most substantial part and should take up most of the space on the page. Employers want to see what kind of work history you have. They will look at your range of experiences, longevity in jobs, and specific tasks you are able to complete. This section may also be called "work experience," "related experience," "employment history," or "employment." No matter what you call this section, some important points to remember are the following:

1. **Describe your duties** as they relate to the position you are seeking.

2. **Emphasize major responsibilities** and indicate increases in responsibility. Include all relevant employment experiences: summer, part-time, internships, cooperative education, or self-employment.

3. **Emphasize skills,** especially those that transfer from one situation to another. The fact that you coordinated a student organization, chaired meetings, supervised others, and managed a budget leads one to suspect that you could coordinate other things as well.

4. **Use descriptive job titles** that provide information about what you did. A "Student Intern" should be more specifically stated as, for example, "Magazine Operations Intern." "Volunteer" is also too general; a title like "Peer Writing Tutor" would be more appropriate.

5. **Create word pictures** by using active verbs to start sentences. Describe *results* you have produced in the work you have done.

A limp description would say something like the following: "My duties included helping with production, proofreading, and editing. I used a word processing package to alter text." An action statement would be stated as follows: "Coordinated and assisted in the creative marketing of brochures and seminar promotions, becoming proficient in WordPerfect."

Remember, an accomplishment is simply a result, a final measurable product that people can relate to. A duty is not a result, it is an obligation—every job holder has duties. For an effective resume, list as many results as you can. To make the most of the limited space you have and to give your description impact, carefully select appropriate and accurate descriptors from the list of action words in Exhibit 2.2.

Exhibit 2.2

Resume Action Verbs

Achieved	Collected	Converted
Acted	Communicated	Coordinated
Administered	Compiled	Corrected
Advised	Completed	Created
Analyzed	Composed	Decreased
Assessed	Conceptualized	Defined
Assisted	Condensed	Demonstrated
Attained	Conducted	Designed
Balanced	Consolidated	Determined
Budgeted	Constructed	Developed
Calculated	Controlled	Directed

continued

continued

Documented	Learned	Received
Drafted	Lectured	Recommended
Edited	Led	Recorded
Eliminated	Maintained	Reduced
Ensured	Managed	Reinforced
Established	Mapped	Reported
Estimated	Marketed	Represented
Evaluated	Met	Researched
Examined	Modified	Resolved
Explained	Monitored	Reviewed
Facilitated	Negotiated	Scheduled
Finalized	Observed	Selected
Generated	Obtained	Served
Handled	Operated	Showed
Headed	Organized	Simplified
Helped	Participated	Sketched
Identified	Performed	Sold
Illustrated	Planned	Solved
Implemented	Predicted	Staffed
Improved	Prepared	Streamlined
Increased	Presented	Studied
Influenced	Processed	Submitted
Informed	Produced	Summarized
Initiated	Projected	Systematized
Innovated	Proposed	Tabulated
Instituted	Provided	Tested
Instructed	Qualified	Transacted
Integrated	Quantified	Updated
Interpreted	Questioned	Verified
Introduced	Realized	

Here are some traits that employers tell us they like to see:

- ❑ Teamwork
- ❑ Energy and motivation
- ❑ Learning and using new skills
- ❑ Demonstrated versatility
- ❑ Critical thinking
- ❑ Understanding how profits are created
- ❑ Displaying organizational acumen

- Communicating directly and clearly, in both writing and speaking
- Risk taking
- Willingness to admit mistakes
- Manifesting high personal standards

SOLUTIONS TO FREQUENTLY ENCOUNTERED PROBLEMS

Repetitive Employment with the Same Employer

EMPLOYMENT: **The Foot Locker,** Portland, Oregon. Summer 1991, 1992, 1993. Initially employed in high school as salesclerk. Due to successful performance, asked to return next two summers at higher pay with added responsibility. Ranked as the #2 salesperson the first summer and #1 the next two summers. Assisted in arranging eye-catching retail displays; served as manager of other summer workers during owner's absence.

A Large Number of Jobs

EMPLOYMENT: Recent Hospitality Industry Experience: Affiliated with four upscale hotel/restaurant complexes (September 1991–February 1994), where I worked part- and full-time as a waiter, bartender, disc jockey, and bookkeeper to produce income for college.

Several Positions with the Same Employer

EMPLOYMENT: Coca-Cola Bottling Co., Burlington, VT, 1991–94. In four years, I received three promotions, each with increased pay and responsibility.

Summer Sales Coordinator: Promoted to hire, train, and direct efforts of add-on staff of 15 college-age route salespeople hired to meet summer peak demand for product.

Sales Administrator: Promoted to run home office sales desk, managing accounts and associated delivery schedules for professional sales force of ten people. Intensive phone work, daily interaction with all personnel, and strong knowledge of product line required.

Route Salesperson: Summer employment to travel and tourism industry sites using Coke products. Met specific schedule demands, used good communication skills with wide variety of customers, and demonstrated strong selling skills. Named salesperson of the month for July and August of that year.

QUESTIONS RESUME WRITERS OFTEN ASK

How Far Back Should I Go in Terms of Listing Past Jobs?

Usually, listing three or four jobs should suffice. If you did something back in high school that has a bearing on your future aspirations for employment, by all means list the job. As you progress through your college career, high school jobs may be replaced on the resume by college employment.

Should I Differentiate between Paid and Nonpaid Employment?

Most employers are not initially as concerned about how much you were paid. They are anxious to know how much responsibility you held in your past employment. There is no need to specify that your work was volunteer if you had significant responsibilities.

How Should I Represent My Accomplishments or Work-Related Responsibilities?

Succinctly, but fully. In other words, give the employer enough information to arouse curiosity, but not so much detail that you leave nothing to the imagination. Besides, some jobs merit more lengthy explanations than others. Be sure to convey any information that can give an employer a better understanding of the depth of your involvement at work. Did you supervise others? How many? Did your efforts result in a more efficient operation? How much did you increase efficiency? Did you handle a budget? How much? Were you promoted in a short time? Did you work two jobs at once or 15 hours per week after high school? Where appropriate, quantify.

Should the Work Section Always Follow the Education Section on the Resume?

Always lead with your strengths. If your past work closely relates to the employment you now seek, put this section after the objective. Or, if you are weak on the academic side but have a surplus of good work experiences, consider reversing the order of your sections to lead with employment, followed by education.

How Should I Present My Activities, Honors, Awards, Professional Societies, and Affiliations?

This section of the resume can add valuable information for an employer to consider if used correctly. The rule of thumb for information in this section is to include only those activities that are in some way relevant to the objective stated on your resume. If you can draw a valid connection between your activities and your objective, include them; if not, leave them out.

Granted, this is hard to do. Center on the championship basketball team or coordinator of the biggest homecoming parade ever held are roles that have meaning for you and represent personal accomplishments you'd like to share. But the resume is a brief document, and the information you provide on it should help the employer make a decision about your job eligibility. Including personal details can be confusing and could hurt your candidacy. Limiting your activity list to a few very significant experiences can be very effective.

If you are applying for a position as a safety officer, your certificate in Red Cross lifesaving skills or CPR would be related and valuable. You would want to include it. If, however, you are applying for a job as a junior account executive in an advertising agency, that information would be unrelated and superfluous. Leave it out.

Professional affiliations and honors should *all* be listed; especially important are those related to your job objective. Social clubs and activities need not be a part of your resume unless you hold a significant office or you are looking for a position related to your membership. Be aware that most prospective employers' principle concerns are related to your employability, not your social life. If you have any, publications can be included as an addendum to your resume.

The focus of the resume is your experience and education. It is not necessary to describe your involvement in activities. However, if your resume needs to be lengthened, this section provides the freedom either to expand on or mention only briefly the contributions you have made. If you have made significant contributions (e.g., an officer of an organization or a particularly long tenure with a group), you may choose to describe them in more detail. It is not always necessary to include the dates of your memberships with your activities the way you would include job dates.

There are a number of different ways in which to present additional information. You may give this section a number of different titles. Assess what you want to list, and then use an appropriate title. Do not use extracurricular activities. This terminology is scholastic, not professional, and therefore not appropriate. The following are two examples:

❑ ACTIVITIES: Society for Technical Communication, Student Senate, Student Admissions Representative, Senior Class Officer

❑ ACTIVITIES:
- Society for Technical Communication Member
- Student Senator
- Student Admissions Representative
- Senior Class Officer

The position you are looking for will determine what you should or should not include. *Always* look for a correlation between the activity and the prospective job.

How Should I Handle References?

The use of references is considered a part of the interview process, and they should never be listed on a resume. You would always provide references to a potential employer if requested to, so it is not even necessary to include this section on the resume if room does not permit. If space is available, it is acceptable to include one of the following statements:

❑ REFERENCES: Furnished upon request.

❑ REFERENCES: Available upon request.

Individuals used as references must be protected from unnecessary contacts. By including names on your resume, you leave your references unprotected. Overuse and abuse of your references will lead to less-than-supportive comments. Protect your references by giving out their names only when you are being considered seriously as a candidate for a given position.

THE FUNCTIONAL RESUME

The functional resume departs from a chronological resume in that it organizes information by specific accomplishments in various settings: previous jobs, volunteer work, associations, etc. This type of resume permits you to stress the substance of your experiences rather than the position titles you have held. (See Exhibit 2.3.) You should consider using a functional resume if you have held a series of similar jobs that relied on the same skills or abilities.

Exhibit 2.3

Functional Resume

FRANK C. BECHARD

Redbud Apartments #18C   266 Chase Avenue
Colby Sawyer College   Winter Park, FL 75426
New London, NH 03765   (714) 555-6666
(603) 555-6666
(Until May 1995)

OBJECTIVE
An entry-level information specialist position that allows me to use my analytical, problem-solving and writing skills.

continued

continued

CAPABILITIES

- Analytical yet creative problem solver
- Strong data base management/spreadsheet software skills
- Skilled report writer and public presenter

SELECTED ACCOMPLISHMENTS

PROBLEM SOLVING: Researched current and accurate sources of information for ongoing research projects. Developed methods and systems for processing survey data results for 23 different projects. Established processing priorities for several overlapping projects; answered questions and resolved problems for library patrons.

COMPUTING: Used SPSS, SAS and Lotus software packages to process data; manipulated digitizers, plotters, and graphics software to create graphics for reports; utilized mainframe and personal computing hardware; helped implement library security system.

COMMUNICATING: Assisted in writing and editing project reports; conducted telephone and door-to-door surveys in the local community; coordinated writing, editing, and computer assignments with three other student research assistants; presented survey findings to several audiences. Helped library patrons locate needed materials.

AWARDS

Awarded select undergraduate fellowship 1993/4
Graduated with highest distinction
Nominated to national honor society

EMPLOYMENT HISTORY

Research Assistant, Central NH Cemetery Project, Colby Sawyer College, New London, NH. Summers 1992–4
Library Information Coordinator, Colby Sawyer Library, New London, NH. 1991–4

EDUCATION

Bachelor of Arts in History
Colby Sawyer College, New London, NH
Additional significant course work in Computer Science

REFERENCES

Provided upon request

The Objective

A functional resume begins with an objective that can be used to focus the contents of the resume.

Specific Accomplishments

Specific accomplishments are listed on this type of resume. Examples of the types of headings used to describe these capabilities might include sales, counseling, teaching, communication, production, management, marketing, or writing. The headings you choose will directly relate to your experience and the tasks that you carried out. Each accomplishment section contains statements related to your experience in that category, regardless of when or where it occurred. Organize the accomplishments and the related tasks you describe in their order of importance as related to the position you seek.

Experience or Employment History

Your actual work experience is condensed and placed after the specific accomplishments section. It simply lists dates of employment, position titles, and employer names.

Education

The education section of a functional resume is identical to that of the chronological resume, but it does not carry the same visual importance because it is placed near the bottom of the page.

References

Because actual reference names are never listed on a resume, this section is optional if space does not permit.

THE TARGETED RESUME

The targeted resume focuses on specific work-related capabilities you can bring to a given position within an organization. (See Exhibit 2.4.) It should be sent to an individual within the organization who makes hiring decisions about the position you are seeking.

The Objective

The objective on this type of resume should be targeted to a specific career or position. It should be supported by the capabilities, accomplishments, and achievements documented in the resume.

Exhibit 2.4

Targeted Resume

CARLA P. MARTINO

Congreve Hall 116
Rollins College
Ann Arbor, MI 86256
(303) 555-6666
(until May 1995)

72 Cherry Street
Stoneham, MA 02192
(617) 555-6666

JOB TARGET

Director of Education for a children's museum

CAPABILITIES

- Design, develop, implement and evaluate interpretive efforts
- Schedule classes, films, workshops, internships
- Collaborate with other institutions
- Provide marketing support
- Recruit and train instructors and docents

ACHIEVEMENTS

- Produced numerous all-campus programs (educational and entertainment)
- Provided research support for award-winning faculty writer
- Operated my own successful children's party business
- Maintained a distinctive GPA throughout college

WORK HISTORY

1993–present (part-time)	*Children's Librarian,* Speare Memorial Library Ann Arbor, MI • Weekly programs with music, puppets, media
1991–93 (summers)	*Children's Program Director,* Stoneham Zoo • Tours, parties, educational visits
1990–92 (summers)	Counselor, YMCA Day Camp, Westwood, MA • Tent counselor and nature teacher

continued

continued

EDUCATION

Bachelor of Arts in History
Rollins College, Ann Arbor, Michigan
Minor: Theatre

Capabilities

Capabilities should be statements that illustrate tasks you believe you are capable of based on your accomplishments, achievements, and work history. Each should relate to your targeted career or position. You can stress your qualifications rather than your employment history. This approach may require research to obtain an understanding of the nature of the work involved and the capabilities necessary to carry out that work.

Accomplishments/Achievements

This section relates the various activities you have been involved in to the job market. These experiences may include previous jobs, extracurricular activities at school, internships, and part-time summer work.

Experience

Your work history should be listed in abbreviated form and may include position title, employer name, and employment dates.

Education

Because this type of resume is directed toward a specific job target and an individual's related experience, the education section is not prominently located at the top of the resume as is done on the chronological resume.

THE BROADCAST LETTER

The broadcast letter is used by some job seekers in place of a resume and cover letter. (See Exhibit 2.5.) The purpose of this type of document is to make a number of potential employers aware of the availability and expertise of the job seeker. Because the broadcast letter is mass-mailed (500–600 employers), the amount of work required may not be worth the return for many people. If you choose to mail out a broadcast letter, you can expect to receive a response from 2–5 percent, at best, of the organizations that receive your letter.

This type of document is most often used by individuals who have an extensive and quantifiable work history. College students often do not have the

Exhibit 2.5

Broadcast Letter

STANTON C. OTIS
27 Highland Links
Coronado, CA 80526
(303) 567-9320

Mr. Robert Tuveson, President   October 15, 1995
Harco Incorporated
2626 East Main Road
Portsmouth, OH 37654

Dear Mr. Tuveson:

I am writing to you because your company may be in need of an assistant or entry-level product manager with my experience, education, and training. My long-term goal is to work in product management in the food industry, developing and marketing new food items. I understand the need for, and look foward with great anticipation to, a period of training and education at corporate headquarters in Indianapolis. I feel confident I can make a strong contribution to your product management staff at Harco. You may be interested in some of my accomplishments:

- My high school employment was in the retail grocery trade where I gained extensive product knowledge and consumer preference sensitivity.

- In college, I worked as a contract researcher for an advertising agency with several food product accounts doing in-store product facing/pricing research.

- Several summers work in the dietary department of our local hospital brought me in contact with vendors and suppliers and I performed numerous detailed cost analyses.

I received my Bachelor of Arts in History from Heidelberg College in Tiffin, Ohio, in May of 1995.

It would be a pleasure to review my qualifications with you in a personal interview at some mutually convenient time. I will call your

continued

---

continued

office at the end of next week to make arrangements. I look forward to discussing career opportunities with Harco Incorporated.

Sincerely,

Stanton C. Otis

---

credentials and work experience to support using a broadcast letter, and most will find it difficult to effectively quantify a slim work history.

A broadcast letter is generally five paragraphs (one page) long. The first paragraph should immediately gain the attention of the reader and state some unusual accomplishment or skill that would be of benefit to the organization. The second paragraph states the reason for the letter. Details of the sender's work history are revealed in the third paragraph. Education and other qualifications or credentials are then described. Finally, the job seeker indicates what he or she will do to follow up on the letter, which usually is a follow-up call 1–2 weeks after the letter is sent.

RESUME PRODUCTION AND OTHER TIPS

If you have the option and convenience of using a laser printer, you may want to initially produce a limited number of copies in case you want or need to make changes on your resume.

Resume paper color should be carefully chosen. You should consider the types of employers who will receive your resume and the types of positions for which you are applying. Use white or ivory paper for traditional or conservative employers, or for higher-level positions.

Black ink on sharply white paper can be harsh on the reader's eyes. Think about an ivory or cream paper that will provide less contrast and be easier to read. Pink, green, and blue tints should generally be avoided.

Many resume writers buy packages of matching envelopes and cover sheet stationery that, although not absolutely necessary, does convey a professional impression.

If you'll be producing many cover letters at home, be sure you have high-quality printing equipment, whether it be computerized or standard typewriter equipment. Learn standard envelope formats for business and retain a copy of every cover letter you send out. You can use it to take notes of any telephone conversations that may occur.

If attending a job fair, women generally can fold their resume in thirds lengthwise and find it fits into a clutch bag or envelope-style purse. Both men and women will have no trouble if they carry a briefcase. For men without a briefcase, carry the resume in a nicely covered legal-size pad holder or fold it in half lengthwise and place it inside your suitcoat pocket, taking care it doesn't "float" outside your collar.

THE COVER LETTER

The cover letter provides you with the opportunity to tailor your resume by telling the prospective employer how you can be a benefit to the organization. It will allow you to highlight aspects of your background that are not already discussed in your resume and that might be especially relevant to the organization you are contacting or to the position you are seeking. Every resume should have a cover letter enclosed when you send it out. Unlike the resume, which may be mass-produced, a cover letter is most effective when it is individually typed and focused on the particular requirements of the organization in question.

A good cover letter should supplement the resume and motivate the reader to review the resume. The format shown in Exhibit 2.6 is only a suggestion to help you decide what information to include in writing a cover letter.

Begin the cover letter with your street address 12 lines down from the top. Leave three to five lines between the date and the name of the person to whom

---

Exhibit 2.6

Cover Letter Format

Your Street Address
Your Town, State, Zip
Phone Number
Date

continued

continued

Name
Title
Organization
Address

Dear _____:

First Paragraph. In this paragraph, state the reason for the letter, name the specific position or type of work you are applying for, and indicate from which resource (career development office, newspaper, contact, employment service) you learned of the opening. The first paragraph can also be used to inquire about future openings.

Second Paragraph. Indicate why you are interested in the position, the company, its products or services, and what you can do for the employer. If you are a recent graduate, explain how your academic background makes you a qualified candidate. Try not to repeat the same information found in the resume.

Third Paragraph. Refer the reader to the enclosed resume for more detailed information.

Fourth Paragraph. In this paragraph, say what you will do to follow up on your letter. For example, state that you will call by a certain date to set up an interview or to find out if the company will be recruiting in your area. Finish by indicating your willingness to answer any questions they may have. Be sure you have provided your phone number.

Sincerely,

Type your name

Enclosure

you are addressing the cover letter. Make sure you leave one blank line between the salutation and the body of the letter and between each paragraph.

After typing "Sincerely," leave four blank lines and type your name. This should leave plenty of room for your signature. A sample cover letter is shown in Exhibit 2.7.

The following are guidelines that will help you write good cover letters:

1. Be sure to type your letter; ensure there are no misspellings.

Exhibit 2.7

Sample Cover Letter

143 Random Way
Shreveport, LA 71130
(318) 555-6666
October 15, 1995

Donna Stivali
Director of Personnel
Louisiana Museum of Transportation
279 Main Street
Shreveport, LA 71130

Dear Ms. Stivali:

In May of 1996, I will graduate from Louisiana State University with a Bachelor of Arts Degree in History. I read of your anticipated opening in *The Times* on Sunday, September 30, 1995, and I am very interested in the possibilities it offers. I am writing to explore the opportunity for employment with the museum.

The ad indicated that you were looking for someone to assist in the overseeing and maintenance of your collection of 18th–20th century river craft, including artifacts and prints. While in college, I did focus on maritime history in my degree work, and although not entirely familiar with the material in your collection, it is very much within my area of interest. In addition to a solid history background, I enrolled in every museum class my college offered and was exposed to museum design, curatorship studies and mounting and cleaning procedures. These courses, combined with my strong academic preparation, should prove valuable in this position.

As you will see from the activity documented on the enclosed resume, I have a high energy level and work experiences that

continued

continued

required significant oral and written communications of a sophisticated order. This particular opening sounds like a wonderful beginning to a museum career.

I would like to meet with you to discuss how my education and experiences would be consistent with your needs. I will contact your office next week to discuss the possibility of an interview. In the meantime, if you have any questions or require additional information, please contact me at my home, (318) 555-6666.

Sincerely,

Kirsten Giebutowski

Enclosure

2. Avoid unusual typefaces, such as script.

3. Address the letter to an individual, using the person's name and title. To obtain this information, call the company. If answering a blind newspaper advertisement, address the letter "To Whom It May Concern" or omit the salutation.

4. Be sure your cover letter directly indicates the position you are applying for and tells why you are qualified to fill it.

5. Send the original letter, not a photocopy, with your resume. Keep a copy for your records.

6. Make your cover letter no more than one page.

7. Include a phone number where you can be reached.

8. Avoid trite language and have someone read it over to react to its tone, content, and mechanics.

9. For your own information, record the date you send out each letter and resume.

CHAPTER THREE

RESEARCHING CAREERS

One common question a career counselor encounters is "What can I do with my degree?" History majors often struggle with this problem because, unlike their fellow students in more applied fields such as accounting, computer science, or health and physical education, there is real confusion about just what kinds of jobs they can do with their degree and what kinds of organizations hire for those positions. An accounting major becomes an accountant. A computer science major can apply for a job as a data analyst. But what does a history major become?

WHAT DO THEY CALL THE JOB YOU WANT?

There is every reason to be unaware. One reason for confusion is perhaps a mistaken assumption that a college education provides job training. In most cases, it does not. Of course, applied fields such as engineering, management, or education provide specific skills for the workplace, whereas most liberal arts degrees simply provide an education. A liberal arts education exposes you to numerous fields of study and teaches you quantitative reasoning, critical thinking, writing, and speaking, all of which can be successfully applied to a number of different job fields. But it still remains up to you to choose a job field and to learn how to articulate the benefits of your education in a way the employer will appreciate.

As indicated in Chapter 1 on self-assessment, your first task is to understand and value what parts of that education you enjoyed and were good at and would continue to enjoy in your life's work. Did your writing courses encourage you in your ability to express yourself in writing? Did you enjoy the research process and did you find your work was well received? Did you enjoy any of your required quantitative subjects like algebra or calculus?

The answers to questions such as these provide clues to skills and interests you bring to the employment market over and above the credential of your degree. In fact, it is not an overstatement to suggest that most employers who demand a college degree immediately look beyond that degree to you as a person and your own individual expression of what you like to do and think you can do for them, regardless of your major.

Collecting Job Titles

The world of employment is a big place, and even seasoned veterans of the job hunt can be surprised about what jobs are to be found in what organizations. You need to become a bit of an explorer and adventurer and be willing to try a variety of techniques to begin a list of possible occupations that might use your talents and education. Once you have a list of possibilities that you are interested in and qualified for, you can move on to find out what kinds of organizations have these job titles.

....

Not every employer seeking to hire a non-classroom educator may be equally desirable to you. Some employment environments may be more attractive to you than others. A history major considering a non-classroom teaching position could do that in a history museum, a governmental agency, a nuclear power facility, an outdoor environmental habitat, a historical reconstruction, or a privately owned historical attraction for tourists. Each of these environments presents a different "culture" with associated norms in the pace of work, the subject matter of interest, and the backgrounds of its employees. Although the job title may be the same, not all locations will present the same "fit" for you.

If you majored in history and enjoyed the in-class presentations you made as part of your degree and developed some good writing skills, you might naturally think law is a possibility for you. You're considering graduate school and a J.D. degree. But history majors with these skills also become governmental managers, advertising executives, trainers, public relations practitioners and bank officers. Each of these job titles can also be found in a number of different settings.

....

Take training, for example. Trainers write policy and procedural manuals and actively teach to assist all levels of employees in mastering various tasks and work-related systems. Trainers exist in all large corporations, banks, consumer goods manufacturers, medical diagnostic equipment firms, sales organizations, and any organization that has processes or materials that need to be presented to and learned by the staff.

In reading job descriptions or want ads for any of these positions, you would find your four-year degree a "must." However, the academic major might be less important than your own individual skills in critical thinking, analysis, report writing, public presentations, and interpersonal communication. Even more important than thinking or knowing you have certain skills is your ability to express those skills concretely and the examples you use to illustrate them to an employer.

The best beginning to a job search is to create a list of job titles you might want to pursue, learn more about the nature of the jobs behind those titles, and then discover what kinds of employers hire for those positions. In the following section, we'll teach you how to build a job title directory to use in your job search.

Developing a Job Title Directory That Works for You

A job title directory is simply a complete list of all the job titles you are interested in, are intrigued by, or think you are qualified for. Combining the understanding gained through self-assessment with your own individual interests and the skills and talents you've acquired with your degree, you'll soon start to read and recognize a number of occupational titles that seem right for you. There are several resources you can use to develop your list, including computer searches, books, and want ads.

Computerized Interest Inventories.   One way to begin your search is to identify a number of jobs that call for your degree and the particular skills and interests you identified as part of the self-assessment process. There are on the market excellent interactive computer career guidance programs to help you produce such selected lists of possible job titles. Most of these are available at high schools and colleges and at some larger town and city libraries. Two of the industry leaders are SIGI and DISCOVER. Both allow you to enter interests, values, educational background, and other information to produce lists of possible occupations and industries. Each of the resources listed here will produce different job title lists. Some job titles will appear again and again, while others will be unique to a particular source. Investigate them all!

Reference Books.   Books on the market that may be available through your local library or career counseling office also suggest various occupations related to a number of majors. The following are only two of the many good books on the market: *What Can I Do with a Major In . . . ? How to Choose and Use Your College Major,* by Lawrence R. Malnig with Anita Malnig, and *The Occupational Thesaurus. What Can I Do with a Major In . . . ?* lists job titles by academic major and identifies those jobs by their *Dictionary of Occupational Titles* (DOT) code (see following discussion).

....

> For history majors, approximately 50 job titles are listed. Some are familiar ones, such as teacher and genealogist, and others are interestingly different, such as ethnologist or art appraiser.
>
> The *Occupational Thesaurus* is another good resource, which essentially lists job title possibilities under general categories. So, if as a history major you discover cataloger as a job title in the book *What Can I Do with a Major in . . . ?,* you can then go to the *Occupational Thesaurus,* which lists scores of jobs under that title. Under "Libraries and Museums," there is a list of over eighteen associated job titles, including technical writing, editing, exhibit preparation, area studies and archival work. So if cataloger was a suggested job title for you, this source adds some depth by suggesting a number of different occupations within that field.

....

Each job title deserves your consideration. Like the layers of an onion, the search for job titles can go on and on! As you spend time doing this activity, you are actually learning more about the value of your degree. What's important in your search at this point is not to become critical or selective, but rather to develop as long a list of possibilities as you can. Every source used will help you add new and potentially exciting jobs to your growing list.

Want Ads.   It has been well publicized that newspaper want ads represent only about 10–15 percent of the current job market. Nevertheless, the Sunday want ads can be a great help to you in your search. Although they may not be the best place to look for a job, they can teach the job seeker much about the job market and provide a good education in job descriptions, duties and responsibilities, active industries, and some indication of the volume of job traffic. For our purposes, they are a good source for job titles to add to your list.

Read the Sunday want ads in a major market newspaper for several Sundays in a row. Circle and then cut out any and all ads that interest you and seem to call for something close to your education and experience. Remember, because want ads are written for what an organization *hopes* to find, you don't have to meet absolutely every criterion. However, if certain requirements are stated as absolute minimums and you cannot meet them, it's best not to waste your time.

A recent examination of *The Boston Sunday Globe* reveals the following possible occupations for a liberal arts major with some computer skills and limited prior work experience. (This is only a partial list of what was available.)

- ❑ Admissions representative
- ❑ Salesperson
- ❑ Compliance director
- ❑ Assistant principal gifts writer
- ❑ Public relations officer

- ❑ Technical writer
- ❑ Personnel trainee
- ❑ GED examiner
- ❑ Direct mail researcher
- ❑ Associate publicist

After performing this exercise for a few Sundays, you'll find you have collected a new library of job titles.

The Sunday want ad exercise is important because these jobs are out in the marketplace. They truly exist, and people with your qualifications are being sought to apply. What's more, many of these advertisements describe the duties and responsibilities of the job advertised and give you a beginning sense of the challenges and opportunities such a position presents. Some will indicate salary, and that will be helpful as well. This information will better define the jobs for you and provide some good material for possible interviews in that field.

Exploring Job Descriptions

Once you've arrived at a solid list of possible job titles that interest you and for which you believe you are somewhat qualified, it's a good idea to do some research on each of these jobs. The preeminent source for such job information is the *Dictionary of Occupational Titles,* or DOT. This directory lists every conceivable job and provides excellent up-to-date information on duties and responsibilities, interactions with associates, and day-to-day assignments and tasks. These descriptions provide a thorough job analysis, but they do not consider the possible employers or the environments in which this job may be performed. So, although a position as public relations officer may be well defined in terms of duties and responsibilities, it does not explain the differences in doing public relations work in a college or a hospital or a factory or a bank. You will need to look somewhere else for work settings.

Learning More about Possible Work Settings

After reading some job descriptions, you may choose to edit and revise your list of job titles once again, discarding those you feel are not suitable and keeping those that continue to hold your interest. Or you may wish to keep your list intact and see where these jobs may be located. For example, if you are interested in public relations and you appear to have those skills and the requisite education, you'll want to know what organizations do public relations. How can you find that out? How much income does someone in public relations make a year and what is the employment potential for the field of public relations?

To answer these and many other good questions about your list of job titles, we will direct you to any of the following resources: *Careers Encyclopedia, Career Information Center, College to Career: The Guide to Job Opportunities,* and the *Occupational Outlook Handbook.* Each of these books, in a different way, will help to put the job titles you have selected into an employer context. *VGM'S Handbook for Business and Management Careers* shows detailed career descriptions for over 50 fields. Entries include complete information on duties and responsibilities for individual careers and detailed entry-level requirements. There is information on working conditions and promotional opportunities as well. Salary ranges and career outlook projections are also provided. Perhaps the most extensive discussion is found in the *Occupational Outlook Handbook,* which gives a thorough presentation of the nature of the work, the working conditions, employment statistics, training, other qualifications, and advancement possibilities as well as job outlook and earnings. Related occupations are also detailed, and a select bibliography is provided to help you find additional information.

Continuing with our public relations example, your search through these reference materials would teach you that the public relations jobs you find attractive are available in larger hospitals, financial institutions, most corporations (both consumer goods and industrial goods), media organizations, and colleges and universities.

Networking to Get the Complete Story

You now have not only a list of job titles but also, for each of these job titles, a description of the work involved and a general list of possible employment settings in which to work. You'll want to do some reading and keep talking to friends, colleagues, teachers, and others about the possibilities. Don't neglect to ask if the career office at your college maintains some kind of alumni network. Often such alumni networks will connect you with another graduate from the college who is working in the job title or industry you are seeking information about. These career networkers offer what assistance they can. For some, it is a full day "shadowing" the alumnus as he or she goes about the job. Others offer partial day visits, tours, informational interviews, resume reviews, job postings, or, if distance prevents a visit, telephone interviews. As fellow graduates, they'll be frank and informative about their own jobs and prospects in their field.

Take them up on their offer and continue to learn all you can about your own personal list of job titles, descriptions, and employment settings. You'll probably continue to edit and refine this list as you learn more about the realities of the job, the possible salary, advancement opportunities, and supply and demand statistics.

In the next section, we'll describe how to find the specific organizations that represent these industries and employers, so that you can begin to make contact.

WHERE ARE THESE JOBS, ANYWAY?

Having a list of job titles that you've designed around your own career interests and skills is an excellent beginning. It means you've really thought about who you are and what you are presenting to the employment market. It has caused you to think seriously about the most appealing environments to work in, and you have identified some employer types that represent these environments.

The research and the thinking that you've done this far will be used again and again. It will be helpful in writing your resume and cover letters, in talking about yourself on the telephone to prospective employers, and in answering interview questions.

Now is a good time to begin to narrow the field of job titles and employment sites down to some specific employers to initiate the employment contact.

Finding Out Which Employers Hire People Like You

This section will provide tips, techniques, and specific resources for developing an actual list of specific employers that can be used to make contacts. It is only an outline that you must be prepared to tailor to your own particular needs and according to what you bring to the job search. Once again, it is important to stress the need to communicate with others along the way exactly what you're looking for and what your goals are for the research you're doing. Librarians, employers, career counselors, friends, friends of friends, business contacts, and bookstore staff will all have helpful information on geographically specific and new resources to aid you in locating employers who'll hire you.

Identifying Information Resources

Your interview wardrobe and your new resume may have put a dent in your wallet, but the resources you'll need to pursue your job search are available for free (although you might choose to copy materials on a machine instead of taking notes by hand). The categories of information detailed here are not hard to find and are yours for the browsing.

Numerous resources described in this section will help you identify actual employers. Use all of them or any others that you identify as available in your geographic area. As you become experienced in this process, you'll quickly figure out which information sources are helpful and which are not. If you live in a rural area, a well-planned day trip to a major city that includes a college career office, a large college or city library, state and federal employment centers, a chamber of commerce office, and a well-stocked bookstore can produce valuable results.

There are many excellent resources available to help you identify actual job sites. They are categorized into employer directories (usually indexed by product lines and geographic location), geographically based directories (designed to highlight particular cities, regions, or states), career-specific directories (e.g., *Sports Market Place,* which lists tens of thousands of firms involved with sports), periodicals and newspapers, targeted job posting publications, and videos. This is by no means meant to be a complete list of resources, but rather a starting point for identifying useful resources.

Working from the more general references to highly specific resources, we will provide a basic list to help you begin your search. Many of these you'll find easily available. In some cases, reference librarians and others will suggest even better materials for your particular situation. Start to create your own customized bibliography of job search references. Use copying services to save time and to allow you to carry away information about organization mission, location, company officers, phone numbers, and addresses.

Employer Directories.   There are many employer directories available to give you the kind of information you need for your job search. Some of our favorites are listed here, but be sure to ask the professionals you are working with to make additional suggestions.

❑ *America's Corporate Families* identifies many major U.S. ultimate parent companies and displays corporate family linkage of subsidiaries and divisions. Businesses can be identified by their industrial code.

❑ *Million Dollar Directory: America's Leading Public and Private Companies* lists about 160,000 companies.

❑ *Moody's* various manuals are intended as guides for investors, so they contain a history of each company. Each manual contains a classification of companies by industries and products.

- *Standard and Poor's Register of Corporations* contains listings for 45,000 businesses, some of which are not listed in the *Million Dollar Directory.*

- *Job Seeker's Guide to Private and Public Companies* profiles 15,000 employers in four volumes, each covering a different geographic region. Company entries include contact information, business descriptions, and application procedures.

- *The Career Guide: Dun's Employment Opportunities Directory* includes more than 5,000 large organizations, including hospitals and local governments. Profiles include an overview and history of the employer as well as opportunities, benefits, and contact names. It contains geographic and industrial indexes and indexes by discipline or internship availability. This guide also includes a state-by-state list of professional personnel consultants and their specialties.

- *Professional's Job Finder/Government Job Finder/Non-Profits Job Finder* are specific directories of job services, salary surveys, and periodical listings in which to find advertisements for jobs in the professional, government, or not-for-profit sector.

- *Opportunities in Nonprofit Organizations* is a VGM career series edition that opens up the world of not-for-profit by helping you match your interest profile to the aims and objectives of scores of nonprofit employers in business, education, health and medicine, social welfare, science and technology, and many others. There is also a special section on fundraising and development career paths.

- *The 100 Best Companies to Sell For* lists companies by industry and provides contact information and describes benefits and corporate culture.

- *The 100 Best Companies to Work For in America* rates organizations on several factors including opportunities, job security, and pay.

- *Companies That Care* lists organizations that the authors believe are family-friendly. One index organizes information by state.

- *Infotrac CD-ROM Business Index* covers business journals and magazines as well as news magazines and can provide information on public and private companies.

- *ABI/INFORM On Disc* (CD-ROM) indexes articles in over 800 journals.

Geographically Based Directories. The Job Bank series published by Bob Adams, Inc. contains detailed entries on each area's major employers, including business activity, address, phone number, and hiring contact name. Many listings specify educational backgrounds being sought in potential employees. Each volume contains a solid discussion of each city's or state's major employment sectors. Organizations are also indexed by industry. Job Bank volumes are available for the following places: Atlanta, Boston, Chicago, Denver, Dallas–Ft. Worth, Florida, Houston, Ohio, St. Louis, San Francisco, Seattle, Los Angeles, New York, Detroit, Philadelphia, Minneapolis, the Northwest, and Washington, D.C.

National Job Bank lists employers in every state, along with contact names and commonly hired job categories. Included are many small companies often overlooked by other directories. Companies are also indexed by industry. This publication provides information on educational backgrounds sought and lists company benefits.

Career-Specific Directories.   VGM publishes a number of excellent series detailing careers for college graduates. In the *Professional Career Series* are guides to careers in the following fields, among others:

- Advertising

- Communications

- Business

- Computers

- Health Care

- High Tech

Each provides an excellent discussion of the industry, educational requirements for jobs, salary ranges, duties, and projected outlooks for the field.

Another VGM series, *Opportunities In . . .,* has an equally wide range of titles relating to your major, such as the following:

- *Opportunities in Banking*

- *Opportunities in Insurance*

- *Opportunities in Sports and Athletics*

- *Opportunities in Journalism*

- *Opportunities in Marketing*

- *Opportunities in Television and Radio*

Sports Market Place (Sportsguide) lists organizations by sport. It also describes trade/professional associations, college athletic organizations, multi-sport publications, media contacts, corporate sports sponsors, promotion/event/athletic management services, and trade shows.

Periodicals and Newspapers. Several sources are available to help you locate which journals or magazines carry job advertisements in your field. Other resources help you identify opportunities in other parts of the country.

❑ *Where the Jobs Are: A Comprehensive Directory of 1200 Journals Listing Career Opportunities* links specific occupational titles to corresponding periodicals that carry job listings for your field.

❑ *Social & Behavioral Sciences Jobs Handbook* contains a periodicals matrix organized by academic discipline and highlights periodicals containing job listings.

❑ *National Business Employment Weekly* compiles want ads from four regional editions of the *Wall Street Journal.* Most are business and management positions.

❑ *National Ad Search* reprints ads from 75 metropolitan newspapers across the country. Although the focus is on management positions, technical and professional postings are also included. *Caution:* Watch deadline dates carefully on listings, because deadlines may have already passed by the time the ad is printed.

❑ *The Federal Jobs Digest* and *Federal Career Opportunities* list government positions.

❑ *World Chamber of Commerce Directory* lists addresses for chambers worldwide, state boards of tourism, convention and visitors' bureaus, and economic development organizations.

This list is certainly not exhaustive; use it to begin your job search work.

Targeted Job Posting Publications. Although the resources that follow are national in scope, they are either targeted to one medium of contact (telephone), focused on specific types of jobs, or are less comprehensive than the sources previously listed.

❑ *Job Hotlines USA* pinpoints over 1,000 hard-to-find telephone numbers for companies and government agencies that use prerecorded job messages and listings. Very few of the telephone numbers listed are toll-free, and sometimes recordings are long, so callers beware!

❑ *The Job Hunter* is a national biweekly newspaper listing business, arts, media, government, human services, health, community-related, and student services job openings.

❑ *Current Jobs for Graduates* is a national employment listing for liberal arts professions, including editorial positions, management opportunities, museum work, teaching, and nonprofit work.

- *Environmental Opportunities* serves environmental job interests nation-wide by listing administrative, marketing, and human resources positions along with education-related jobs and positions directly related to a degree in an environmental field.

- *Y National Vacancy List* shows YMCA professional vacancies, including development, administration, programming, membership, and recreation postings.

- *ARTSearch* is a national employment service bulletin for the arts, including administration, managerial, marketing, and financial management jobs.

- *Community Jobs* is an employment newspaper for the nonprofit sector that provides a variety of listings, including project manager, canvas director, government relations specialist, community organizer, and program instructor.

- *College Placement Council Annual: A Guide to Employment Opportunities for College Graduates* is an annual guide containing solid job-hunting information and, more importantly, displaying ads from large corporations actively seeking recent college graduates in all majors. Company profiles provide brief descriptions and available employment opportunities. Contact names and addresses are given. Profiles are indexed by organization name, geographic location, and occupation.

Videos.   You may be one of the many job seekers who like to get information via a medium other than paper. Many career libraries, public libraries, and career centers in libraries carry an assortment of videos that will help you learn new techniques and get information helpful in the job search. A small sampling of the multitude of videos now available includes the following:

- *The Skills Search* (20 min.) discusses three types of skills important in the workplace, how to present the skills in an interview, and how to respond to problem questions.

- *Effective Answers to Interview Questions* (35 min.) presents two real-life job seekers and shows how they realized the true meaning of interview questions and formulated positive answers.

- *Employer's Expectations* (33 min.) covers three areas that are important to all employers: appearance, dependability, and skills.

❑ *The Tough New Labor Market of the 1990s* (30 min.) presents labor market facts as well as suggestions on what job seekers should do to gain employment in this market.

❑ *Dialing for Jobs: Using the Phone in the Job Search* (30 min.) describes how to use the phone effectively to gain information and arrange interviews by following two new graduates as they learn and apply techniques.

Locating Information Resources

An essay by John Case that appeared in the *Boston Globe* (August 25, 1993) alerts both new and seasoned job seekers that the job market is changing, and the old guarantees of lifelong employment no longer hold true. Some of our major corporations, which were once seen as the most prestigious of employment destinations, are now laying off thousands of employees. Middle management is especially hard hit in downsizing situations. On the other side of the coin, smaller, more entrepreneurial firms are adding employees and realizing enormous profit margins. The geography of the new job market is unfamiliar, and the terrain is much harder to map. New and smaller firms can mean different kinds of jobs and new job titles. The successful job seeker will keep an open mind about where he or she might find employment and what that employment might be called.

In order to become familiar with this new terrain, you will need to undertake some research, which can be done at any of the following locations:

❑ Public libraries

❑ Business organizations

❑ Employment agencies

❑ Bookstores

❑ Career libraries

Each one of these places offers a collection of resources that will help you get the information you need.

As you meet and talk with service professionals at all these sites, be sure to let them know what you're doing. Inform them of your job search, what you've already accomplished, and what you're looking for. The more people who know you're job seeking, the greater the possibility that someone will have information or know someone who can help you along your way.

Public Libraries. Large city libraries, college and university libraries, and even well-supported town library collections contain a variety of resources to help you conduct a job search. It is not uncommon for libraries to have separate "vocational choices" sections with books, tapes, and associated materials relating to job search and selection. Some are now even making resume creation software available for use by patrons.

Some of the publications we name throughout this book are expensive reference items that are rarely purchased by individuals. In addition, libraries carry a wide range of newspapers and telephone yellow pages as well as the usual array of books. If resources are not immediately available, many libraries have loan arrangements with other facilities and can make information available to you relatively quickly.

Take advantage of not only the reference collections, but also the skilled and informed staff. Let them know exactly what you are looking for, and they'll have their own suggestions. You'll be visiting the library frequently, and the reference staff will soon come to know who you are and what you're working on. They'll be part of your job search network!

Business Organizations.   Chambers of Commerce, Offices of New Business Development, Councils on Business and Industry, Small Business Administration (SBA) offices, and professional associations can all provide geographically specific lists of companies and organizations that have hiring needs. They also have an array of other available materials, including visitors' guides and regional fact books that provide additional employment information.

These agencies serve to promote local and regional businesses and ensure their survival and success. Although these business organizations do not advertise job openings or seek employees for their members, they may be very aware of staffing needs among their member firms. In your visits to each of these locations, spend some time with the personnel getting to know who they are and what they do. Let them know of your job search and your intentions regarding employment. You may be surprised and delighted at the information they may provide.

Employment Agencies.   Employment agencies, including state and federal employment offices, professional "head hunters" or executive search firms, and some private career counselors can provide direct leads to job openings. Don't overlook these resources. If you are mounting a complete job search program and want to ensure that you are covering the potential market for employers, consider the employment agencies in your territory. Some of these organizations work contractually with several specific firms and may have access that is unavailable to you. Others may be particularly well informed about supply and demand in particular industries or geographic locations.

In the case of professional (commercial) employment agencies, which include those executive recruitment firms labeled "head hunters," you should be cautious about entering into any binding contractual agreement. Before doing so, be sure to get the information you need to decide whether their services can be of use to you. Questions to ask include the following: Who pays the fee when employment is obtained? Are there any other fees or costs associated with this service? What is their placement rate? Can you see a list of previous clients and can you talk to any for references? Do they typically work with entry-level job seekers? Do they tend to focus on particular kinds of employment or industries?

A few cautions are in order, however, when you work with professional agencies. Remember, the professional employment agency is, in most cases, paid by the hiring organization. Naturally, their interest and attention is largely directed to the employer, not to the candidate. Of course, they want to provide good candidates to guarantee future contracts, but they are less interested in the job seeker than the employer.

For teacher candidates, there are a number of good placement firms that charge the prospective teacher, not the employer. This situation has evolved over time as a result of supply and demand and financial structuring of most school systems, which cannot spend money on recruiting teachers. Usually these firms charge a nonrefundable administrative fee and, upon successful placement, require a fee based on percentage of salary, which may range from 10–20 percent of annual compensation. Often, this can be repaid over a number of months. Check your contract carefully.

State and federal employment offices are no-fee services that maintain extensive "job boards" and can provide detailed specifications for each job advertised and help with application forms. Because government employment application forms are detailed, keep a master copy along with copies of all additional documentation (resumes, educational transcripts, military discharge papers, proof of citizenship, etc.). Successive applications may require separate filings. Visit these offices as frequently as you can, because most deal with applicants on a "walk-in" basis and will not telephone prospective candidates or maintain files of job seekers. Check your telephone book for the address of the nearest state and federal offices.

One type of employment service that causes much confusion among job seekers is the outplacement firm. Their advertisements tend to suggest they will put you in touch with the "hidden job market." They use advertising phrases such as "We'll work with you until you get that job," or "Maximize your earnings and career opportunities." In fact, if you read the fine print on these ads, you will notice these firms must state they are "Not an employment agency." These firms are, in fact, corporate and private outplacement counseling agencies whose work involves resume editing, counseling to provide leads for jobs, interview skills training, and all the other aspects of hiring preparation. They do this for a fee, sometimes in the thousands of dollars, which is paid by you, the client. Some of these firms have good reputations and provide excellent materials and techniques. Most, however, provide a service you as a college student or graduate can receive free from your alma mater or through a reciprocity agreement between your college and a college or university located closer to your current address.

Bookstores. Any well-stocked bookstore will carry some job search books that are worth buying. Some major stores will even have an extensive section devoted to materials, including excellent videos, related to the job search process. Several possibilities are listed in following sections. You will also find copies of local newspapers and business magazines. The one advantage that is provided by resources purchased at a bookstore is that you can read and work with the information in the comfort of your own home and do not have to conform to the hours of operation of a library, which can present real difficulties if you are working full time as you seek employment. A few minutes spent browsing in a bookstore might be a beneficial break from your job search activities and turn up valuable resources.

Career Libraries. Career libraries, which are found in career centers at colleges and universities and sometimes within large public libraries, contain a unique blend of the job search resources housed in other settings. In addition, career libraries often purchase a number of job listing publications, each of which targets a specific industry or type of job. You may find job listings specifically for entry-level positions for liberal arts majors. Ask about job posting newsletters or newspapers specifically focused on careers in the area that most interests you. Each center will be unique, but you are certain to discover some good sources of jobs.

Most college career libraries now hold growing collections of video material on specific industries and on aspects of your job search process, including dress and appearance, how to manage the luncheon or dinner interview, how to be effective at a job fair, and many other specific titles. Some larger corporations produce handsome video materials detailing the variety of career paths and opportunities available in their organizations.

Some career libraries also house computer-based career planning and information systems. These interactive computer programs help you to clarify your values and interests and will combine that with your education to provide possible job titles and industry locations. Some even contain extensive lists of graduate school programs.

One specific kind of service a career library will be able to direct you to is computerized job search services. These services, of which there are many, are run by private companies, individual colleges, or consortiums of colleges. They attempt to match qualified job candidates with potential employers. The candidate submits a resume (or an application) to the service. This information (which can be categorized into hundreds of separate "fields" of data) is entered into a computer database. Your information is then compared with the information from employers about what they desire in a prospective employee. If there is a "match" between what they want and what you have indicated you can offer, the job search service or the employer will contact you directly to continue the process.

Computerized job search services can complement an otherwise complete job search program. They are *not,* however, a substitute for the kinds of activities described in this book. They are essentially passive operations that are random in nature. If you have not listed skills, abilities, traits, experiences, or education *exactly* as an employer has listed its needs, there is simply no match.

Consult with the staff members at the career libraries you use. These professionals have been specifically trained to meet the unique needs you present. Often you can just drop in and receive help with general questions, or you may want to set up an appointment to speak one-on-one with a career counselor to gain special assistance.

Every career library is different in size and content, but each can provide valuable information for the job search. Some may even provide some limited counseling. If you have not visited the career library at your college or alma mater, call and ask if these collections are still available for your use. Be sure to ask about other services that you can use as well.

If you are not near your own college as you work on your job search, call the career office and inquire about reciprocal agreements with other colleges that are closer to where you live. Very often, your own alma mater can arrange for you to use a limited menu of services at another school. This typically would include access to a career library and job posting information and might include limited counseling.

CHAPTER FOUR

NETWORKING

etworking is the process of deliberately establishing relationships to get career-related information or to alert potential employers that you are available for work. Networking is critically important to today's job seeker for two reasons: it will help you get the information you need, and it can help you find out about *all* of the available jobs.

Getting the Information You Need

Networkers will review your resume and give you candid feedback on its effectiveness. They will talk about the job you are looking for and give you a candid appraisal of how they see your strengths and weaknesses. If they have a good sense of the industry or the employment sector for that job, you'll get their feelings on future trends in the industry as well. Some networkers will be very candid about salaries, job hunting techniques, and suggestions for your job search strategy. Many have been known to place calls right from the interview desk to friends and associates that might be interested in you. Each networker will make his or her own contribution, and each will be valuable.

Because organizations must evolve to adapt to current global market needs, the information provided by decision makers within various organizations will be critical to your success as a new job market entrant. For example, you might learn about the concept of virtual organizations from a networker. Virtual organizations are those that are temporarily established to take advantage of fast-changing opportunities and then dissolved. This concept is being discussed and implemented by chief executive officers of many organizations, including Corning, Apple, and Digital. Networking can help you find out about this and other trends currently affecting the industries under your consideration.

Finding Out about All of the Available Jobs

Secondly, not every job that is available at this very moment is advertised for potential applicants to see. This is called the *hidden job market.* Only 15–20 percent of all jobs are formally advertised, which means that 80–85 percent of available jobs do not appear in published channels. Networking will help you become more knowledgeable about all the employment opportunities available during your job search period.

Although someone you might talk to today doesn't know of any openings within his or her organization, tomorrow or next week or next month an opening may occur. If you've taken the time to show an interest in and knowledge of their organization, if you've shown the company representative how you can help achieve organizational goals and that you can fit into the organization, you'll be one of the first candidates considered for the position.

Networking: A Proactive Approach

Networking is a proactive rather than a reactive approach. You, as a job seeker, are expected to initiate a certain level of activity on your own behalf; you cannot afford to simply respond to jobs listed in the newspaper. Being proactive means building a network of contacts that includes informed and interested decision makers who will provide you with up-to-date knowledge of the current job market and increase your chances of finding out about employment opportunities appropriate for your interests, experience, and level of education.

An old axiom of networking says, "You are only two phone calls away from the information you need." In other words, by talking to enough people, you will quickly come across someone who can offer you help. Start with your professors. Each of them probably has a wide circle of contacts. In their work and travel they might have met someone who can help you or direct you to someone who can.

Control and the Networking Process

In deliberately establishing relationships, the process of networking begins with you in control—*you* are contacting specific individuals. As your network expands and you establish a set of professional relationships, your search for information or jobs will begin to move outside of your total control. A part of the networking process involves others assisting you by gathering information for you or recommending you as a possible job candidate. As additional people become a part of your networking system, you will have less knowledge about activities undertaken on your behalf; you will undoubtedly be contacted by individuals whom you did not initially approach. If you want to function effectively in surprise situations, you must be prepared at all times to talk with strangers about the informational or employment needs that motivated you to become involved in the networking process.

PREPARING TO NETWORK

In deliberately establishing relationships, maximize your efforts by organizing your approach. Five specific areas in which you can organize your efforts include reviewing your self-assessment, reviewing your research on job sites and organizations, deciding who it is you want to talk to, keeping track of all your efforts, and creating your self-promotion tools.

Review Your Self-Assessment

Your self-assessment is as important a tool in preparing to network as it has been in other aspects of your job search. You have carefully evaluated your personal traits, personal values, economic needs, longer-term goals, skill base, preferred skills, and underdeveloped skills. During the networking process you will be called upon to communicate what you know about yourself and relate it to the information or job you seek. Be sure to review the exercises that you completed in the self-assessment section of this book in preparation for networking. We've explained that you need to assess what skills you have acquired from your major that are of general value to an employer and to be ready to express those in ways employers can appreciate as useful in their own organizations.

Review Researching Job Sites and Organizations

In addition, individuals assisting you will expect that you'll have at least some background information on the occupation or industry of interest to you. Refer to the appropriate sections of this book and other relevant publications to acquire the background information necessary for effective networking. They'll explain how to identify not only the job titles that might be of interest to you, but also what kinds of organizations employ people to do that job. You will develop some sense of working conditions and expectations about duties and responsibilities—all of which will be of help in your networking interviews.

Decide Who It Is You Want to Talk To

Networking cannot begin until you decide who it is that you want to talk to and, in general, what type of information you hope to gain from your contacts. Once you know this, it's time to begin developing a list of contacts. Five useful sources for locating contacts are described here.

College Alumni Network.   Most colleges and universities have created a formal network of alumni and friends of the institution who are particularly interested in helping currently enrolled students and graduates of their alma mater gain employment-related information.

....

Because history is a classic degree program, you'll find an abundance of history graduates spanning the full spectrum of possible employment. Just the diversity of employment evidenced by such an alumni list should be encouraging and informative to the history graduate. Among such a diversified group, there are likely to be scores you would enjoy talking with and perhaps could meet.

....

It is usually a simple process to make use of an alumni network. You need only visit the alumni or career office at your college or university and follow the procedure that has been established. Often, you will simply complete a form indicating your career goals and interests and you will be given the names of appropriate individuals to contact. In many cases, staff members will coach you on how to make the best use of the limited time these alumni contacts may have available for you.

Alumni networkers may provide some combination of the following services: day-long shadowing experiences, telephone interviews, in-person interviews, information on relocating to given geographic areas, internship information, suggestions on graduate school study, and job vacancy notices.

....

What a valuable experience! If you are interested in a government position, you may be concerned about your history degree and its relevance for certain federal positions. Spending a day with an alumnus in government service whose academic credentials include the same degree you are seeking, asking questions about their preparedness for the job, and observing firsthand how they have transferred their academic skills to their new job, will be a far better career decision criteria for you than any reading on the subject could possibly provide.

In addition to your own observations, the alumnus will have his or her own perspective on the relevancy of your degree to a government career and which settings may utilize more of your skills and attributes and which may not.

....

Present and Former Supervisors. If you believe you are on good terms with present or former job supervisors, they may be an excellent resource for providing information or directing you to appropriate resources that would have information related to your current interests and needs. Additionally, these supervisors probably belong to professional organizations, which they might be willing to utilize to get information for you.

....

If, for example, you were interested in working as a guide or interpreter at a historic site, such as a reconstructed town or village, and you are currently working on the wait staff of a local restaurant, talk with your supervisor or the owner. He or she may belong to the local Chamber of Commerce, whose director might have information on members affiliated with historical operations in your area. You would probably be able to obtain the names and telephone numbers of those people, which would allow you to begin the networking process.

....

Employers in Your Area.   Although you may be interested in working in a geographic location different from the one where you currently reside, don't overlook the value of the knowledge and contacts those around you are able to provide. Use the local telephone directory and newspaper to identify the types of organizations you are thinking of working for or professionals who have the kinds of jobs you are interested in. Recently, a call made to a local hospital's financial administrator for information on working in health care financial administration yielded more pertinent information on training seminars, regional professional organizations, and potential employment sites than a national organization was willing to provide.

Employers in Geographic Areas Where You Hope to Work.   If you are thinking about relocating, identifying prospective employers or informational contacts in this new location will be critical to your success. Many resources are available to help you locate contact names. These include the yellow pages directory, the local newspapers, local or state business publications, and local Chambers of Commerce.

Professional Associations and Organizations.   Professional associations and organizations can provide valuable information in several areas: career paths that you may not have considered, qualifications relating to those career choices, publications that list current job openings, and workshops or seminars that will enhance your professional knowledge and skills. They can also be excellent sources for background information on given industries: their health, current problems, and future challenges.

There are several excellent resources available to help you locate professional associations and organizations that would have information to meet your needs. Two especially useful publications are the *Encyclopedia of Associations* and the *National Trade and Professional Associations of the United States.*

Keep Track of All Your Efforts

It can be difficult, almost impossible, to remember all the details related to each contact you make during the networking process, so you will want to develop a record-keeping system that works for you. Formalize this process by using a notebook or index cards to organize the information you gather. Begin by creating a list of the people or organizations you want to contact. Record the contact's name, address, telephone number, and what information you hope to gain. Each entry might look something like this:

Contact Name	Address	Phone #	Purpose
Mr. Tim Keefe	Wrigley Bldg.		
Dir. of Mines	Suite 72	555-8906	Resume screen

Once you have created this initial list, it will be helpful to keep more detailed information as you begin to actually make the contacts. Using the Network Contact Record form in Exhibit 4.1, keep good information on all your network contacts. They'll appreciate your recall of details of your meetings and conversations, and the information will help you to focus your networking efforts.

Exhibit 4.1

Network Contact Record

Name: Be certain your spelling is absolutely correct.

Title: Pick up a business card to be certain of the correct title.

Employing organization: Note any parent company or subsidiaries.

Business mailing address: This is often different from the street address.

Business telephone number: Include area code/alternative numbers/fax.

Source for this contact: Who referred you, and what is their relationship?

continued

---

continued

Date of call or letter: Use plenty of space here to record multiple phone calls or visits, other employees you may have met, names of secretaries/ receptionists, etc.

Content of discussion: Keep enough notes here to remind you of the substance of your visits and telephone conversations in case some time elapses between contacts.

Follow-up necessary to continue working with this contact:
Your contact may request that you send them some materials or direct you to contact an associate. Note any such instructions or assignments in this space.

Name of additional networker: Here you would record the names
Address: and phone numbers of additional
Phone: contacts met at this employer's
Name of additional networker: site. Often you will be introduced to
Address: many people, some of whom may
Phone: indicate a willingness to help in
Name of additional networker: your job search.
Address: ——————————————
Phone: ——————————————

Date thank-you note written: May help to date your next contact.

Follow-up action taken: Phone calls, visits, additional notes.

Other miscellaneous notes: Record any other additional interaction you may find is important to remember in working with this networking client. You will want this form in front of you when telephoning or just before and after a visit.

Create Your Self-Promotion Tools

There are two types of promotional tools that are used in the networking process. The first is a resume and cover letter, and the second is a one-minute "infomercial," which may be given over the telephone or in person.

Techniques for writing an effective resume and cover letter are covered in Chapter 2. Once you have reviewed that material and prepared these important documents, you will have created one of your self-promotion tools.

The one-minute infomercial will demand that you begin tying your interests, abilities, and skills to the people or organizations you want to network with. Think about your goal for making the contact to help you understand what you should say about yourself. You should be able to express yourself easily and convincingly. If, for example, you are contacting an alumna of your institution to obtain the names of possible employment sites in a distant city, be prepared to discuss why you are interested in moving to that location, the types of jobs you are interested in, and the skills and abilities you possess that will make you a qualified candidate.

To create a meaningful one-minute infomercial, write it out, practice it if it will be a spoken presentation, rewrite it, and practice it again if necessary until expressing yourself comes easily and is convincing.

Here's a simplified example of an infomercial for use over the telephone:

· ·

Hello, Mr. Lilla? My name is Allison Parks. I am a recent graduate of West Coast College, and I wish to enter the information specialist field. I feel confident I have many of the skills I understand are valued in information management. I have a strong background in history, with some good research and computer skills to go along with that degree. What's more, I am thorough and exacting and work well under pressure, which I understand can be a real advantage in this business!

Mr. Lilla, I'm calling you because I still need more information about the information specialist field. I'm hoping you'll have the time to sit down with me for about half an hour and discuss your perspectives on careers in information management with me. There are so many possible employers to approach, and I am seeking some advice on which might be the best bet for my particular combination of skills and experiences.

Would you be willing to do that for me? I would greatly appreciate it. I am available most mornings, if that's convenient for you.

· ·

Other effective self-promotion tools include portfolios for those in the arts, writing professions, or teaching. Portfolios show examples of work, photographs of projects or classroom activities, or certificates and credentials that are job related. There may not be an opportunity to use the portfolio during an interview, and it is not something that should be left with the organization. It is designed to be explained and displayed by the creator. However, during some networking meetings, there may be an opportunity to illustrate a point or strengthen a qualification by exhibiting the portfolio.

BEGINNING THE NETWORKING PROCESS

Set the Tone for Your Contacts

It can be useful to establish "tone words" for any communications you embark upon. Before making your first telephone call or writing your first letter, decide what you want your contact to think of you. If you are networking to try to obtain a job, your tone words might include works like *genuine, informed,* and *self-knowledgeable.* When trying to acquire information, your tone words may have a slightly different focus, such as *courteous, organized, focused,* and *well spoken.* Use the tone words you establish for your contacts to guide you through the networking process.

Honestly Express Your Intentions

When contacting individuals, it is important to be honest about your reasons for making the contact. Establish your purpose in your own mind and be able and ready to articulate it concisely. Determine an initial agenda, whether it be informational questioning or self-promotion, present it to your contact, and be ready to respond immediately. If you don't adequately prepare before initiating your contacts, you may find yourself at a disadvantage if you're asked to immediately begin your informational interview or self-promotion during the first phone conversation or visit.

Start Networking within Your Circle of Confidence

Once you have organized your approach—by utilizing specific researching methods, creating a system for keeping track of the people you will contact, and developing effective self-promotion tools—you are ready to begin networking. The best place to begin networking is by talking with a group of people you trust and feel comfortable with. This group is usually made up of your family, friends, and career counselors. No matter who is in this inner circle, they will have a special interest in seeing you succeed in your job search. In addition, because they will be easy to talk to, you should try taking some risks in terms of practicing your information-seeking approach. Gain confidence in talking about the strengths you bring to an organization and the underdeveloped skills you feel hinder your candidacy. Be sure to review the section on self-assessment for tips on approaching each of these areas. Ask for critical but constructive feedback from the people in your circle of confidence on the letters you write and the one-minute infomercial you have developed. Evaluate whether you want to make the changes they suggest, then practice the changes on others within this circle.

Stretch the Boundaries of Your Networking Circle of Confidence

Once you have refined the promotional tools you will use to accomplish your networking goals, you will want to make additional contacts. Because you will not know most of these people, it will be a less comfortable activity to undertake. The practice that you gained with your inner circle of trusted friends should have prepared you to now move outside of that comfort zone.

It is said that any information a person needs is only two phone calls away, but the information cannot be gained until you (1) make a reasonable guess about who might have the information you need and (2) pick up the telephone to make the call. Using your network list that includes alumni, instructors, supervisors, employers, and associations, you can begin preparing your list of questions that will allow you to get the information you need. Review the question list shown below and then develop a list of your own.

Questions You Might Want to Ask

1. In the position you now hold, what do you do on a typical day?

2. What are the most interesting aspects of your job?

3. What part of your work do you consider dull or repetitive?

4. What were the jobs you had that led to your present position?

5. How long does it usually take to move from one step to the next in this career path?

6. What is the top position to which you can aspire in this career path?

7. What is the next step in *your* career path?

8. Are there positions in this field that are similar to your position?

9. What are the required qualifications and training for entry-level positions in this field?

10. Are there specific courses a student should take to be qualified to work in this field?

11. What are the entry-level jobs in this field?

12. What types of training are provided to persons entering this field?

13. What are the salary ranges your organization typically offers to entry-level candidates for positions in this field?

14. What special advice would you give a person entering this field?

15. Do you see this field as a growing one?

16. How do you see the content of the entry-level jobs in this field changing over the next two years?

17. What can I do to prepare myself for these changes?

18. What is the best way to obtain a position that will start me on a career in this field?

19. Do you have any information on job specifications and descriptions that I may have?

20. What related occupational fields would you suggest I explore?

21. How could I improve my resume for a career in this field?

22. Who else would you suggest I talk to, both in your organization and in other organizations?

Questions You Might Have to Answer

In order to communicate effectively, you must anticipate questions that will be asked of you by the networkers you contact. Review the list below and see if you can easily answer each of these questions. If you cannot, it may be time to revisit the self-assessment process.

1. Where did you get my name, or how did you find out about this organization?

2. What are your career goals?

3. What kind of job are you interested in?

4. What do you know about this organization and this industry?

5. How do you know you're prepared to undertake an entry-level position in this industry?

6. What course work have you taken that is related to your career interests?

7. What are your short-term career goals?

8. What are your long-term career goals?

9. Do you plan to obtain additional formal education?

10. What contributions have you made to previous employers?

11. Which of your previous jobs have you enjoyed the most, and why?

12. What are you particularly good at doing?

13. What shortcomings have you had to face in previous employment?

14. What are your three greatest strengths?

15. Describe how comfortable you feel with your communication style.

General Networking Tips

Make Every Contact Count.   Setting the tone for each interaction is critical. Approaches that will help you communicate in an effective way include politeness, being appreciative of time provided to you, and being prepared and thorough. Remember, *everyone* within an organization has a circle of influence, so be prepared to interact effectively with each person you encounter in the networking process, including secretarial and support staff. Many information or job seekers have thwarted their own efforts by being rude to some individuals they encountered as they networked because they made the incorrect assumption that certain persons were unimportant.

Sometimes your contacts may be surprised at their ability to help you. After meeting and talking with you, they might think they have not offered much in the way of help. A day or two later, however, they may make a contact that would be useful to you and refer you to it.

With Each Contact, Widen Your Circle of Networkers.   Always leave an informational interview with the names of at least two more people who can help you get the information or job that you are seeking. Don't be shy about asking for additional contacts; networking is all about increasing the number of people you can interact with to achieve your goals.

Make Your Own Decisions.   As you talk with different people and get answers to the questions you pose, you may hear conflicting information or get conflicting suggestions. Your job is to listen to these "experts" and decide what information and which suggestions will help you achieve *your* goals. Only implement those suggestions that you believe will work for you.

SHUTTING DOWN YOUR NETWORK

As you achieve the goals that motivated your networking activity—getting the information you need or the job you want—the time will come to inactivate all or parts of your network. As you do so, be sure to tell your primary supporters about your change in status. Call or write to each one of them and give them as many details about your new status as you feel is necessary to maintain a positive relationship.

Because a network takes on a life of its own, activity undertaken on your behalf will continue even after you cease your efforts. As you get calls or are contacted in some fashion, be sure to inform these networkers about your change in status, and thank them for assistance they have provided.

Information on the latest employment trends indicates that workers will change jobs or careers several times in their lifetime. If you carefully and thoughtfully conduct your networking activities now, you will have solid experience when you need to network again.

CHAPTER FIVE

INTERVIEWING

ertainly, there can be no one part of the job search process more fraught with anxiety and worry than the interview. Yet seasoned job seekers welcome the interview and will often say, "Just get me an interview and I'm on my way!" They understand that the interview is crucial to the hiring process and equally crucial for them, as job candidates, to have the opportunity of a personal dialogue to add to what the employer may already have learned from a resume, cover letter, and telephone conversations.

Believe it or not, the interview is to be welcomed, and even enjoyed! It is a perfect opportunity for you, the candidate, to sit down with an employer and express yourself and display who you are and what you want. Of course, it takes thought and planning and a little strategy; after all, it *is* a job interview! But it can be a positive, if not pleasant, experience and one you can look back on and feel confident about your performance and effort.

For many new job seekers, a job, any job, seems a wonderful thing. But seasoned interview veterans know that the job interview is an important step for both sides—the employer and the candidate—to see what each has to offer and whether there is going to be a "fit" of personalities, work styles, and attitudes. And it is this concept of balance in the interview, that both sides have important parts to play, that holds the key to success in mastering this aspect of the job search strategy.

Try to think of the interview as a conversation between two interested and equal partners. You both have important, even vital, information to deliver and to learn. Of course, there's no denying the employer has some leverage, especially in the initial interview for recruitment or any interview scheduled by the candidate and not the recruiter. That should not prevent the interviewee from seeking to play an equal part in what should be a fair exchange of information. Too often the untutored candidate allows the interview to become one-sided. The employer asks all the questions and the candidate simply responds. The ideal would be for two mutually interested parties to sit down and discuss possibilities for each. For this is a *conversation of significance,* and it requires pre-interview preparation, thought about the tone of the interview, and planning of the nature and details of the information to be exchanged.

PREPARING FOR THE INTERVIEW

Most initial interviews are about 30 minutes long. Given the brevity, the information that is exchanged ought to be important. The candidate should be delivering material that the employer cannot discover on the resume and, in turn, the candidate should be learning things about the employer that he or she could not otherwise find out. After all, if you have only 30 minutes, why waste time on information that is already published? Not all the information exchanged is factual, and both sides will learn much from what they see of each other, as well. How the candidate looks, speaks, and acts is important to the employer. The employer's attention to the interview and awareness of the candidate's resume, the setting, and the quality of information presented are important to the candidate.

Just as the employer has every right to be disappointed when a prospect is late for the interview, looks unkempt, and seems ill prepared to answer fairly standard questions, the candidate may be disappointed with an interviewer who isn't ready for the meeting, hasn't learned the basic resume facts, and is constantly interrupted for telephone calls. In either situation, there's good reason to feel let down.

There are many elements to a successful interview, and some of them are not easy to describe or prepare for. Sometimes there is just a chemistry between interviewer and interviewee that brings out the best in both, and a good exchange takes place. But there is much the candidate can do to pave the way for success in terms of his or her resume, personal appearance, goals, and interview strategy—each of which we will discuss. However, none of this preparation is as important as the time and thought the candidate gives to personal self-assessment.

Self-Assessment
Neither a stunning resume nor an expensive, well-tailored suit can compensate for candidates who do not know what they want, where they are going, or why they are interviewing with a particular employer. Self-assessment, the process by which we begin to know and acknowledge our own particular blend of education, experiences, needs, and goals is not something that can be sorted out the weekend before a major interview. Of all the elements of interview preparation, this one requires the longest lead time and cannot be faked.

Because the time allotted for most interviews is brief, it is all the more important for job candidates to understand and express succinctly why they are there and what they have to offer. This is not a time for undue modesty or for braggadocio, either; but it is a time for a compelling, reasoned statement of why you feel that you and this employer might make a good match. It means you have to have thought about your skills, interests, and attributes; related those to your life experiences and your own history of challenges and opportunities; and determined what that indicates about your strengths, preferences, values, and areas needing further development.

A common complaint of employers is that many candidates didn't take advantage of the interview time, didn't seem to know why they were there or what they wanted. When asked to talk about themselves and their work-related skills and attributes, employers don't want to be faced with shyness or embarrassed laughter; they need to know about you so they can make a fair determination of you and your competition. If you lose the opportunity to make a case for your employability, you can be certain the person ahead of you has or the person after you will, and it will be on the strength of those impressions that the employer will hire.

If you need some assistance with self-assessment issues, refer to Chapter 1. Included are suggested exercises that can be done as needed, such as making up an experiential diary and extracting obvious strengths and weaknesses from past experiences. These simple, pen-and-paper assignments will help you look at past activities as collections of tasks with accompanying skills and responsibilities. Don't overlook your high school or college career office, as well. Many offer personal counseling on self-assessment issues and may provide testing instruments such as the Myers-Briggs Type Indicator (MBTI)®, the Harrington-O'Shea Career Decision Making® System (CDM), the Strong Interest Inventory (SII)®, or any of a wide selection of assessment tools that can help you clarify some of these issues prior to the interview stage of your job search.

The Resume

Resume preparation has been discussed in detail, and some basic examples of various types were provided. In this section, we want to concentrate on how best to use your resume in the interview. In most cases, the employer will have seen the resume prior to the interview, and, in fact, it may well have been the quality of that resume that secured the interview opportunity.

An interview is a conversation, however, and not an exercise in reading. So, if the employer hasn't seen your resume and you have brought it along to the interview, wait until asked or until the end of the interview to offer it. Otherwise, you may find yourself staring at the back of your resume and simply answering "Yes" and "No" to a series of questions drawn from that document.

Sometimes an interviewer is not prepared and does not know or recall the contents of the resume and may use the resume to a greater or lesser degree as a "prompt" during the interview. It is for you to judge what that may indicate about the individual doing the interview or the employer. If your interviewer seems surprised by the scheduled meeting, relies on the resume to an inordinate degree, and seems otherwise unfamiliar with your background, this lack of preparation for the hiring process could well be a symptom of general management disorganization or may simply be the result of poor planning on the part of one individual. It is your responsibility as a potential employee to be aware of these signals and make your decisions accordingly.

....

In any event, it is perfectly acceptable for you to get the conversation back to a more interpersonal style by saying something like, "Mr. Smith, you might be interested in some recent experience I gained in a volunteer position at our local historical society that is not detailed on my resume. May I tell you about it?" This can return the interview to two people talking to each other, not one reading and the other responding.

....

By all means, bring at least one copy of your resume to the interview. Occasionally, at the close of an interview, an interviewer will express an interest in circulating a resume to several departments, and you could then offer to provide those. Sometimes, an interview appointment provides an opportunity to meet others in the organization who may express an interest in you and your background, and it may be helpful to follow that up with a copy of your resume. Our best advice, however, is to keep it out of sight until needed or requested.

Appearance

Although many of the absolute rules that once dominated the advice offered to job candidates about appearance have now been moderated significantly, conservative is still the watchword unless you are interviewing in a fashion-related industry. For men, conservative translates into a well-cut dark suit with appropriate tie, hosiery, and dress shirt. A wise strategy for the male job seeker looking for a good but not expensive suit would be to try the men's department of a major department store. They usually carry a good range of sizes, fabrics, and prices; offer professional sales help; provide free tailoring; and have associated departments for putting together a professional look.

For women, there is more latitude. Business suits are still popular, but they have become more feminine in color and styling with a variety of jacket and skirt lengths. In addition to suits, better quality dresses are now worn in many environments and, with the correct accessories, can be most appropriate. Company literature, professional magazines, the business section of major newspapers, and television interviews can all give clues about what is being worn in different employer environments.

Both men and women need to pay attention to issues such as hair, jewelry, and make-up; these are often what separates the candidate in appearance from the professional work force. It seems particularly difficult for the young job seeker to give up certain hair styles, eyeglass fashions, and jewelry habits, yet those can be important to the employer, who is concerned with your ability to successfully make the transition into the organization. Candidates often find the best strategy is to dress conservatively until they find employment. Once employed and familiar with the norms within your organization, you can begin to determine a look that you enjoy, works for you, and fits your organization.

Choose clothes that suit your body type, fit well, and flatter you. Feel good about the way you look! The interview day is not the best for a new hairdo, a new pair of shoes, or any other change that will distract you or cause you to be self-conscious. Arrive a bit early to avoid being rushed, and ask the receptionist to direct you to a restroom for any last-minute adjustments of hair and clothes.

Employer Information

Whether your interview is for graduate school admission, an overseas corporate position, or a reporter position with a local newspaper, it is important to know something about the employer or the organization. Keeping in mind that the interview is relatively brief and that you will hopefully have other interviews with other organizations, it is important to keep your research in proportion. If secondary interviews are called for, you will have additional time to do further research. For the first interview, it is helpful to know the organization's mission, goals, size, scope of operations, etc. Your research may uncover recent areas of challenge or particular successes that may help to fuel the interview. Use the "Where Are These Jobs, Anyway?" section of Chapter 3, your library, and your career or guidance office to help you locate this information in the most efficient way possible. Don't be shy in asking advice of these counseling and guidance professionals on how best to spend your preparation time. With some practice, you'll soon learn how much information is enough and which kinds of information are most useful to you.

INTERVIEW CONTENT

We've already discussed how it can help to think of the interview as an important conversation—one that, as with any conversation, you want to find pleasant and interesting and leaves you with a good feeling. But because this conversation is especially important, the information that's exchanged is critical to its success. What do you want them to know about you? What do you need to know about them? What interview technique do you need to particularly pay attention to? How do you want to manage the close of the interview? What steps will follow in the hiring process?

Except for the professional interviewer, most of us find interviewing stressful and anxiety-provoking. Developing a strategy before you begin interviewing will help you relieve some stress and anxiety. One particular strategy that has worked for many and may work for you is interviewing by objective. Before you interview, write down 3–5 goals you would like to achieve for that interview. They may be technique goals: smile a little more, have a firmer handshake, be sure to ask about the next stage in the interview process before I leave, etc. They may be content-oriented goals: find out about the company's current challenges and opportunities, be sure to speak of my recent research writing experiences or foreign travel, etc. Whatever your goals, jot down a few of them as goals for this interview.

Most people find that, in trying to achieve these few goals, their interviewing technique becomes more organized and focused. After the interview, the most common question friends and family ask is, "How did it go?" With this technique, you have an indication of whether you met *your* goals for the meeting, not just some vague idea of how it went. Chances are, if you accomplished what you wanted to, it informed the quality of the entire interview. As you continue to interview, you will want to revise your goals to continue improving your interview skills.

Now, add to the concept of the significant conversation the idea of a beginning, a middle, and a closing and you will have two thoughts that will give your interview a distinctive character. Be sure to make your introduction warm and cordial. Say your full name (and if it's a difficult-to-pronounce name, help the interviewer to pronounce it) and make certain you know your interviewer's name and how to pronounce it. Most interviews begin with some "soft talk" about the weather, chat about the candidate's trip to the interview site, national events, etc. This is done as a courtesy, to relax both you and the interviewer, to get you talking, and to generally try to defuse the atmosphere of excessive tension. Try to be yourself, engage in the conversation, and don't try to second-guess the interviewer. This is simply what it appears to be—casual conversation.

Once you and the interviewer move on to exchange more serious information in the middle part of the interview, the two most important concerns become your ability to handle challenging questions and your success at asking meaningful ones. Interviewer questions will probably fall into one of three categories: personal assessment and career direction, academic background, and knowledge of the employer. The following are some examples of questions in each category:

Personal Assessment and Career Direction

1. How would you describe yourself?

2. What motivates you to put forth your greatest effort?

3. In what kind of work environment are you most comfortable?

4. What do you consider to be your greatest strengths and weaknesses?

5. How well do you work under pressure?

6. What qualifications do you have that make you think you will be successful in this career?

7. Will you relocate? What do you feel would be the most difficult aspect of relocating?

8. Are you willing to travel?

9. Why should I hire you?

Academic Assessment

1. Why did you select your college or university?

2. What changes would you make at your alma mater?

3. What led you to choose your major?

4. What subjects did you like best and least? Why?

5. If you could, how would you plan your academic study differently? Why?

6. Describe your most rewarding college experience.

7. How has your college experience prepared you for this career?

8. Do you think that your grades are a good indication of your ability to succeed with this organization?

9. Do you have plans for continued study?

Knowledge of the Employer

1. If you were hiring a graduate of your school for this position, what qualities would you look for?

2. What do you think it takes to be successful in an organization like ours?

3. In what ways do you think you can make a contribution to our organization?

4. Why did you choose to seek a position with this organization?

The interviewer wants a response to each question but is also gauging your enthusiasm, preparedness, and willingness to communicate. In each response you should provide some information about yourself that can be related to the employer's needs. A common mistake is to give too much information. Answer each question completely, but be careful not to run on too long with extensive details or examples.

Questions about Underdeveloped Skills

Most employers interview people who have met some minimum criteria of education and experience. They interview candidates to see who they are, to learn what kind of personality they exhibit, and to get some sense of how this person might fit into the existing organization. It may be that you are asked about skills the employer hopes to find and that you have not documented. Maybe it's grant-writing experience, knowledge of the European political system, or a knowledge of the film world.

To questions about skills and experiences you don't have, answer honestly and forthrightly and try to offer some additional information about skills you do have. For example, perhaps the employer is disappointed you have no grant-writing experience. An honest answer may be as follows:

> No, unfortunately, I was never in a position to acquire those skills. I do understand something of the complexities of the grant-writing process and feel confident that my attention to detail, careful reading skills, and strong writing would make grants a wonderful challenge in a new job. I think I could get up on the learning curve quickly.

The employer hears an honest admission of lack of experience but is reassured by some specific skill details that do relate to grant writing and a confident manner that suggests enthusiasm and interest in a challenge.

For many liberal arts majors, questions about their possible contribution to an employer's organization can prove challenging. Because your education has not included specific training for a job, you need to review your academic record and select capabilities you have developed in your major that an employer can appreciate. For example, perhaps you read well and can analyze and condense what you've read into smaller, more focused pieces. That could be valuable. Or maybe you did some serious research and you know you have valuable investigative skills. Your public speaking might be highly developed and you might use visual aids appropriately and effectively. Or maybe your skill at correspondence, memos, and messages is effective. Whatever it is, you must take it out of the academic context and put it into a new, employer-friendly context so your interviewer can best judge how you could help the organization.

Exhibiting knowledge of the organization will, without a doubt, show the interviewer that you are interested enough in the available position to have done some legwork in preparation for the interview. Remember, it is not necessary to know every detail of the organization's history, but rather to have a general knowledge about why it is in business and how the industry is faring.

Sometime during the interview, generally after the midway point, you'll be asked if you have any questions for the interviewer. Your questions will tell the employer much about your attitude and your desire to understand the organization's expectations so you can compare it to your own strengths. The following are some selected questions you might want to ask:

1. What are the main responsibilities of the position?

2. What are the opportunities and challenges associated with this position?

3. Could you outline some possible career paths beginning with this position?

4. How regularly do performance evaluations occur?

5. What is the communication style of the organization? (meetings, memos, etc.)

6. Describe a typical day for me in this position.

7. What kinds of opportunities might exist for me to improve my professional skills within the organization?

8. What have been some of the interesting challenges and opportunities your organization has recently faced?

Most interviews draw to a natural closing point, so be careful not to prolong the discussion. At a signal from the interviewer, wind up your presentation, express your appreciation for the opportunity, and be sure to ask what the next stage in the process will be. When can you expect to hear from them? Will they be conducting second-tier interviews? If you're interested and haven't heard, would they mind a phone call? Be sure to collect a business card with the name and phone number of your interviewer. On your way out, you might have an opportunity to pick up organizational literature you haven't seen before.

With the right preparation—a thorough self-assessment, professional clothing, and employer information, you'll be able to set and achieve the goals you have established for the interview process.

CHAPTER SIX

NETWORKING OR INTERVIEWING FOLLOW-UP

 uite often, there is a considerable time lag between interviewing for a position and being hired, or, in the case of the networker, between your phone call or letter to a possible contact and the opportunity of a meeting. This can be frustrating. "Why aren't they contacting me?" "I thought I'd get another interview, but no one has telephoned." "Am I out of the running?" You don't know what is happening.

CONSIDER THE DIFFERING PERSPECTIVES

Of course, there is another perspective—that of the networker or hiring organization. Organizations are complex, with multiple tasks that need to be accomplished each day. Hiring is but one discrete activity that does not occur as frequently as other job assignments. The hiring process might have to take second place to other, more immediate organizational needs. Although it may be very important to you and it is certainly ultimately significant to the employer, other issues such as fiscal management, planning and product development, employer vacation periods, or financial constraints, may prevent an organization or individual within that organization from acting on your employment or your request for information as quickly as you or they would prefer.

USE YOUR COMMUNICATION SKILLS

Good communication is essential here to resolve any anxieties, and the responsibility is on you, the job or information seeker. Too many job seekers and networkers offer as an excuse that they don't want to "bother" the organization by writing letters or calling. Let us assure you here and now, once and for all, that if you are troubling an organization by over-communicating, someone will indicate that situation to you quite clearly. If not, you can only assume you are a worthwhile prospect and the employer appreciates being reminded of your availability and interest in them. Let's look at follow-up practices in both the job interview process and the networking situation separately.

FOLLOWING UP ON THE EMPLOYMENT INTERVIEW

A brief thank-you note following an interview is an excellent and polite way to begin a series of follow-up communications with a potential employer with whom you have interviewed and want to remain in touch. It should be just that—a thank-you for a good meeting. If you failed to mention some fact or experience during your interview that you think might add to your candidacy, you may use this note to do that. However, this should be essentially a note whose overall tone is appreciative and, if appropriate, indicative of a continuing interest in pursuing any opportunity that may exist with that organization. It is one of the few pieces of business correspondence that may be handwritten, but always use plain, good-quality, monarch-size paper.

If, however, at this point you are no longer interested in the employer, the thank-you note is an appropriate time to indicate that. You are under no obligation to identify any reason for not continuing to pursue employment with that organization, but if you are so inclined to indicate your professional reasons (pursuing other employers more akin to your interests, looking for greater income production than this employer can provide, a different geographic location than is available, etc.), you certainly may. It should not be written with an eye to negotiation, for it will not be interpreted as such.

As part of your interview closing, you should have taken the initiative to establish lines of communication for continuing information about your candidacy. If you asked permission to telephone, wait a week following your thank-you note, then telephone your contact simply to inquire how things are progressing on your employment status. The feedback you receive here should be taken at face value. If your interviewer simply has no information, he or she will tell you so and indicate whether you should call again and when. Don't be discouraged if this should continue over some period of time.

If during this time something occurs that you think improves or changes your candidacy (some new qualification or experience you may have had), including any offers from other organizations, by all means telephone or write to inform the employer about this. In the case of an offer from a competing but less desirable or equally desirable organization, telephone your contact, explain what has happened, express your real interest in the organization, and inquire whether some determination on your employment might be made before you must respond to this other offer. If the organization is truly interested in you, they may be moved to make a decision about your candidacy. Equally possible is the scenario in which they are not yet ready to make a decision and so advise you to take the offer that has been presented. Again, you have no ethical alternative but to deal with the information presented in a straightforward manner.

When accepting other employment, be sure to contact any employers still actively considering you and inform them of your new job. Thank them graciously for their consideration. There are many other job seekers out there just like you who will benefit from having their candidacy improved when others bow out of the race. Who knows, you might, at some future time, have occasion to interact professionally with one of the organizations with whom you sought employment. How embarrassing to have someone remember you as the candidate who failed to notify them of taking a job elsewhere!

In all of your follow-up communications, keep good notes of who you spoke with, when you called, and any instructions that were given about return communications. This will prevent any misunderstandings and provide you with good records of what has transpired.

Following Up on the Network Contact

Far more common than the forgotten follow-up after an interview is the situation where a good network contact is allowed to lapse. Good communications are the essence of a network, and follow-up is not so much a matter of courtesy here as it is a necessity. In networking for job information and contacts, you are the active network link. Without you, and without continual contact from you, there is no network. You and your need for employment is often the only shared element between members of the network. Because network contacts were made regardless of the availability of any particular employment, it is incumbent upon the job seeker, if not simple common sense, that unless you stay in regular communication with the network, you will not be available for consideration should some job become available in the future.

This brings up the issue of responsibility, which is likewise very clear. The job seeker initiates network contacts and is responsible for maintaining those contacts; therefore, the entire responsibility for the network belongs with him or her. This becomes patently obvious if the network is left unattended. It very shortly falls out of existence, as it cannot survive without careful attention by the networker.

A variety of ways are open to you to keep the lines of communication open and to attempt to interest the network in you as a possible employee. You are limited only by your own enthusiasm for members of the network and your creativity. However, you as a networker are well advised to keep good records of whom you have met and spoken with in each organization. Be sure to send thank-you notes to anyone who has spent any time with you, be it a quick tour of a department or a sit-down informational interview. All of these communications should, in addition to their ostensible reason, add some information about you and your particular combination of strengths and attributes.

You can contact your network at any time to convey continued interest, to comment on some recent article you came across concerning an organization, to add information about your training or changes in your qualifications, to ask advice or seek guidance in your job search, or to request referrals to other possible network opportunities. Sometimes just a simple note to network members reminding them of your job search, indicating that you have been using their advice, and noting that you are still actively pursuing leads and hope to continue to interact with them is enough to keep communications alive.

Because networks have been abused in the past, it's important that your conduct be above reproach. Networks are exploratory options, they are not back-door access to employers. The network works best for someone who is exploring a new industry or making a transition into a new area of employment and who needs to find information or to alert people to their search activity. Always be candid and direct with contacts in expressing the purpose of your call or letter and your interest in their help or information about their organization. In follow-up contacts, keep the tone professional and direct. Your honesty will be appreciated, and people will respond as best they can if your qualifications appear to meet their forthcoming needs. The network does not owe you anything, and that tone should be clear to each person you meet.

FEEDBACK FROM FOLLOW-UPS

A network contact may prove to be miscalculated. Perhaps you were referred to someone and it became clear that your goals and their particular needs did not make a good match. Or the network contact may simply not be in a position to provide you with the information you are seeking. Or in some unfortunate situations, the contact may become annoyed by being contacted for this purpose. In such a situation, many job seekers simply say "Thank you" and move on.

If the contact is simply not the right contact, but the individual you are speaking with is not annoyed by the call, it might be a better tactic to express regret that the contact was misplaced and then express to the contact what you are seeking and ask for their advice or possible suggestions as to a next step. The more people who are aware you are seeking employment, the better your chances of connecting, and that is the purpose of a network. Most people in a profession have excellent knowledge of their field and varying amounts of expertise on areas near to or tangent to their own. Use their expertise and seek some guidance before you dissolve the contact. You may be pleasantly surprised.

Occasionally, networkers will express the feeling that they have done as much as they can or provided all the information that is available to them. This may be a cue that they would like to be released from your network. Be alert to such attempts to terminate, graciously thank the individual by letter, and move on in your network development. A network is always changing, adding and losing members, and you want the network to be composed of only those who are actively interested in supporting your interests.

A Final Point on Networking for History Majors

In any field a history major might consider as a potential career path, your contacts will be critically evaluating all your written and oral communications. For some job seekers, this may be more crucial than others. Many of the jobs in the career paths that follow do, however, emphasize communication skills. This should be a welcome demand, as your study of history has involved writing papers, research reports and some classroom presentations—all of which have helped polish your communication style.

In your telephone communications, interview presentation, follow-up correspondence, and ability to deal with negative feedback, your written and spoken use of English will be part of the portfolio of impressions you create in those you meet along the way.

CHAPTER SEVEN

JOB OFFER CONSIDERATIONS

or many recent college graduates, the thrill of their first job and, for some, the most substantial regular income they have ever earned seems an excess of good fortune coming at once. To question that first income or be critical in any way of the conditions of employment at the time of the initial offer seems like looking a gift horse in the mouth. It doesn't seem to occur to many new hires even to attempt to negotiate any aspect of their first job. And, as many employers who deal with entry-level jobs for recent college graduates will readily confirm, the reality is that there simply isn't much movement in salary available to these new college recruits. The entry-level hire generally does not have an employment track record on a professional level to provide any leverage for negotiation. Real negotiations on salary, benefits, retirement provisions, etc., come to those with significant employment records at higher income levels.

Of course, the job offer is more than just money. It can be comprised of geographic assignment, duties and responsibilities, training, benefits, health and medical insurance, educational assistance, car allowance or company vehicle, and a host of other items. All of this is generally detailed in the formal letter that presents the final job offer. In most cases, this is a follow-up to a personal phone call from the employer representative who has been principally responsible for your hiring process.

That initial telephone offer is certainly binding as a verbal agreement, but most firms follow up with a detailed letter outlining the most significant parts of your employment contract. You may certainly choose to respond immediately at the time of the telephone offer (which would be considered a binding oral contract), but you will also be required to formally answer the letter of offer with a letter of acceptance, restating the salient elements of the employer's description of your position, salary, and benefits. This ensures that both parties are clear on the terms and conditions of employment and remuneration and any other outstanding aspects of the job offer.

Is This the Job You Want?

Most new employees will write this letter of acceptance back, glad to be in the position to accept employment. If you've worked hard to get the offer, and the job market is tight, other offers may not be in sight, so you will say "Yes, I accept!" What is important here is that the job offer you accept be one that does fit your particular needs, values, and interests as you've outlined them in your self-assessment process. Moreover, it should be a job that will not only use your skills and education, but also challenge you to develop new skills and talents.

Jobs are sometimes accepted too hastily, for the wrong reasons and without proper scrutiny by the applicant. For example, an individual might readily accept a sales job only to find the continual rejection by potential clients unendurable. An office worker might realize within weeks the constraints of a desk job and yearn for more activity. Employment is an important part of our lives. It is, for most of our adult lives, our most continuous productive activity. We want to make good choices based on the right criteria.

If you have a low tolerance for risk, a job based on commission will certainly be very anxiety provoking. If being near your family is important, issues of relocation could present a decision crisis for you. If you're an adventurous person, a job with frequent travel would provide needed excitement and be very desirable. The importance of income, the need to continue your education, your personal health situation—all of these have an impact on whether the job you are considering will ultimately meet your needs. Unless you've spent some time understanding and thinking about these issues, it will be difficult to evaluate offers you do receive.

More importantly, if you make a decision that you cannot tolerate and feel you must leave that job, you will then have both unemployment and self-esteem issues to contend with. These will combine to make the next job search tough going, indeed. So make your acceptance a carefully considered decision.

Negotiating Your Offer

It may be that there is some aspect of your job offer that is not particularly attractive to you. Perhaps there is no relocation allotment to help you move your possessions and this presents some financial hardship for you. It may be that the medical and health insurance is less than you had hoped. Your initial assignment may be different than you expected, either in its location or in the duties and responsibilities that comprise it. Or it may simply be that the salary is less than you anticipated. Other considerations may be your official starting date of employment, vacation time, evening hours, dates of training programs or schools, etc.

If you are considering not accepting the job because of some item or items in the job offer "package" that do not meet your needs, you should know that most employers emphatically wish that you would bring that issue to their attention. It may be that the employer can alter it to make the offer more agreeable for you. In some cases, it cannot be changed. In any event, the employer would generally like to have the opportunity to try to remedy a difficulty rather than risk losing a good potential employee over an issue that might have been resolved. After all, they have spent time and funds in securing your services, and they certainly deserve an opportunity to resolve any possible differences.

Honesty is the best approach in discussing any objections or uneasiness you might have over the employer's offer. Having received your formal offer in writing, contact your employer representative and indicate your particular dissatisfaction in a straightforward manner. For example, you might explain that, while very interested in being employed by this organization, the salary (or any other benefit) is less than you have determined you require. State the terms you do need, and listen to the response. You may be asked to put this in writing, or you may be asked to hold off until the firm can decide on a response. If you are dealing with a senior representative of the organization, one who has been involved in hiring for some time, you may get an immediate response or a solid indication of possible outcomes.

Perhaps the issue is one of relocation. Your initial assignment is in the Midwest, and because you had indicated a strong West Coast preference, you are surprised at the actual assignment. You might simply indicate that, while you understand the need for the company to assign you based on its needs, you are disappointed and had hoped to be placed on the West Coast. You could inquire if that were still possible and, if not, would it be reasonable to expect a West Coast relocation in the future.

If your request is presented in a reasonable way, the employer will not see this as jeopardizing your offer. If they can agree to your proposal, they will. If not, they will simply tell you so, and you may choose to continue your candidacy with them or remove yourself from consideration as a possible employee. The choice will be up to you.

Some firms will adjust benefits within their parameters to meet the candidate's need if at all possible. If a candidate requires a relocation cost allowance, he or she may be asked to forgo tuition benefits for the first year to accomplish this adjustment. An increase in life insurance may be adjusted by some other benefit trade-off; perhaps a family dental plan is not needed. In these decisions, you are called upon, sometimes under time pressure, to know how you value these issues and how important each is to you.

Many employers find they are more comfortable negotiating for candidates who have unique qualifications or who bring especially needed expertise to the organization. Employers hiring large numbers of entry-level college graduates may be far more reluctant to accommodate any changes in offer conditions. They are well supplied with candidates with similar education and experience, so that if rejected by one candidate, they can draw new candidates from an ample labor pool.

COMPARING OFFERS

With only about 40 percent of recent college graduates employed three months after graduation, many graduates do not get to enjoy the experience of entertaining more than one offer at a time. The conditions of the economy, the job seekers' particular geographic job market, and their own needs and demands for certain employment conditions may not provide more than one offer at a time. Some job seekers may feel that no reasonable offer should go unaccepted, for the simple fear there won't be another.

In a tough job market, or if the job you seek is not widely available, or when your job search goes on too long and becomes difficult to sustain financially and emotionally, it may be necessary to accept an offer. The alternative is continued unemployment. Even here, when you feel you don't have a choice, you can at least understand that in accepting this particular offer, there may be limitations and conditions you don't appreciate. At the time of acceptance, there were no other alternatives, but the new employee can begin to use that position to gain the experience and talent to move toward a more attractive position.

Sometimes, however, more than one offer is received at one time, and the candidate has the luxury of choice. If the job seeker knows what he or she wants and has done the necessary self-assessment honestly and thoroughly, it may be clear that one of the offers conforms more closely to those expressed wants and needs.

However, if, as so often happens, the offers are similar in terms of conditions and salary, the question then becomes which organization might provide the necessary climate, opportunities, and advantages for your professional development and growth. This is the time when solid employer research and astute questioning during the interviews really pays off. How much did you learn about the employer through your own research and skillful questioning? When the interviewer asked during the interview, "Now, I'm sure you must have many questions?" did you ask

the kinds of questions that would help resolve a choice between one organization and another? Just as an employer must decide among numerous applicants, so must the applicant learn to assess the potential employer. Both are
partners in the job search.

RENEGING ON AN OFFER

An especially disturbing occurrence for employers and career counseling professionals is when a student formally (either orally or by written contract)
accepts employment with one organization and later reneges on the agreement
and goes with another employer.

There are all kinds of rationalizations offered for this unethical behavior.
None of them satisfies. The sad irony is that what the job seeker is willing to
do to the employer—make a promise and then break it—he or she would be
outraged to have done to them—have the job offer pulled. It is a very bad
way to begin a career. It suggests the individual has not taken the time to do
the necessary self-assessment and self-awareness exercises to think and judge
critically. The new offer taken may, in fact, be no better or worse than the one
refused. Job candidates should be aware that there have been incidents of legal action following job candidates reneging on an offer. This adds a very sour
note to what should be a harmonious beginning of a lifelong adventure.

CHAPTER EIGHT

THE GRADUATE SCHOOL CHOICE

he reasons for continuing one's education in graduate school can be as varied and unique as the individuals electing this course of action. Many continue their studies at an advanced level because they simply find it difficult to end the educational process. They love what they are learning and want to learn more and continue their academic exploration.

Continuing to work with a particular subject, such as the cultural, social and political foundations of modern Europe, and thinking, studying and writing critically on what others have discovered, can provide excitement, challenge and serious work. Some history majors have loved this aspect of their academic work and want to continue that activity.

Others go on to graduate school for purely practical reasons. They have examined employment prospects in their field of study and all indications are that a graduate degree is required. For example, you have a B.A. in history and you have not obtained teaching certification, and many of the museum jobs you're interested in seem to demand at least a master's degree. You sense your opportunities to be directly involved with history without advanced work will be limited.

Alumni who are working in the fields you are considering can be a good source of what degree level the field demands. Ask your college career office for some alumni names and give them a telephone call. Prepare some questions on specific job prospects in their field at each degree level. A thorough examination of the marketplace and talking to employers and professors will give you a sense of the scope of employment for a bachelor's, master's, or doctoral degree.

College teaching will require an advanced degree. The more senior museum positions will require an advanced education and perhaps some particular specialization in a subject area.

CONSIDER YOUR MOTIVES

The answer to the question of "Why graduate school?" is a personal one for each applicant. Nevertheless, it is important to consider your motives carefully. Graduate school involves additional time out of the employment market, a high degree of critical evaluation, significant autonomy as you pursue your studies, and considerable financial expenditure. For some students in doctoral programs, there may be additional life choice issues, such as relationships, marriage, and parenthood that may present real challenges while in a program of study. You would be well advised to consider the following questions as you think about your decision to continue your studies.

Are You Postponing Some Tough Decisions by Going to School?

Graduate school is not a place to go to avoid life's problems. There is intense competition for graduate school slots and for the fellowships, scholarships, and financial aid available. This competition means extensive interviewing, resume submission, and essay writing that rivals corporate recruitment. Likewise, the graduate school process is a mentored one in which faculty stay aware of and involved in the academic progress of their students and continually challenge the quality of their work. Many graduate students are called upon to participate in teaching and professional writing and research as well.

In other words, this is no place to hide from the spotlight. Graduate students work very hard and much is demanded of them individually. If you elect to go to graduate school to avoid the stresses and strains of the "real world," you will find no safe place in higher academics. Vivid accounts, both fiction and nonfiction, have depicted quite accurately the personal and professional demands of graduate school work.

The selection of graduate studies as a career option should be a positive choice—something you *want* to do. It shouldn't be selected as an escape from other, less attractive or more challenging options, nor should it be selected as the option of last resort (i.e., "I can't do anything else; I'd better just stay in school."). If you're in some doubt about the strength of your reasoning about continuing in school, discuss the issues with a career counselor. Together you can clarify your reasoning, and you'll get some sound feedback on what you're about to undertake.

On the other hand, staying on in graduate school because of a particularly poor employment market and a lack of jobs at entry-level positions has proven to be an effective "stalling" strategy. If you can afford it, pursuing a graduate degree immediately after your undergraduate education gives you a year or two to "wait out" a difficult economic climate while at the same time acquiring a potentially valuable credential.

Have You Done Some "Hands-on" Reality Testing?

There are experiential options available to give some reality to your decision-making process about graduate school. Internships or work in the field can give you a good idea about employment demands, conditions, and atmosphere.

Perhaps, as a history major, you're considering a graduate program. A summer position teaching history in a continuing education program or working as a historic guide will bring home some of the reality of a teaching career. You will struggle with explaining concepts and planning effective lessons. After only one exposure, you will have a stronger concept of the pace of the job, one's interaction with colleagues, and opportunities for personal development. Talking to people and asking questions is invaluable in helping you understand the objective of your graduate study.

For history majors who wish to specialize in history as an archivist or in museum work, the opportunity to do some kind of reality testing will be invaluable. It demonstrates far more authoritatively than any other source what your skills are, how they can be put to use, and what aspects of your academic preparation you rely on. It has been well documented that liberal arts majors do well in occupations once they identify them. Internships and co-op experiences speed that process up and prevent the frustrating and expensive process of investigation many graduates begin only after graduation.

....

Do You Need an Advanced Degree to Work in Your Field?

Certainly there are fields such as law, psychiatry, medicine, and college teaching that demand advanced degrees. Is the field of employment you're considering one that also puts a premium on an advanced degree? You may be surprised. Read the want ads in a number of major Sunday newspapers for positions you would enjoy. How many of those require an advanced degree?

Retailing, for example, has always put a premium on what people can do, rather than how much education they have had. Successful people in retailing come from all academic preparations. A Ph.D. in English may bring only prestige to the individual employed as a magazine researcher. It may not bring a more senior position or better pay. In fact, it may disqualify you for some jobs because an employer might believe you will be unhappy to be overqualified for a particular position. Or your motives in applying for the work may be misconstrued, and the employer might think you will only be working at this level until something better comes along. None of this may be true for you, but it comes about because you are working outside of the usual territory for that degree level.

When economic times are especially difficult, we tend to see stories featured about individuals with advanced degrees doing what is considered unsuitable work, such as the Ph.D. in English driving a cab or the Ph.D. in chemistry waiting tables. Actually, this is not particularly surprising when you consider that as your degree level advances, the job market narrows appreciably. At any one time, regardless of economic circumstances, there are only so many jobs for your particular level of expertise. If you cannot find employment for your advanced degree level, chances are you will be considered suspect for many other kinds of employment and may be forced into temporary work far removed from your original intention.

Before making an important decision such as graduate study, learn your options and carefully consider what you want to do with your advanced degree. Ask yourself whether it is reasonable to think you can achieve your goals. Will there be jobs when you graduate? Where will they be? What will they pay? How competitive will the market be at that time, based on current predictions?

If you're uncertain about the degree requirements for the fields you're interested in, you should check a publication such as the U.S. Department of Labor's *Occupational Outlook Handbook.* Each entry has a section on training and other qualifications that will indicate clearly what the minimum educational requirement is for employment, what degree is the standard, and what employment may be possible without the required credential.

For example, for physicists and astronomers, a doctoral degree in physics or a closely related field is essential. Certainly this is the degree of choice in academic institutions. However, the *Occupational Outlook Handbook* also indicates what kinds of employment may be available to individuals holding a master's or even a bachelor's degree in physics.

Have You Compared Your Expectations of What Graduate School Will Do for You with What It Has Done for Alumni of the Program You're Considering?

Most colleges and universities perform some kind of postgraduate survey of their students to ascertain where they are employed, what additional education they have received, and what levels of salary they are enjoying. Ask to see this information either from the university you are considering applying to or from your own alma mater, especially if it has a similar graduate program. Such surveys often reveal surprises about occupational decisions, salaries, and work satisfaction. This information may affect your decision.

The value of self-assessment (the process of examining and making decisions about your own hierarchy of values and goals) is especially important in this process of analyzing the desirability of possible career paths involving graduate education. Sometimes a job requiring advanced education seems to hold real promise but is disappointing in salary potential or numbers of opportunities available. Certainly, it is better to research this information before embarking on a program of graduate studies. It may not change your mind about your decision, but by becoming better informed about your choice, you become better prepared for your future.

Have You Talked with People in Your Field to Explore What You Might Be Doing after Graduate School?

In pursuing your undergraduate degree, you will have come into contact with many individuals trained in the field you are considering. You might also have the opportunity to attend professional conferences, workshops, seminars, and job fairs where you can expand your network of contacts. Talk to them all! Find out about their individual career paths, discuss your own plans and hopes, and get their feedback on the reality of your expectations, and heed their advice about your prospects. Each will have a unique tale to tell, and each will bring a different perspective on the current marketplace for the credentials you are seeking. Talking to enough people will make you an expert on what's out there.

Are You Excited by the Idea of Studying the Particular Field You Have in Mind?

This question may be the most important one of all. If you are going to spend several years in advanced study, perhaps engendering some debt or postponing some life-style decisions for an advanced degree, you simply ought to enjoy what you're doing. Examine your work in the discipline so far. Has it been fun? Have you found yourself exploring various paths of thought? Do you read in your area for fun? Do you enjoy talking about it, thinking about it, and sharing it with others? Advanced degrees often are the beginning of a lifetime's involvement with a particular subject. Choose carefully a field that will hold your interest and your enthusiasm.

It is fairly obvious by now that we think you should give some careful thought to your decision and take some action. If nothing else, do the following:

- ❑ Talk and question (remember to listen!)

- ❑ Reality-test

- ❑ Soul-search by yourself or with a person you trust

FINDING THE RIGHT PROGRAM FOR YOU: SOME CONSIDERATIONS

There are several important factors in coming to a sound decision about the right graduate program for you. You'll want to begin by locating institutions that offer appropriate programs, examining each of these programs and their requirements, undertaking the application process by obtaining catalogs and application materials, visiting campuses if possible, arranging for letters of recommendation, writing your application statement, and finally following up on your applications.

Locate Institutions with Appropriate Programs

Once you decide on a particular advanced degree, it's important to develop a list of schools offering such a degree program. Perhaps the best source of graduate program information are Peterson's *Guides to Graduate Study*. Use these guides to build your list. In addition, you may want to consult the College Board's *Index of Majors and Graduate Degrees*, which will help you find graduate programs offering the degree you seek. It is indexed by academic major and then categorized by state.

Now, this may be a considerable list. You may want to narrow the choices down further by a number of criteria: tuition, availability of financial aid, public versus private institutions, U.S. versus international institutions, size of student body, size of faculty, application fee (this varies by school; most fall within the $10–$75 range), and geographic location. This is only a partial list; you will have your own important considerations. Perhaps you are an avid scuba diver and you find it unrealistic to think you could pursue graduate study for a number of years without being able to ocean dive from time to time. Good! That's a decision and it's honest. Now, how far from the ocean is too far, and what schools meet your other needs? In any case, and according to your own criteria, begin to build a reasonable list of graduate schools that you are willing to spend the time investigating.

Examine the Degree Programs and Their Requirements

Once you've determined the criteria by which you want to develop a list of graduate schools, you can begin to examine the degree program requirements, faculty composition, and institutional research orientation. Again, using a resource such as Peterson's *Guides to Graduate Study* can reveal an amazingly rich level of material by which to judge your possible selections.

In addition to degree programs and degree requirements, entries will include information about application fees, entrance test requirements, tuition, percentage of applicants accepted, numbers of applicants receiving financial aid, gender breakdown of students, numbers of full- and part-time faculty, and often gender breakdown of faculty as well. Numbers graduating in each program and research orientations of departments are also included in some entries. There is information on graduate housing, student services, and library, research, and computer facilities. A contact person, phone number, and address are also standard pieces of information in these listings. In addition to the standard entries, some schools pay an additional fee to place full-page, more detailed program descriptions. The location of such a display ad, if present, would be indicated at the end of the standard entry.

It can be helpful to draw up a chart and enter relevant information about each school you are considering in order to have a ready reference on points of information that are important to you.

Undertake the Application Process

The Catalog.   Once you've decided on a selection of schools, send for catalogs and applications. It is important to note here that these materials might take many weeks to arrive. Consequently, if you need the materials quickly, it might be best to telephone and explain your situation to see whether the process can be speeded up for you. Also, check a local college or university library, which might have current and complete college catalogs in a microfiche collection. These microfiche copies can provide you with helpful information while you wait for your own copy of the graduate school catalog or bulletin to arrive.

When you receive your catalogs, give them a careful reading and make notes of issues you might want to discuss on the telephone or in a personal interview, if that's possible. Does the course selection have the depth you had hoped for?

....

If you are interested in graduate work in history, for example, in addition to graduate courses centered around geographical areas, time period and specific events, consider colloquiums, directed research opportunities and specialized seminars.

....

What is the ratio of faculty to the required number of courses for your degree? How often will you encounter the same faculty member as an instructor?

If, for example, your program offers a practicum or off-campus experience, who arranges this? Does the graduate school select a site and place you there, or is it your responsibility? What are the professional affiliations of the faculty? Does the program merit any outside professional endorsement or accreditation?

Critically evaluate the catalogs of each of the programs you are considering. List any questions you have and ask current or former teachers and colleagues for their impressions as well.

The Application.   Preview each application thoroughly to determine what you need to provide in the way of letters of recommendation, transcripts from undergraduate schools or any previous graduate work, and personal essays that may be required. Make a notation for each application of what you need to complete that document.

Additionally, you'll want to determine entrance testing requirements for each institution and immediately arrange to complete your test registration. For example, the Graduate Record Exam (GRE) and the Graduate Management Admission Test (GMAT) each have 3–4 weeks between the last registration date and the test date. Your local college career office should be able to provide you with test registration booklets, sample test materials, information on test sites and dates, and independent test review materials that might be available commercially.

Visit the Campus If Possible

If time and finances allow, a visit, interview, and tour can help make your decision easier. You can develop a sense of the student body, meet some of the faculty, and hear up-to-date information on resources and the curriculum. You will have a brief opportunity to "try out" the surroundings to see if they fit your needs. After all, it will be home for a while. If a visit is not possible but you have questions, don't hesitate to call and speak with the dean of the graduate school. Most are more than happy to talk to candidates and want them to have the answers they seek. Graduate school admission is a very personal and individual process.

Arrange for Letters of Recommendation

This is also the time to begin to assemble a group of individuals who will support your candidacy as a graduate student by writing letters of recommendation or completing recommendation forms. Some schools will ask you to provide letters of recommendation to be included with your application or sent directly to the school by the recommender. Other graduate programs will provide a recommendation form that must be completed by the recommender. These graduate school forms vary greatly in the amount of space provided for a written recommendation. So that you can use letters as you need to, ask your recommenders to address their letters "To Whom It May Concern," unless one of your recommenders has a particular connection to one of your graduate schools or knows an official at the school.

Choose recommenders who can speak authoritatively about the criteria important to selection officials at your graduate school. In other words, choose recommenders who can write about your grasp of the literature in your field of study, your ability to write and speak effectively, your class performance, and your demonstrated interest in the field outside of class. Other characteristics that graduate schools are interested in assessing include your emotional maturity, leadership ability, breadth of general knowledge, intellectual ability, motivation, perseverance, and ability to engage in independent inquiry.

When requesting recommendations, it's especially helpful to put the request in writing. Explain your graduate school intentions and express some of your thoughts about graduate school and your appreciation for their support. Don't be shy about "prompting" your recommenders with some suggestions of what you would appreciate being included in their comments. Most recommenders will find this direction helpful and will want to produce a statement of support that you can both stand behind. Consequently, if your interaction with one recommender was especially focused on research projects, he or she might be best able to speak of those skills and your critical thinking ability. Another recommender may have good comments to make about your public presentation skills.

Give your recommenders plenty of lead time in which to complete your recommendation, and set a date by which they should respond. If they fail to meet your deadline, be prepared to make a polite call or visit to inquire if they need more information or if there is anything you can do to move the process along.

Whether or not you are providing a graduate school form or asking for an original letter to be mailed, be sure to provide an envelope and postage if the recommender must mail the form or letter directly to the graduate school.

Each recommendation you request should provide a different piece of information about you for the selection committee. It might be pleasant for letters of recommendation to say that you are a fine, upstanding individual, but a selection committee for graduate school will require specific information. Each recommender has had a unique relationship with you, and their letters should reflect that. Think of each letter as helping to build a more complete portrait of you as a potential graduate student.

Write Your Application Statement

....

For the history major, this should be an exciting and challenging assignment and one you should be able to complete successfully. Certainly, any required essays on a graduate application for history will weigh heavily in the decision process of the graduate school admissions committee.

....

An excellent source to help in thinking about writing this essay is *How to Write a Winning Personal Statement for Graduate and Professional School* by Richard J. Stelzer. It has been written from the perspective of what graduate school selection committees are looking for when they read these essays. It provides helpful tips to keep your essay targeted on the kinds of issues and criteria that are important to selection committees and that provide them with the kind of information they can best utilize in making their decision.

Follow Up on Your Applications

After you have finished each application and mailed it along with your transcript requests and letters of recommendation, be sure to follow up on the progress of your file. For example, call the graduate school administrative staff to see whether your transcripts have arrived. If the school required your recommenders to fill out a specific recommendation form that had to be mailed directly to the school, you will want to ensure that they have all arrived in good time for the processing of your application. It is your responsibility to make certain that all required information is received by the institution.

Researching Financial Aid Sources, Scholarships, and Fellowships

Financial aid information is available from each school, so be sure to request it when you call for a catalog and application materials. There will be several lengthy forms to complete, and these will vary by school, type of school (public versus private), and state. Be sure to note the deadline dates for these important forms.

There are many excellent resources available to help you explore all of your financial aid options. Visit your college career office or local public library to find out about the range of materials available. Two excellent resources include Peterson's *Grants for Graduate Students* and the Foundation Center's *Foundation Grants to Individuals*. These types of resources generally contain information that can be accessed by indexes including field of study, specific eligibility requirements, administering agency, and geographic focus.

Evaluating Acceptances

If you apply to and are accepted at more than one school, it is time to return to your initial research and self-assessment to evaluate your options and select the program that will best help you achieve the goals you set for pursuing graduate study. You'll want to choose a program that will allow you to complete your studies in a timely and cost-effective way. This may be a good time to get additional feedback from professors and career professionals who are familiar with your interests and plans. Ultimately, the decision is yours, so be sure you get answers to all the questions you can think of.

Some Notes about Rejection

Each graduate school is searching for applicants who appear to have the qualifications necessary to succeed in its program. Applications are evaluated on a combination of undergraduate grade point average, strength of letters of recommendation, standardized test scores, and personal statements written for the application.

A carelessly completed application is one reason many applicants are denied admission to a graduate program. To avoid this type of needless rejection, be sure to carefully and completely answer all appropriate questions on the application form, focus your personal statement given the instructions provided, and submit your materials well in advance of the deadline. Remember that your test scores and recommendations are considered a part of your application, so they must also be received by the deadline.

If you are rejected by a school that especially interests you, you may want to contact the dean of graduate studies to discuss the strengths and weaknesses of your application. Information provided by the dean will be useful in reapplying to the program or applying to other, similar programs.

PART TWO

THE CAREER PATHS

CHAPTER NINE

INTRODUCTION TO THE HISTORY CAREER PATHS

There's no denying the excitement and lure of history. The events, the personalities, the discoveries, and the continuing mysteries are endlessly fascinating. David Macaulay, the children's author and illustrator, has done much to invigorate young people's appreciation of the history of architecture through his magnificent books and incredibly detailed drawings of medieval cathedrals, the pyramids and famous bridges. Other recent books on the history of knitting, the Gulf War, skiing, or girlhood embroidery indicate the popularity of specialization and detail among history enthusiasts.

HISTORY AND TECHNOLOGY

An article in *The Chronicle of Higher Education* (January 12, 1994) illustrates at one and the same time the relevance of studying history, the excitement and interest in applying new technology to examining the past, a glimpse into the future of the academic study of history and a suggestion of the controversy all this change can entail. The article outlines the use of media, especially CD-ROMs and on-line data bases, for making documents, data and even the sights and sound of history available to even larger audiences.

Increasingly, textbooks housed on CD-ROM contain simulations and role-playing exercises that allow students to experience how history actually takes place and to participate in the choices and decision-making of those they study, resulting in greater engagement with, interest in and understanding of the forces that shaped the present. Student response is positive and the visual and auditory enhancement of learning is entirely consistent with the preferred medium of information and entertainment transfer.

Though *The Chronicle* article speaks of a generational gap that currently exists between faculty who are not computer literate and those who are as a determinant in the use of these new technologies, especially the many history Internet databases that are in use, other issues involve the cost of subscribing to these items and the growing amount of storage space these data bases demand. Currently, the storage and computer use are being supplied by university computer administrators but that may change. Some scholars question the reliability and authenticity of electronically retrieved documents. Many issues remain to be solved, but the future for history is certain to include electronic *and* printed resources.

For archivists and curators and information specialists of all kinds, technology makes new demands on budgets for acquisitions, as new technology is never inexpensive. Information storage and retrieval will be altered as we learn the best ways to store, preserve and make this material available to the public. Accuracy and reliability of information sourcing will come under new scrutiny and will add to the critical review of these materials by information specialists.

History Is Full of Controversy

History is not without controversy, as you know full well from your studies. That controversy will continue into the future, as has been suggested in the discussion on advanced technology. Political controversy exists as well. In an editorial for *The Chronicle of Higher Education* (March 16, 1994), James B. Gardner, acting executive director of the American Historical Association, and Page Putnam Miller, director of the National Coordinating Committee for the Promotion of History, issue a vigorous warning to the White House. They expect the President to make a considered choice for the position of Archivist of the United States and ensure that whoever is chosen has the following qualifications:

> "demonstrated professional expertise in history, archival theory and practice, or a related field; national stature among archivists, historians, and other professionals concerned with the integrity of federal records; successful experience in administering programs with responsibility for cultural or informational resources; and demonstrated understanding of archival concerns and of the role of historical research in documenting federal policies, programs, and actions."

Why the concern? The federal archivist is responsible for the housing, preservation and availability of federal records to scholars, legislators and the general public. He or she also oversees the presidential libraries, regional archives and other records centers. With the Freedom of Information Act and the interest of journalists in past administrations, military actions and, most recently, governmental involvement in the use of radiation experiments on human subjects, it is critical that the archivist be above politics and of unimpeachable integrity.

TURN AROUND AND LOOK AT THE FUTURE FOR HISTORY MAJORS!

Because history is concerned with "the memory of things said and done," it is, as with so many liberal arts majors, often targeted by those questioning its career relevance. The following chapters will fully illustrate the wonderful opportunities available to you with this valuable degree. They give you detailed information on which you can begin to travel your own career path and write your own personal career history. The five options described in this book include:

1. Non-Classroom Education

2. Curatorship

3. Information Specialization

4. Business Administration and Management

5. Teaching

Think of the implications of just the new technology for the career paths we outline. For educators of all kinds, classroom teachers as well as interpreters and guides, these new technologies allow history to truly come alive in sight and sound for learners. The use and ability to draw from these on-line systems and CD-ROM technologies will have a corresponding demand for in-service training for all types of instructors as they learn to master this technology and bring it to their students and their classroom, be it a traditional learning site or a field experience.

Begin exploring for yourself the innumerable byways offered up by each of the paths described here.

CHAPTER TEN

PATH 1: NON-CLASSROOM EDUCATION

an you picture yourself in any of these scenes?

Scene 1. A room full of noisy, excited children are visiting you for the morning at the State Historical Society where you, in costume, walk them through room after room of carefully reconstructed period living arrangements. You tell them stories of the people who may have lived there and what they did, and you explain the significance and utility of everything from a niddy-noddy to a priceless pendulum clock brought over by a family on their perilous voyage to America.

Scene 2. A group of professional needlework artists from abroad are visiting the museum/historic house/collection of which you are the docent for textiles. They are filled with admiration and ask challenging questions about the provenance of the pieces, the fabric composition, the dyes used in the wool and the availability of design motifs. All your research and study is on display in a lively and sophisticated exchange of information.

Scene 3. Watch out! Leading people on tours of indoor and outdoor environmental exhibits that include nature trails and aquatic exhibits takes careful footing and a whole new range of other skills on top of that! If you like the outdoors and enjoy sharing what you know with visitors, building exhibits and writing grants, maybe you can see yourself here.

For you history majors who want to educate, teach and guide others, but not in the classroom, this career path offers all the rich rewards of teaching, often in a less-structured environment and with a volunteer audience that's enthusiastic and interested. What's more, you'll continue learning yourself. You will discover in this career path that traditional education continues to redefine itself. Education now extends far, far beyond classroom walls and most importantly draws on the resources of specialists in every area of human endeavor as collaborators and consultants in the educational process. You can join that select group of specialists that consults with the classroom teacher.

We now understand how important it is for young learners in the elementary and middle school years to listen to and hear from role models with expertise in many fields. Different voices and different points of view help students develop their own critical thinking skills. Seeing different personalities, ages and cultures present important information may be just the role modeling an individual student needs to consider their own career path. Classroom visits by outside experts are now commonplace. Each day, school hallways across America are visited by storytellers, naturalists, artists, poets, judges, tradespeople, craftsmen, farmers and other occupational and educational representatives. These talented people want to share what they know and appreciate with a new and eager audience.

Enthusiasm is certainly important, but understanding how to structure and deliver information appropriate to varying grade levels and developmental stages is equally so. Third graders will enjoy dressing up and acting out playlets from the Pilgrim's first Thanksgiving while seventh graders will find Early American farming techniques (including the use of fish as fertilizer!) more fascinating. The older grades are also more interested in and better able to handle the realities of Pilgrim/Native American relations or the cold, hard truth that the first Thanksgiving did not include turkey!

Knowing what you want to accomplish, what you hope your groups will learn, means setting goals and learning outcomes and planning appropriate exercises to encourage that learning. To assess your accomplishments and your growing expertise, you'll want some kind of evaluation instrument, however simple. This could range from the hysterical cheering following "Did you have a good time?" to a simple form for older students or adults to fill out. Teaching aids, use of media, and additional reading lists will all help the classroom teacher expand and build on your lessons.

For the classroom teacher, your expertise as a visitor brings a whole new dimension of learning to the students. It's exciting for the school teacher to see the changes in response and adaptability of students to a different instructor. Each student comes to you with a clean slate, consequently you treat them differently than the teachers who know their academic and behavioral history. In addition to your specialized content knowledge, your presence, your voice, your orientation to the material and your interaction with the class helps these young pupils prepare for other learning experiences and other teachers.

In the high school years, as students begin to become increasingly concerned with the future, possible college choices or vocational options, the opportunity to see and meet role models from a variety of occupations is a window on the world. In addition to the reason for your visit, you also present a role model as a working man or woman in an area of employment many students might not have heard of. Perhaps you are a representative from a natural history museum who has been invited to do a program for high school juniors. Your topic is "Whale Bone Carvings of Eighteenth-Century New England Whalers." Perhaps you'll bring along some atmosphere; a recording of waves crashing and water lapping against the side of the hull of the wooden whaling vessel. Perhaps some faintly heard sea chanties. You darken the classroom and light some candles or effect the dim light of lanterns to demonstrate the conditions under which some of these magnificent carvings were created. Of course, you'll bring samples to pass about and maybe give students the opportunity to try their hand at carving something themselves out of a comparable material.

Before they know it, you will have told them of the location of some of the important collections of seafarers' memorabilia in the United States, the economics of whaling, the great oil painters of ships and the fishing industry, the seacoast towns of New England and the Pacific Northwest, the literature of Herman Melville and even the distinctive knitted designs on fishermans' guernsey sweaters for the macabre purpose of helping to identify a drowned body when recognition was no longer possible!

Literature, museum studies, economics, social and cultural anthropology, art, craft, and history all prove rich fodder for young minds and a visit such as the one described can leave an indelible impression. What's also important for your temporary students is that they meet and see educators from outside the classroom whose expertise is solid but whose pupils are constantly changing. They see someone creating a career from something they love. They begin to understand learning can happen everywhere and throughout life. Your visit may suggest possibilities for exploration they had not imagined. What's most important is that they gain from you the insight that learning does not have to take place in a classroom. Your students may be inspired to develop interests and avocational or educational pursuits that will be with them their entire lives as a source of true enrichment and pleasure.

High schools and colleges increasingly want students out of the classroom and interacting with the "real world" and its representatives. Rather than see a film on Shaker life, a visit to a Shaker community will have far more impact, as the guide demonstrates the infinite productivity and ingenuity of this religious sect that, though short-lived, remains a testament to their love of God through their architecture, tools, furniture and a way of life. The restored communities at Pleasant Hill, Kentucky; Sabbathday Lake, Maine; and Enfield and Canterbury, New Hampshire are each a university of material about religion, social structure, ingenuity, spirituality, joy, communal living, productivity and purity.

The broadening mission of education is one of the principle motivations behind this collaboration with educators from outside the classroom. Teachers realize that they cannot do it all by themselves, and that there are scores of talented individuals who will work with them to excite these young minds with a variety of topics. You will be seen as a professional colleague and an important part of the educational network.

There is yet another valuable reason behind our growing dependence upon educators whose arena is not in the schools. We increasingly realize the fragility and vulnerability of our planet and its people. Never have our resources and our heritage been more important to us and more subject to the stresses and strains of humanity. The preservation of the condor, the maintenance and restoration of great architecture, all the perishable remains of culture are vulnerable. We now understand the importance of protecting our historic sites, of preserving our natural wetlands, of providing resources for our natural flora and fauna and of recognizing and celebrating the rich legacy of all our ancestors and their contributions and impact on our present lives.

The role the non-classroom educator plays is vital and, like the ripples across the pond that follow any disturbance of the water's surface, you often cannot and will not know the full effects of your interaction with your learners. Depending upon your setting and your presentation you may inspire hobbies, personal study regimens, or entire changes in a way of living. Whatever your effect, you will assuredly enhance and enlarge what has been learned through the traditional classroom and bring to life with a special vividness a new learning experience.

DEFINITION OF THE CAREER PATH

One of the most exciting aspects of using your history background in non-classroom education is the incredible and unlimited variety of settings, instructional modes and subject areas. With no difficulty whatsoever, the following brief list of possibilities was assembled from a variety of easily accessible job listings.

Museum Educator. Work with preschool children. 25 hrs/wk. Resume/ ltr to Smithsonian Early Enrichment Center, National Museum of American History, . . .

continued

---

continued

Educator. Bachelors degree in science, history or education-related field, 3 yrs museum experience required. Submit cover ltr/resume to (specialty museum) . . .

Coordinator of School & Youth Programs. Sustain, create, implement, oversee youth educational programs, curricula, tours, activities & outreach programs for youth of all ages. Hire, train, schedule, coach, evaluate museum teachers. Serve as liaison with regional educational institutions; develop & operate teacher institute; prepare teacher newsletters. Requirements: creativity, high academic standards; strong writing & communication skills; strong organizational skills; two years experience teaching history in a museum setting; MA in history, anthropology, folklore, education, or related field; IBM word-processing useful.

Education Specialist. Museum w/decorative arts collection and historic house. Plan family programs, liaison w/teachers, manage classroom outreach program, develop interpretive materials, write grants. Flex schedule including some weekend work. Req BA history/art/museum studies/museum educ. Low 20's, benes. Resume/ltr/refs to Director of Education (state historical society) . . .

Counselor Naturalist. To teach environmental day camp for Grades K–6. Prepare lesson plans & materials, lead activities, check in & supervise campers. May have opportunity to work with staff on natural history interpretation for the public. BA/BS with strong biology, marine biology, history, or natural history background.

Program Coordinator. Under direction of curator of education, assist in the implementation of programs to promote greater use of museum's resources in college teaching. 3 yr/grant funded position. BA required, MA in art history preferred, museum education experience preferred; maturity, interpersonal skills & attention to detail essential. Send letter & resume to (college) . . .

Nature Education Instructor. 37 wks/yr, 3 yrs. Deliver tours, teach in K–12 classrooms. Req 2 yrs natural history/environmental teach exp. Resume/ltr to (wildlife sanctuary) . . .

Outdoor Education Instructor. Seasonal. Established 5-day resident program serving grades 5–8. Teach pioneer living, ropes courses,

continued

continued
natural history. Req rel BA/BS. $175/wk, room & board. Resume/ltr to (outdoor education center) . . .

Interpretive Guide. Explain/suggest hiking and sites, liaison between staff and guests. Req learn about Tarahumara Indians and natural history of Copper Canyon Lodges. Send ltr/resume to . . .

Interpreter/Caretaker. (private museum) noted as the birthplace of America's foremost portrait painter and for its operational 18th century water powered snuff mill. Located in rural community. Active interpretation program goes on from early spring to late fall. Small boats avail. for recreational use. Year round position w/housing provided. Salary negotiable. Good communication skills a must. Record keeping, garden maintenance, grounds keeping, general maintenance are all phases of the job. Submit resume to Trustees, . . .

Field Interpreter. Design programs focusing on natural and cultural history of the region. Req rel BA/BS, 2–3 yrs exp developing/interpreting experiential learning programs, know NW natural/cultural history & ecology, current CPR/first aid cert. Pref MA/MS, teach cert. $58/day, lodging & meals, benes. Resume/ltr to . . .

Coordinator of Interpretation and Visitor Services. Research, develop, implement, sustain, evaluate interpretive materials and strategies; interview, hire, train, schedule, coach, evaluate interpreters; design and oversee visitor orientation. Requirements: significant supervisory experience; excellent interpersonal skills; imagination and high scholarly standards; strong writing and communications skills; strong organizational skills; four yrs exp in history or related field; MA in history, anthro, folklore or related field. IBM wordprocessing useful. Letter/resume to . . .

Gallery Assistant. At the Old State House, assist in daily operations of the museum in areas of interpretation, visitors services, monitoring of galleries. Gallery Assistant is in daily contact with the public in the galleries or visitor orientation area. Also works directly with Department of Public Programs and volunteers. Responsibilities: interpretation, answering questions and assisting general visitors and

continued

continued
school programs; building operations, set-up and preparation for
events including some evening hours; visitor services, providing
access for visitors with special needs, monitoring galleries for exhibition problems, and assisting at the information desk. Candidate
should possess mature people-handling skills, enjoy area history and
working with audiences of all ages. Job involves walking up and down
a winding staircase many times a day. Weekend and some holiday
hours required. Letter and resume to . . .

Museum Assistant. Seasonal position. Work w/museum docents to
conduct tours and interpret exhibits, care for and maintain
serpentarium and marine systems. Ltr/resume to (conservancy
organization) . . .

With such a varied list of job announcements (including some that we are
certain you wish you could apply for!), you might well ask, is there any com-
monality? What are the linking elements in the career of the non-classroom
educator? What kinds of general statements can be made about so many different positions? Consider the following:

Focused Fields of Study. Unlike your classroom counterparts, you can focus
quite specifically on a period in history, a particular person, a piece of architec-
tural history, an environmental domain (wetland, forest, etc.) and develop
your acumen in that regard.

Age-Specific Populations. In most of the ads listed above, there are definite
age parameters, which may appeal to you if you have had experience working
with particular age groups.

Sense of Excitement and Adventure. In most situations, a visit to where you
work is a highlight or treat for your clientele, be it schoolchildren or family
outing. Your audiences will be enthusiastic and you will find that atmosphere
infects you as well.

Levels of Activity. Many of these postings indicate or suggest heightened
levels of activity and some make explicit statements about walking, stairs and
other physical demands. Some of this is discussed in the section that follows.
Here, the important point to remember is that your classroom is more interactive, and may involve more movement and energy than a traditional setting.

WORKING CONDITIONS

How does having your own apartment on the grounds of a historic home and gardens sound? Or, can you imagine spending your day helping animated young schoolchildren to appreciate the life of a colonial family? Maybe your interest is in designing curricula, planning events or organizing programs for young people of all ages. Some history majors would love to work outside, educating others about our natural history, the environment or Native American customs.

The working conditions in this career path are defined by each individual position, and very often you will find some mention of schedule, hours, accommodation, and targeted populations in the job posting itself. Your self-assessment is important here as you will need to match your own wants and needs, skills and abilities against the varying demands of each position. There are many working conditions to consider as you explore the world of non-classroom education. Consider each of the following sections to see how well the job seems to "fit."

Public Presentations

How much public presentation does the job require and how do you feel about that? How successful has that kind of activity been for you in the past? Will presentations be throughout the day or will they be punctuation marks in a day filled with other activities? Will you enjoy "being on" as much as the job requires or will you find that role fatiguing?

Curriculum Development/Program Planning

If curriculum development and program planning is a job requirement, how will that suit you? That means research, writing, and probably significant collaboration to develop effective programs.

Teamwork

What team experiences have you had with important activities to judge your ability in this new role? Have you tended to be a "loner" or autonomous worker in past jobs or do you enjoy being part of a larger work unit? Will this behind the scenes work be satisfying to you or will you be anxious to be with the public?

Irregular Hours

Because many facilities that seek to educate the public are open both during the school week for educational trips and on weekends for family excursions, non-school educational positions frequently require some weekend hours.

Continuing Education

Another important factor to seriously consider is the continuing education demands of these positions. As with any educator role, the teachers themselves must continue to learn. You'll be pursuing your own self-education, year round, on the time period, peoples or artifacts your job deals with, in addition to conferences, seminars and formal training programs to increase your expertise in the field. A teacher, by virtue of his or her profession, must remain a student.

Versatility and Unpredictability

The watchword of jobs such as these is "expect the unexpected." Your classroom is open to anyone and the public is a mysterious variable. Each group you lead will be different and though you will come to expect and be wonderfully adept at answering those famous questions, each day will bring new challenges in the public's behavior, understanding of what you are trying to communicate and appreciation for your field. The non-classroom educator must enjoy the unpredictability of the public equally as much as they enjoy their subject matter.

TRAINING AND QUALIFICATIONS

You probably have many questions about your readiness for any of these positions. As you read the job ads we have cited in this career path, chances are quite high that you've seen more than one job that sounds "perfect." You are probably wishing the authors had listed exactly where that job was located! By the time you read this chapter, those particular jobs have been filled. Never fear, for each day, each week, and each month bring more positions onto the market in this growing and exciting field.

Your questions remain, however. Your history study in college has been typically broad and though you have favorite topics and periods, they don't coincide with any of these jobs. Is that a problem? Absolutely not!

In almost every situation you've seen advertised, be it historic home, children's museum, private collection, National Park position, or environmental center, your study skills will be put to new use as you master the research, historical background, personalities and artifacts associated with your new employment.

In the case of tours, you will probably find "scripts" prepared that you may tailor to suit your individual style of presentation, and you may enjoy a period of training from your predecessor or another employee who has done this job. In most cases, your interpretation is limited only by your own willingness to research your subject and incorporate that material into your teaching and a corresponding need to be accurate with your facts and pay attention to details.

EARNINGS

Earnings packages for non-classroom educators vary dramatically and may include important conditions of employment that need to be weighed against your salary. There may be room and/or board, there may be long days out-of-doors, there may be continual stair-climbing as you lead visitors on tours. Weigh your needs, the job demands, and the experience you'll gain carefully before making a decision.

The range is amazingly wide, from minimum wage tour guides to National Park positions with entry level salaries of approximately $24,000 plus benefits. The size of the employer has much to do with entry level salary ranges. The Smithsonian has History Education Specialist positions for bachelor degree candidates that cite a range of $27,789–$35,123 with most entry level candidates falling at the mid-point within that range. A smaller institution, perhaps a state historical society with a comprehensive education program, would have starting salaries for educators in the mid to high 20s. Some historical sites with local or regional appeal hire costumed interpreters at hourly wages, approximating an annual salary in the high teens.

It's difficult to make sweeping generalizations about a field where required training, job demands, activity level and possible prerequisites vary so dramatically from site to site. What is encouraging is that the field of non-classroom education is increasingly recognized for its value and importance in conveying information that profoundly affects the recipient's learning through channels outside the traditional classroom setting.

CAREER OUTLOOK

The career outlook for the talented non-classroom educator is excellent. Be it restored Shaker village, historic mill reconstruction, art gallery, museum education programs of all types, wetlands reclamation project or costumed interpretation, the variety, number and scope of these professions continues to grow as Americans become increasingly interested in what is educational, entertaining, and enjoyable as a pastime.

Gone are the days where the public will suffer a self-guided tour with printed literature. Though many still prefer this, many others opt for a guide, a docent, an interpreter, or an information coordinator to make their experience worthwhile. For young people, this often means interactive programs. For adults, it frequently means specific answers to countless questions that have real meaning for the person asking them. No matter what the age or experience, the addition of your role as a non-classroom educator heightens and enhances the experience for everyone!

The authors wish that they could append to this volume even a small part of the great number of job listings they have perused in the category of non-classroom education. To do so would make this a multi-volume set, for there are thousands! But they are not all equal. Pay varies, as do hours and, in some cases, seasonality. Many will use your history expertise in a very direct way, others will make additional demands on your interests and experience beyond your major.

Strategy for Finding the Jobs

If you can't picture yourself sitting behind a desk for most of your workday, you can use your degree in history to work in a non-classroom educational setting. Outlined below is a four-pronged strategy you can implement to position yourself more competitively in the marketplace. Consider undertaking these tasks:

Learn about Educational Theory and Process

Unless you have been granted or are eligible for teacher certification, you will want to learn more about educational theory and the educational process. Because many of the positions outlined in this path either oversee or provide educational programming, it is important to know how to reach the audiences you are trying to educate.

Gain an understanding of the differences in learning styles for different ages and how to appeal to the various ways in which we all learn. There are a number of methods you can use to acquire this information.

1. Become a critical observer of other non-classroom educators. When you attend meetings, workshops, seminars or even watch educational television, note how information is conveyed, how media is employed to illustrate certain points, and what techniques are used to assess learning outcomes.

2. Read. There are some excellent library resource books on how to construct education programs that include setting reasonable learning goals, developing learning activities to further those goals, and testing or evaluating for learning outcomes that you expect from your presentation. Create your own bibliography of good instructional books and put it in your portfolio. Be ready to discuss your own position on effective designs for learning.

3. Enroll in a continuing education course or professional seminar on conducting effective workshops. These are often full-day programs that cover all aspects of effective program design and delivery, and you will be able to document this formal training on your resume. It might also stimulate you to do some further study on your own.

4. Think also about acquiring some good media technology skills. Too often, the presenter's inability with an overhead projector or VCR can mar an otherwise strong program. Your college or university or local high school may have a media specialist on the staff who would be willing to volunteer some time to acquaint you with the most common equipment and how to operate it effectively.

Acquire a Specialized Knowledge That Complements Your Study of History

As you have seen in the job descriptions threaded throughout the discussion of this career path, some require knowledge in areas not covered in a traditional history curriculum. Some positions require a knowledge of art history, natural history, or the environment, while others ask for computer or media skills. The academic minor you choose could play a critical role in helping you acquire the specialized knowledge you'll need to gain employment in certain types of positions.

If you have already graduated, consider taking continuing education courses at a nearby college or university to enhance your skills. Or consider adding to your portfolio of skills by attending a one-time seminar or workshop. Many professional associations notify members of and offer training and educational opportunities in this more-intensive, shorter format. Check the association information at the end of this path for those organizations that offer seminars, workshops or other training opportunities.

Do an Internship or Volunteer Your Time in the Type of Setting in which You Hope to Work

There are a range of settings in which non-classroom educational programs are offered, and each requires a specialized knowledge. Your academic work is important, but gaining actual work experience in the field is also critical to your job search success. By gaining work experience in a specific type of setting you will be able to test your decision by seeing if you like the work, you will gain hands-on experience to add to your resume, and you will make important contacts who may be willing to help you in your search for professional employment.

Some excellent resources which will help you locate actual internships, as well as help you understand the types of employers that work with interns, include the newsletter *InternAmerica,* the latest edition of Peterson's *Internships,* and *The National Directory of Internships.* There are many, many additional resources available, so be sure to ask the career professional or librarian you are working with for other titles.

Use Both Reactive and Proactive Job Search Techniques

Your job search should begin with a review of published job listings. You'll get a good sense of the types of jobs that are available and the range of titles used to describe these jobs. In addition, you'll become intimately familiar with duties associated with each type of job, and the salary range for the geographic area you're examining. Some sources for actual job listings can be found in the section listing professional associations. Other excellent job listings include:

- ❑ *Current Jobs in Art*

- ❑ *Community Jobs*

- ❑ *Current Jobs for Graduates*

- ❑ *The Job Hunter*

- ❑ *Environmental Opportunities*

- ❑ *Earth Work*

- ❑ *Aviso: A Monthly Dispatch from the American Association of Museums*

Using information contained in this path and in the job descriptions you read, you'll be able to create a focused resume that describes how you can help accomplish the goals of the organizations you are approaching, and learn to speak directly to employer needs in an interview situation.

But don't limit your search to simply responding to job advertisements. Be sure to use your college alumni network to begin developing contacts who are currently employed at the type of organization you would like to work for. Use other techniques described in the networking chapter of this book to enhance your proactive job search activities.

POSSIBLE EMPLOYERS

Museums are, of course, one of the major employers for non-classroom educators. But have you considered the other types of employers that hire people to educate the public about their histories, mission, or collections? Read on and find out more about some of them, including zoological parks, aquariums, wildlife refuges and bird sanctuaries; arboretums, botanical and aquatic gardens, conservatories, and horticultural societies; outdoor education centers; camps; and national and state parks.

Museums

Profile.   Have you ever investigated all of the different types of museums that exist in the United States? There is an institution for nearly every interest. Most often art comes to mind when we hear the word museum, but educational programs, walking tours, films, lectures or slide shows are also offered at textile museums, children's museums, military museums, arboretums, wildlife refuges, circus museums, mappariums, and sports museums.

The American Association of Museums categorizes institutions into one of fourteen groups. They include:

- ❑ Art museums

- ❑ Children's museums

- ❑ College and university museums

- ❑ Company museums

- ❑ Exhibit areas

- ❑ General museums

- ❑ History museums

- ❑ Libraries having collections of books

- ❑ Libraries having collections other than books

- ❑ National and state agencies, councils and commissions

- ❑ Nature centers

- ❑ Park museums and visitor centers

- ❑ Science museums

- ❑ Specialized museums

History and specialized museums may be of particular interest to the history major; these types of facilities are divided into several sub-categories in *The Official Museum Directory.*

Under the history category of museums you will find, of course, history museums, but you will also see military museums, preservation projects, as well as history agencies, councils, commissions and research institutes. Be sure to review *The Official Museum Directory* for a complete listing of their members in this category.

Agricultural museums to horological museums displaying timepieces, industrial museums to woodcarving museums, all are found in the specialized museum classification. If you have a hobby or special interest, you may be able to combine your specialized knowledge with your work in a non-classroom educational environment.

Help in Locating These Employers. If you would like to explore one of these categories of museums, the best source is the latest edition of *The Official Museum Directory.* Institutions are indexed by state and by category of institution. In addition, other listings of interest are provided, including:

❑ Federal agencies providing museum support

❑ Regional arts organizations

❑ State arts agencies

❑ State humanities councils

Other useful resources which can be used to help you locate potential employers include your local and regional yellow pages (look under Museums), and state or regional directories of non-profit organizations (call your local chamber of commerce to determine whether they know of such a directory for your area). Or talk with a representative of a state or regional museum association. The regions are:

❑ New England Museum Association, Boston, Massachusetts

❑ Mid-Atlantic Association of Museums, Newark, Delaware

❑ Southeastern Museums Conference, Baton Rouge, Louisiana

❑ Midwest Museum Conference, St. Louis, Missouri

❑ Mountain-Plains Museum Association, Manitou Springs, Colorado

❑ Western Museums Association, Los Angeles, California

Zoological Parks, Aquariums, Wildlife Refuges and Bird Sanctuaries

Profile. If your interests lie in helping the general public understand the impact of historical events and human experiences on the living creatures with whom we share the world, you may be interested in getting involved in educational programming efforts offered at zoos, aquariums, wildlife refuges and bird sanctuaries. There are people who work as guides at sites all around the United States, leading groups of interested nature and animal lovers on zoo or aquarium tours, nature walks, and wildlife education tours.

Help in Locating These Employers. An excellent resource for locating zoos and aquariums is *Zoological Parks and Aquariums in the Americas* published by the

American Association of Zoological Parks and Aquariums. This directory lists facilities by state and provides contact information, and also describes the species and specimens that can be found at the facility, as well as visitor information. *The Official Museum Directory* also lists these types of organizations, and can provide a contact name, mailing address, telephone number and background information.

Wildlife refuge and bird sanctuary educators are, for the most part, public sector employees. The federal government, as well as state and local governments, hire workers to educate the public through various education programs. Three federal agencies that hire this type of educator include the National Park Service, the U.S. Fish and Wildlife Service, and the Bureau of Land Management. State departments or agencies that may provide employment opportunities include environmental protection, fish and wildlife, forestry, natural resources, and parks and recreation. Local governments that include a parks and recreation department may also hire workers for non-classroom teaching positions. A book titled, *Guide to the National Wildlife Refuges* by Laura and William Riley, lists more than 475 sites. A description of each refuge is provided, as well as directions for locating the site, hours of operation, what can be seen and done there, and contact information if you would like to learn more.

Some excellent resources which can help you navigate the maze of government employment include: *The Complete Guide to Public Employment, Opportunities in State and Local Government Careers,* and *Government Job Finder.*

Many non-profit organizations which were established to protect animal life also run educational programs. Listings of non-profit organizations involved in this type of effort can be found in *Great Careers: The Fourth of July Guide to Careers, Internships, and Volunteer Opportunities in the Nonprofit Sector.* You'll also want to review *The Directory of National Environmental Organizations.* It contains a subject index that includes animal rights and animal welfare groups, education, endangered species, and wildlife preservation.

The National Audubon Society has two publications you will want to review if you are interested in working at one of their eighty-two sanctuaries. Call the Society and ask for their Sanctuary Brochure or Sanctuary Booklet. Both provide contact information; the brochure is free, but there is a small charge for the booklet.

Arboretums, Botanical and Aquatic Gardens, Conservatories, and Horticultural Societies

Profile.   Have you ever enjoyed walking a trail of rising and sinking boards floating on a mass of sphagnum moss surrounded by shoulder high autumn-hued vegetation? Have you ever gasped at the beauty of a Bird of Paradise? Or enjoyed smelling the rich perfume of a mock-orange tree in bloom? You *can* combine your love for, or interest in living botanical environments with your history degree to educate people who share these same interests.

Help in Locating These Employers. Your career or public library will probably have on hand a reference book entitled *North American Horticulture: A Reference Guide*. Use it to become familiar with possible employment sites. If you are interested in working at a botanical garden, you can join the American Association of Botanical Gardens and Arboreta to obtain a copy of their membership directory which will list employers of each member. *The Official Museum Directory* also contains contact information for these types of facilities, and the *Directory of National Environmental Organizations* contains a section listing organizations concerned with preserving and protecting oceans and marine environments.

Outdoor Education Centers

Profile. Have you ever participated in a leadership training program that included a ropes course, or visited a center that offered a year-round program in environmental education? Both of these types of settings are included in what we are calling outdoor education. Each type of facility employs workers who are dedicated to the mission of the organization, and many of these people have bachelors degrees. A recent review of the credentials of an adventure center's employees revealed that nine of the sixteen had either a BA or a BS, and a deep commitment to outdoor education.

Help in Locating These Employers. Employment opportunities exist in many places and are called by different names, so be sure to follow up on lots of different leads. There are year-round environmental education centers that employ people like yourself, and you can locate them by contacting the North American Association for Environmental Education located in Troy, Ohio. You can also contact the Educational Resources Information Center (ERIC) Center for Environmental Education at Ohio State University or use ERIC resources (often housed on CD-ROMs) at your college or public library. Additionally, each state has a Department of Natural Resources, or Environmental Protection, or Environmental Education, and they often offer ongoing educational programs. Check with these agencies or with your state personnel office to find out about job vacancies. Environmental issues are a major concern in our society, and there is much being written about careers in this area, so be sure to ask for assistance in locating the many additional resources available to you.

Camps

Profile. Camping is an American tradition; there are summer resident and day camps, church camps, and travel and trip camps sponsored under public and private auspices. If you are interested in becoming a part of the educational efforts provided through the camping experience, many opportunities are available, especially during the summer months. Year-round opportunities are not as abundant, but are available.

Help in Locating These Employers. One resource to begin with is the *Guide to Accredited Camps* published by the American Camping Association. This guide provides contact information that you can use to find out about jobs that are, primarily, available during the summer months. Another publication, called *Summer Opportunities in Marine and Environmental Science* by Joy Herriott and Betty G. Herrin, contains information on camp programs which you could use to explore employment opportunities in non-classroom educational efforts.

National and State Parks

Profile. Nearly every national and state park has a visitor center which is the focal point for educational programs. Our park systems employ people to educate individuals and groups who visit the park about special features found there—spouting geysers at Yellowstone National Park, mammoth redwoods at Yosemite National Park, Stone-face Old Man of the Mountain at Franconia Notch State Park, and lofty sand dunes at Cape Hatteras National Seashore. Many individuals begin their government career in national or state parks as summer park rangers. Those who "pay their dues" have the advantage of previous government employment as they are being considered for available full-time openings.

Help in Locating These Employers. Each year the U.S. Department of the Interior, National Park Service, advertises seasonal park ranger positions by notifying career offices across the country. Information on locations offering employment, and application forms are available through these offices, as well as federal job information centers. Competition for these entry-level jobs is keen, so begin your search early, carefully complete the application, and follow up with the parks you are most interested in. Full-time positions are advertised in publications such as *Federal Jobs Digest.* If you would like additional information on securing government employment, be sure to review *Government Job Finder* or the *Complete Guide to Public Employment.*

POSSIBLE JOB TITLES

Job titles in non-classroom educational programming will vary depending on the type of employer and role within the educational effort (administering versus teaching), but often-seen job titles include the following:

Administrative assistant
Coordinator of interpretation
    and visitor services
Coordinator of school and
    youth programs
Director of education (museum)
Director of educational
    programs
Director of visitor services
Education coordinator
Education specialist
Educational programs
    coordinator
Educator
Environmental education
    instructor/teacher
Executive director

Field instructor
Interpreter
Interpreter/caretaker
Interpretive guide
Museum assistant
Museum educator
Nature education instructor
Nature interpreter
Outdoor education instructor
Outreach assistant
Park ranger
Programs coordinator
Project planner and coordinator
School programs assistant
Urban park ranger

RELATED OCCUPATIONS

A variety of skills are used by the non-classroom educator, and many of these skills are directly transferable to a variety of other jobs. You know these jobs require designing, organizing and implementing programs; making public presentations; and acting as a public relations representative. Review the list below, and for those position titles that are unfamiliar to you, do some investigating to see if they are jobs possibilities you should consider.

Career Counselor
Caseworker
Classroom teacher
Conference coordinator
Educational equipment and supplies salesperson
Financial Aid Counselor
Human resources professional
Librarian
Public relations specialist
Training specialist
Travel agent

PROFESSIONAL ASSOCIATIONS

Many different professional associations have been listed here, and some of them provide services or publications that you might like to use. Contact those you want to find out more about and ask them to send you information. If you are currently a student, you may be able to initially join the organization for a modest student membership fee. Make sure you know what benefits you'll get from joining a particular association and ask specifically how the organization can help you in your job search. Many provide job listings in their newsletter, or they may have a job placement service available to members. Read on and think about whether membership would benefit you in your job search.

American Association of Botanical Gardens and Arboreta
786 Church Road
Wayne, PA 19087
Members/Purpose: Directors and staffs of botanical gardens, arboreta, institutions maintaining or conducting horticultural courses, and others.
Journal/Publication: *AABGA Newsletter; Public Garden;* internship directory, salary survey.
Job Listings: See *AABGA Newsletter;* call organization for job hotline number.

American Association for Museum Volunteers
c/o American Association of Museums
1225 I Street, NW, Suite 200
Washington, DC 20005
Members/Purpose: Affiliate committee of the American Association of Museums. Serves as forum and source of information for museum volunteers.
Journal/Publication: *AAMV Newsletter; Directory of Museum Volunteer Programs; Museum Volunteer Handbook.*

American Association of Museums
1225 I Street, NW, Suite 200
Washington, DC 20005
Members/Purpose: Art, history, and science museums, art associations and centers, historic houses and societies, preservation projects, planetariums, zoos, aquariums, botanical gardens, college and university museums and others interested in the museum field.
Journal/Publication: *Aviso; Museum News; The Official Museum Directory.*
Job Listings: Maintains placement service for museum professionals; see *Aviso* for employment opportunities in museums.

❧ American Association for State and Local History
530 Church Street, Suite 600
Nashville, TN 37219
Members/Purpose: Organization of educators, historians, writers, and other individuals; state and local historical societies; agencies and institutions interested in improving the study of state and local history in the U.S. and Canada, and assisting historical organizations in improving their public services.
Training: Conducts seminars and workshops.
Journal/Publication: *Directory of Historical Societies and Agencies in the U.S. and Canada; History News; History News Dispatch.*

American Association of Zoo Keepers
Topeka Zoological Park
635 SW Gage Blvd.
Topeka, KS 66606
Members/Purpose: Professional members are zoo keepers and aquarists; affiliate members are other zoo employees and volunteers; associate members are students and other interested persons. Disseminates information about the care of wild animals, birds, reptiles, and marine life found in captivity.
Training: Conducts specialized education and research programs.
Journal/Publication: *Animal Keepers Forum;* directory; conference proceedings.
Job Listings: See *Animal Keepers Forum.*

American Association of Zoological Parks and Aquariums
Oglebay Park
Route 88
Wheeling, WV 26003
Members/Purpose: Zoological park and aquarium personnel; individuals interested in promoting zoos and aquariums for educational and scientific interpretation of nature and animal conservation and for public recreation and cultural pursuits.
Journal/Publication: Annual conference proceedings; *AAZPA Communique; Zoological Parks and Aquariums in the Americas.*
Job Listings: See *AAZPA Communique.*

American Camping Association
5000 State Road 67 North
Martinsville, IN 46151
Members/Purpose: Camp owners, directors, counselors, camps, businesses, and students interested in organized summer camp. Offers information services in several areas including educational programs.

Journal/Publication: *Guide to Accredited Camps; Camping Magazine; Facilities for Conferences, Retreats and Outdoor Education.*

Job Listings: Sponsors placement service.

American Federation of Arts

41 East 65th Street

New York, NY 10021

Members/Purpose: Service organization comprising not-for-profit art museums committed to fostering art appreciation in the U.S. Seeks to broaden public knowledge and appreciation of the visual arts through art, video, and film exhibits, which travel to museums, university art galleries, and other cultural and media centers.

Training: Administrates the Museum Management Institute.

Journal/Publication: *AFA Newsletter.*

American Horticultural Society

7931 East Boulevard Drive

Alexandria, VA 22308

Members/Purpose: Amateur and professional gardeners.

Journal/Publication: *American Horticulturist; American Horticulturist: News Edition.*

Job Listings: Offers internships.

American Park Rangers Association

3801 Biscayne Blvd.

Miami, FL 33130

Members/Purpose: National, state, county, and municipal park rangers who serve in general educational and law enforcement capacities.

Training: Has available a national guide to park ranger training services.

Journal/Publication: *American Park Ranger Newsletter; The Police Times.*

American Park and Recreation Society

1800 Silas Deane Highway, No. 1

Rocky Hill, CT 06067

Members/Purpose: Professional park and recreation directors who provide cultural, physical, and intellectual opportunities in recreational settings throughout the country.

Training: Conducts educational sessions and research symposia at annual congressional meetings.

Journal/Publication: *APRS National Resource Directory; Keeping You Current* (newsletter); *Programmer's Information Network.*

Association of Art Museum Directors

41 East 65th Street

New York, NY 10021

Members/Purpose: Chief staff officers of major art museums.

Journal/Publication: *Professional Practices in Art Museums; Museum Schools and Studio Related Programs; Art Museum Salary Survey.*

Association for Living Historical Farms and Agricultural Museums
Route 14, Box 214
Santa Fe, NM 87505

Members/Purpose: Provides a central repository of information on plants, animals, tools, and implements used in farming in the past; assists farms and museums in securing information; accredits living historical farms and museums; joins in publicizing the farms and museums.

Journal/Publication: Convention proceedings; *Living Historical Farms Bulletin;* membership list.

Association of North American Museums, Libraries, Archives, Cultural Centers, and Fraternal Organizations
6500 South Pulaski Road
Chicago, IL 60629

Members/Purpose: North American ethnic museums, other museums, historical societies, libraries, archives, fraternal organizations, universities, university libraries, and cultural centers. Functions as vehicle for other ethnic and non-ethnic groups to become viable art and education centers in their communities.

Training: Sponsors seminars and exhibits.

Intermuseum Conservation Association
Allen Art Building
Oberlin, OH 44074

Members/Purpose: Performs the examination and treatment of works of art, inspection and maintenance of collections, and research and education in art conservation technology.

Training: Conducts seminars for museum professionals.

Job Listings: Has newsletter with job listings for members.

International Council for Bird Preservation, U.S. Section
c/o World Wildlife Fund
1250 24th Street, NW
Washington, DC 20037

Members/Purpose: Organizations interested in conservation of birds; associate members are individuals providing financial support for conservation activities of the council. Promotes conservation and study of birds on an international basis.

Training: Conducts educational activities.

Journal/Publication: *Bird Conservation; Bulletin; World Birdwatch.*

National Aquarium Society
U.S. Department of Commerce Bldg., Room B-037
14th Street and Constitution Avenue, NW
Washington, DC 20230
Members/Purpose: Objectives are to: operate the National Aquarium; conduct and encourage research; develop educational programs for the public; provide information regarding aquariums; cooperate with other aquarium and wildlife societies.
Journal/Publication: *Fish Lines.*

National Association for Interpretation
P.O. Box 1892
Ft. Collins, CO 80522
Members/Purpose: Specialists who prepare exhibits and conduct programs at information centers maintained by public and private institutions; persons engaged in education programs at museums, zoos, parks, arboretums, botanical gardens, historical sites, schools and camps. Seeks to advance education and develop skills in interpreting the natural, historical, and cultural environment.
Training: Provides national training opportunities; conducts regional training workshops.
Journal/Publication: Directory of members; *Legacy.*
Job Listings: Provides information on job opportunities through employment hotlines and listings.

National Association of Professional Environmental Communicators
500 N. Michigan Avenue, Suite 1400
Chicago, IL 60611
Members/Purpose: Environmental communicators in academe, government, industry, the arts and other fields.
Journal/Publication: *NAPEC Quarterly; NAPEC News.*

National Audubon Society
700 Broadway
New York, NY 10003
Members/Purpose: Persons interested in ecology, energy, and the conservation and restoration of natural resources, with emphasis on wildlife, wildlife habitats, soil, water, and forests.
Journal/Publication: *American Birds; Audubon; Audubon Activist; Wildlife Report.*

National Conference of State Historic Preservation Officers
Hall of States
444 North Capitol Street, NW, Suite 342
Washington, DC 20001

Members/Purpose: Officers and deputy officers appointed by the governor in each of the states and territories. Provides an exchange of information about state and federal preservation program administration.
Training: Offers periodic training sessions.
Journal/Publication: *NCSHPO/Alert; NCSHPO/News;* directory.

National Society for Park Resources
2775 South Quincy Street
Alexandria, VA 22206
Members/Purpose: A professional branch of the National Recreation and Park Association. Park resource managers, planners, designers, rangers, and maintenance persons; nature interpreters and persons concerned with the preservation and use of natural, recreational, historic, and cultural resources.
Training: Conducts educational seminars and training institutes.
Journal/Publication: *Park Practice Program* series; *Parks and Recreation Magazine; Recreation and Parks Law Reporter.*
Job Listings: *Park and Recreation Opportunities Job Bulletin.*

National Wildlife Federation
1400 16th Street, NW
Washington, DC 20036
Members/Purpose: Federation of state and territorial conservation organizations and associate members, including individual conservationist-contributors. Encourages the intelligent management of the life-sustaining resources of the earth and promotes greater appreciation of these resources, their community relationship, and wise use.
Journal/Publication: *Conservation Directory; Conservation Exchange; EYAS* (newsletter); *International Wildlife; The Leader; National Wildlife; Survey of Compensation in the Fields of Fish and Wildlife Management.*

National Wildlife Refuge Association
10824 Fox Hunt Lane
Potomac, MD 20854
Members/Purpose: Conservation clubs, National Audubon Society chapters, birding groups, NWR employees and retirees and interested individuals. Seeks to protect the integrity of the National Wildlife Refuge System and to increase public understanding and appreciation of it.
Training: Conducts education and information programs.
Journal/Publication: *Blue Goose Flyer.*

Natural Science for Youth Foundation
130 Azalea Drive
Roswell, GA 30075

Members/Purpose: Sponsors natural science centers, junior nature museums, native animal parks, and trailside museums. Provides information service.
Training: Conducts training courses in museum and nature center management.
Journal/Publication: Conference proceedings; *Directory of Natural Science Centers; Natural Science Center News; Opportunities.*
Job Listings: Maintains museum and placement service; see publication *Opportunities.*

North American Association for Environmental Education
1255 23rd Street, NW, Suite 400
Washington, DC 20037
Members/Purpose: Individuals associated with colleges, public schools, nature centers, government agencies, and environmental organizations; associates include students in environmental education and environmental studies.
Journal/Publication: *The Environmental Communicator;* newsletter.

Outdoor Education Association
c/o Dr. Edward J. Ambry
143 Fox Hill Road
Denville, NJ 07834
Members/Purpose: Persons interested in promotion of outdoor and environmental education. Advocates outdoor living and learning as an integral part of school and organization programs.
Journal/Publication: *Extending Education.*

Wilderness Education Association
Department of Rec. Resources
Colorado State University
Fort Collins, CO 80523
Members/Purpose: Trains and certifies outdoor leaders; operates in affiliation with 21 colleges, universities and outdoor programs.
Training: Offers training to employers, administrative agencies, insurance companies and the public.
Journal/Publication: *WEA Legend; WEA Affiliate Handbook.*
Job Listings: Job referral service for members.

Wildlife Conservation Fund of America
801 Kingsmill Parkway
Columbus, OH 43229-1137
Members/Purpose: Conservation organizations representing 1 million members. To protect the heritage of the American sportsman to hunt, fish, and trap; and to protect scientific wildlife management practices.
Journal/Publication: *Protect What's Right* (newsletter).

CHAPTER ELEVEN

PATH 2: CURATORIAL AND ARCHIVAL MANAGEMENT

not uncommon question asked of the history major is, "Well, what are you going to do with *that* degree after you graduate?" As this book amply demonstrates, there's no lack of opportunities to build a career on the history degree. It has always been a superb beginning for careers in teaching, business administration and management, information specialization and a variety of non-classroom educational roles. Another very fertile area of employment for a history major is curatorial and archival work. Though one of the most obvious uses of a degree in history, curatorial work is often overlooked by the history major as the province of art students, and archival work as the province of library or information science graduates. After reading this career path, you may want to answer that infamous question, "What are you going to do with a history degree?" with "I'm going to become a curator!" or, "I've decided to become an archivist!"

Get ready to explain who curators and archivists are and what they do. That's okay, it's a perfect opportunity. Too many people associate curators and archivists with boxes of specimens, exhibit materials, and piles of old paper. We envision them working on long tables in rooms down long corridors, well behind the scenes. Nothing could be further from the truth.

It would be a mischaracterization to think of curators and archivists simply as custodians of the past. Of course both these professions acquire objects and works, they document them as to origin, composition, provenance, age and condition, and they store them for scholars and researchers and for rotation on display. They ensure the preservation of artifacts through temperature and humidity control and scientific conservation methods, and they display and maintain these pieces for our enjoyment, wonder and edification.

But today's curator/archivist is much, much more. They are environmentalists, historians, teachers, explorers, trainers, and impresarios. Think about these roles and review excerpts from some recently advertised jobs.

Environmentalists

Just as curators and archivists have become adept at correcting and stopping ravages of civilization in the form of dirt, smog, fumes, acid rain and other ills on the artifacts they collect and display, they have been frequently called out of the work site to consult with municipal officials, private collectors, and the federal government on how best to preserve and maintain our existing cultural heritage. **"Responsibilities include processing and cataloging archival collections from various parks in the southeast region of the National Park System."**

Historians

Your position might be entitled "Historic Preservation Curator" or "Associate Director for Historic Resources," but whether or not the word "history" appears in your job title, it is very present in your work. In addition to many positions requiring you to have a history degree, there may be stipulations as to your mastery of historical facts, literature and art of a particular period. **"Candidates should be well versed in American material cultural studies or a related field . . ."**

Teachers

People visit collections and museums to learn. The curatorial and archival staffs can be among the best teachers. They have intimate knowledge of their collections and can make what was previously confusing or misunderstood, coherent and explainable. They are knowledgeable and adept at connecting events, personalities, literature and art so that we begin to understand the times, the people and their expressive efforts. **". . . coordinate living history, school and public programs; develop and refine historic interpretation."**

Explorers

Curators and archivists are breaking new ground each year as they stretch the traditional definitional boundaries of their jobs. New kinds of museums (computer museums, discovery museums, indigenous peoples collections) and new locations all around the world require risk takers and adventuresome types in a field where that has not been the traditional association. ". . . join a creative staff working in an exciting, cutting-edge environment—humor and flexibility a plus."

Trainers

Exhibits are often so rich with information and detail that, without a trained guide, we would only skim the surface and leave with only a superficial understanding of what is being presented. Consequently, curators need to be skilled trainers, bringing together groups with leadership and strong interpersonal skills to enliven, entertain and educate. "Opportunity for skilled communicator with demonstrated leadership to oversee guide and volunteer programs, including supervision, training, administration."

Impresarios

In a world where so much else competes for our time and discretionary income, the curator/archivist has had to become skillful at capturing our attention. Marketing, museum reproductions, off-site gift shops, catalogs, licensing agreements, leasing of museum sites for public events, and most of all, the advertising and public relations surrounding important touring collections has become a necessary skill for the curator/archivist who wants to see their collection survive and grow. "World's first bicultural museum open in the Capital city on a magnificent waterfront site in February 1998. It will be an exciting and challenging public experience expressing the perspectives of our country's peoples. It will be a must-see attraction for residents and visitors from overseas. The principal measure of this success will be the Museum's ability to attract large visitor numbers from diverse and new audiences."

For the purpose of this career path, we have brought these two positions, curator and archivist together, because for the history major there is more in common between the positions than there are differences. In fact, you will find some job postings for both curators and archivists that read almost identically. But are they the same? No, they are not, although they do share many of the same concerns. Let's begin with some generally accepted definitions:

Curator.   Those engaged in operating exhibiting institutions (museums, botanical gardens, arboretums, art galleries, zoos) who direct activities concerned with acquisition, instruction, exhibition, and safekeeping of primarily three-dimensional objects; research and publication; and public service.

Archivist.   Individuals concerned with the identification, preservation, and use of records of enduring historical value. Archivists work for the government, colleges and universities, historical societies, museums, libraries, businesses and religious institutions. They work with records of all types, including letters and diaries, photographs, films, sound recordings, maps, manuscripts and machine-readable records.

A Variety of Employment Settings

What's particularly exciting for you as a history major in pursuing curatorial and archival positions is the variety of settings in which you can work. Your first thought may well be a major museum or collection in a downtown urban area. Of course, the United States does have a significant number of important museums located in major cities and those institutions do have large staffs. However, all across this country and, in fact, the world are restored historic homes, specialized collections, smaller museums, art galleries, complete recreations of historic working villages and towns, children's discovery centers and countless ethnic and indigenous peoples exhibitions. All of these require curators and archivists, as well as other types of staff positions you may find equally intriguing.

The following list demonstrates the infinite variety of collections and structure available to the history major contemplating a career in curatorship or archives. This does not aspire to being a complete list; it would be impossible to stay abreast of the constantly changing world of exhibits, collections, museums and site re-creations. The authors recently came across a published "call for interested applicants for the development of a new museum dedicated to Civil War medicine."

Maritime Museums
Whaling Museums
College and University Museum Collections
Museums of Art
Children's Museums
Museums of Photography/Moving Image
Computer Museums
Collections built around the home and/or work of famous people
Natural History Museums
Recreated villages
Historic Houses
Antiquarian and Landmark Societies
Centers of Science and Industry
Art Conservation Laboratories
Historical Societies

continued

> continued
>
> Centers for Curatorial Studies
> State Museums
> Private collections
> Oral History Centers

Each item in this list represents not only employment possibilities, especially when the generic type of institution cited is multiplied by states, regions, or countries, but also by sharp differences in degree of focus. Some museums hold broad, expansive collections of art, sculpture, furnishings, maps, films and other items that require curators and archivists to be equally talented and adept in a variety of areas. In these museums (a state historical collection provides a good example) you will need to know prints, furniture, fabric, and paintings.

Specialized museums or smaller, more focused collections (a museum devoted to transportation or contemporary art) will, by necessity, demand not breadth but depth in their faculty and require applicants to come to the position with considerable expertise in their material.

Explore the following list and, better yet, explore some of the wonderful job posting newsletters available through your career office or through the associations mentioned at the close of this chapter. The New England Museum Association of the American Association of Museums publishes *NEMA News* and the American Association of Museums itself publishes *AVISO* with editorial content and job listings. As with all such specialized job listing publications, reading the job announcements will indicate how competitive you are in the marketplace and suggest many possible paths your career may take as you grow and develop within it.

A Growing Need for Professionals

In our own country, we continue to find areas of our culture that cry out for the skilled work of curatorial and archival professionals. Some of the most recent controversy in the film industry has been over the major studios' storage arrangements for the motion picture legacy of this country. Concerns over possible deterioration of that corpus of work, which many agree to be one of the world's richest film traditions, has led to new initiatives in restoration, preservation, cataloging and storage. A print of a film of Sir Richard Burton in his stage production of Hamlet was only recently discovered by his widow. It is of such importance that it will be restored and released as a commercial venture. Burton's stage Hamlet was considered one of the definitive interpretations of this role and, until this film's discovery, was known only to the collective memory of those who attended his performances on the stage. We now have a new and important resource for students of acting, directing, set design, theatrical lighting, theatre history, and biographers of Sir Richard.

The newly restored National Park Service facility at Ellis Island has brought together the efforts of numerous curators and archivists eager to help tell the story of U.S. immigration in the very buildings in which it took place. One can even still walk "The Stairs of Separation" where immigrants, newly screened in the great Registry Hall, were shunted to railway passage and freedom, holding facilities for medical or documentation purposes, or, tragically, deportation back to their homelands. The curators and archivists of this exhibit have provided not only exhibit rooms filled with wonderful photographs but magnificent displays of artifacts such as steamship passage tickets, passport photos, great dramatic displays of actual immigrant trunks of every variety of composition, and actual recordings of immigrants describing their heartache at leaving their homeland and their fear, trepidation and joy in arriving in the New World.

But this exhibit is not just about preserving the legacy of our great diversity as a country. It records and preserves our future as well. On this recent visit to Ellis Island, the authors were able to enter the name of one of their co-workers into a computer data bank which then displayed their colleague's entire family portrait with information on their country of origin and current home city and state. Our identification with and our ties to our immigrant forebears continues to be celebrated!

DEFINITION OF THE CAREER PATH

Curators and archivists must want to connect, through their collections, with the public. They have stories to share about the objects they preserve and they truly must enjoy and welcome that sharing. The following job advertisement for a curator is indicative of the qualification demands museum administrators must ask of professionals seeking curator/archivist positions.

Curator of Interpretive Programs. Primary responsibility for the interpretive programs concerned with the exhibitions and collections of the gallery and for the integration of the gallery with the intellectual, teaching, and research prerogatives of a major research university. **Responsibilities include: creating discussion on campus and in the community pertaining to the exhibitions and collections on view; making the art and the ideas and cultural context they**

continued

> continued
>
> **represent accessible to a diverse constituency; organization of international symposia, lecture series, courses, film series, discussion groups, docent training; and other educational programs.**

Let's look at two other job postings that reveal even more surprising and interesting facts about the curator/archivist position.

> *Curator.* Famous personage birthplace seeks curator. Qualifications include background in American History or Political Science, strong writing and computer skills, knowledge of museum principles, and the ability to work as part of a team. Responsibilities include: creating and mounting temporary exhibitions, developing the museum collection, care and storage of objects, visitor services for groups of varying sizes and collection management.
>
> *Project Archivist.* (State historical society) seeks Project Archivist for 2 yr, grant-funded project to process selected manuscript collections of national importance. Duties include: arrange collections; write finding aids; catalog using the MARC/AMC format & microcomputer; develop processing manual; work with volunteers; and write summary of collections processed for publication. Qualifications include MLS degree with one yr archival experience or archival certification; or BA with 4 yrs archival experience or 2 yrs of archival experience and certification. Experience using MARC/AMC format and OCLC is highly desirable. Good organizational & communication skills, knowledge of archival preservation techniques, and ability to work independently and supervise untrained volunteers is desirable. Starting salary $22,500 + generous benefits. Position expected to become permanent. Send letter, resume, references to . . .

Looking at actual job advertisements such as those shown above are a window on the reality of the jobs you seek. How many of you reading these job announcements would have realized the importance of computer skills? If you stop to think about it, the collection and retrieval of data, similar to research you did in college, is intrinsic to the study of history and one of the foremost skills you bring to any of the career paths outlined in this book. The computer adds a level of technology that allows you to work faster, smarter and more efficiently than you otherwise might. If you're interested in curatorial and archival positions, you'll want to ensure that you acquire the necessary computer skills. In the section that follows on qualifications, we discuss this and other important and necessary attributes you'll want to acquire before leaving college and which will help you compete for entry-level work.

What else do these ads tell us about the jobs? Developing exhibits, helping to guide visitors through a historic home, working on the computer, and caring for and documenting collections all add up to a busy, diverse and active career. It's a far cry from how many people think of a curator's or archivist's job. The role of the curator/archivist is to help us to understand what has gone before. The new museum in Washington, D.C., dedicated to the horrors of the Holocaust is a preeminent example of how the curator/archivist can reach out and deeply touch the public's sensitivity, compassion and understanding through their choice, placement and siting of objects in a collection.

Both of these jobs are more about the present than the past. It's about bringing the past into the present, communicating it and making it real, immediate and helpful to us. It is not an exercise in simply displaying artifacts under glass for visitors to pass by in varying stages of bewilderment. Real exhibits explain, dramatize and make understandable what seems at first to be remote and obscure.

Each of us can remember a history instructor who made the subject real for us. Someone whose knowledge, passion and understanding of the human element brought home to us the reality of a period, an event, or the lives of individuals. They brought to the classroom not just the textbook, but their own outside reading, special materials including films, drawings, charts, overhead projections, tools or equipment that made what had passed seem still with us. Think of curators and archivists as superb history teachers to the world.

The advertisements cited above announced that the job holder will help in exhibit design. Design is an area that can help us appreciate and understand the past as well as the objects featured. Perhaps you are helping to mount an exhibit of Egyptian artifacts discovered in the ancient pyramids. Exhibit room walls and public foyers might be repainted to resemble the magnificent frescoes of the tombs, helping exhibit visitors to appreciate the color, symbolism and figurative motifs of the time. The exhibit itself might be dimly lit overall, with effective spotlighting on the objects, as if the exhibit-goers were discovering the artifacts themselves in the vaults of the pyramids, adding to the excitement and drama of the collection and helping people to focus on the intricacy, detail and beauty of the pieces being displayed.

More and more often, we find special children's sections of exhibits, where young people can roll their sleeves up and participate in making art, working inventions, or touching and feeling objects on display. It might be an opportunity to make or paint your own papyrus or sleep on a Japanese futon or experience the inside of an old model diesel submarine. One of the best demonstrations a historian can make to graphically demonstrate the changes in physiques over the centuries is to have adult men and women today try to fit into the dresses or suits of men and women from the period about 1890. People were, on the average, shorter and thinner, with smaller waists and chests. A size "small" in 1890 was far, far, smaller than a size "small" today.

BEGIN BUILDING YOUR CAREER

Here are a few lines from a job posting that says much about how you begin to acquire and build your expertise: "Internship starts with an intensive orientation to all aspects of the museum, after which interns gradually assume responsibility and become integral part of the staff."

The road to a successful career in either curatorship or archival studies is a lengthy process of building expertise and experiences. Extensive study, field trips, the opportunity to mount or catalog a collection, each of these experiences enriches your professional life and will add elements to your resume that may be important for promotion or job change.

As you learn more about your job and the dimensions it offers you in terms of a career, you may find yourself moving along a specific career path within this field. Let's look at some of the traditional positions, highlighting their duties and responsibilities and role in the overall function of an institution.

Interns. The beginning of many careers, an internship is really an opportunity to explore, to observe and, quite frankly, to make mistakes! Once in a while, the authors will have one of their career clients return from an internship vowing, "I'll never do that for a living!" That's okay, in fact, that's a valuable lesson learned with very little risk. It's much better to take an internship for little or no money and a limited time period and learn you don't like the job than to seek career employment and all the changes that go with it only to be unhappy.

Internships that expose workers to all aspects of museum programming, administration and operations make for the best experiences.

Entry-Level Curators. Curators are charged with the care and stewardship of some element of a collection. To ensure not only good accessibility to the collection they maintain, but a high quality exhibit, curators must understand preservation and maintenance methods for their specialty (metalwork, prints, oil paintings, models, fabrics, etc.), and develop, implement and supervise interpretive programs.

Curators. Professional curators are true scholars who, in addition to many of the duties listed under entry-level curatorship, both speak and write frequently on their chosen field. As this is often a management position, they must also develop strong organizational, budgetary and supervisory talents to schedule and train staff, maintain operating budgets and deal with a variety of support personnel. Additional skills may involve grant writing, connoisseurship, research, and buying and selling elements to enhance the collections.

Entry-Level Archivists.   The duties of the archivist involve maintaining control, both physical and intellectual, over noncurrent permanent records of individuals, groups, institutions and governments. Entry-level requirements will include computer capabilities, physical abilities in lifting up to 50 pounds, and communication skills for working with other team members and serving the public.

Archivists.   A professional archivist understands the historical context in which given records were created, how those records were used and their relationships to other sources. The variety of media on which these records are found changes along with improvements in technology and now include films, video and sound recordings, computer tapes, and video and optical disks. Archivists also have duties relating to administration, management, marketing, and public relations.

Registrars.   A strong computer background will be important for today's museum registrar. This is the position charged with creating and maintaining records for all objects that both enter and leave the collection. They assign record numbers, complete accession sheets, number objects, assist in packing, unpacking, shipping of loan objects, maintain donor forms and complete computer records on all objects. They must be well-versed in handling and storage techniques and have significant computer skills, including data base management and spreadsheet familiarity.

Preparators.   The preparator is responsible for installing and disassembling exhibits. They plan and direct fabrication, installation, and disassembly of both permanent and temporary museum exhibits. In addition, they administer budgets, personnel and operations of their department. The chief preparator reports directly to the chief curator or director of the facility.

Directors/Administrators.   Museums, collections, galleries, historic homes and outdoor sites all need experienced administrators to act as chief operating officers, administering the budget, overseeing programming, collections and exhibits, implementing and initiating a strong development program, directing planning activities, supervising staff and representing the institution to outside publics.

The history graduate very often doesn't think of curator/archivist positions as an employment opportunity following graduation. Hopefully, the discussion in this career path will lead you to take a serious look at the wonderful careers in these fields that will make use of and build upon your history degree and, more importantly, the curiosity and fascination with the past that led you to your degree in the first place! But, just as you might not have thought much about these kinds of jobs, you probably haven't been exposed to many job advertisements for curatorial/archival positions. We've tried to include several throughout our discussion to illustrate some points. Before moving on to the requisite training and qualifications needed for the field, let's look at a few more entry-level position ads.

Curator of Collections. Bachelors degree in history, art history or related field, knowledge of museum practices & record management, experience as curator required; resume to (university) . . .

Museum Worker. Collect/classify museum items; req min BA incl coursework in history/museum studies/rel field, 1 yr exp. Pref MA museum studies/history/archaeology. $20,661–32,017. Resume/ltr to (county personnel dept) . . .

Assistant Registrar/Preparator. Active museum seeks assistant registrar to help manage collections, prepare to move, and move collections to new exhibition facility. Process new accessions and accession back-log; photograph these objects; prepare objects for move and for exhibition. Also inventory, pack, move collections to new museum, process loans. Some travel required. Seeks applicants who are highly motivated & self directed, have at least 2 yrs museum registration experience. Object preparation & computer skills desired. Send letter, resume, 3 references (historical society) . . .

Curatorial Associate. University library. Responsible for providing references services in university archives to clientele of university staff, faculty & students, as well as to general public. Answer inquiries received by mail & telephone, service at the reference desk is a daily function. Supervise reference support staff & student assistants. Position requires understanding of the central coordinating & service role of reference dept in maintaining good communication among various users of collections. Minimum requirements: MLS and/or MA in American History & 3–5 yrs relevant exp. Cover letter/resume . . .

Archivist/Curator of Library Collections. Historic association, a small museum and library located in . . . seek full-time professional archivist to lead major project to reorganize archives, library, and two-dimen-

continued

continued

sional collections. Direct a major project to expand & reorganize the library, develop new inventory & cataloguing systems, & establish appropriate policies & procedures for the daily operations of the library. Degree in archives mgt/history & two yrs experience working with archival collections. MLS, foreign language skills, and a sense of humor preferred but not required. Send resume, cover letter, salary requirements to . . .

Archivist. The National Park Service anticipates filling the position of archivist GS-1420-11 (salary range $33,623–$43,712 per annum). This is a term position, not to exceed four years. Responsibilities include processing and cataloging archival collections from various parks in designated regions of the National Park System. Applications (Standard Form 171) must be received by . . .

Assistant Archivist. Maintain library/archives/material, provide CD-ROM/WESTLAW tech training and service, assist staff and public w/rsrch questions. Req BA/equiv, records mgmt/rel exp, able to lift and move 50 lbs. 20 hrs/wk, $13.96/hr + benes. Resume/letter to (state bar association).

WORKING CONDITIONS

The world of curators and archivists is as diverse as your interests. A good demonstration of the variety that exists is contained in the following ads.

Curator/Administrator: 18th c historic house. PR, grant writing, volunteer development, advancement of educ/curatorial goals. Req rel BA, computer skills. Resume/ltr . . .

or

Museum Technician/Registrar: Maintain permanent collection at Cultural Center (New Mexico). Req BA humanities/fine arts/educ, know textiles. Resume/ltr/transcripts . . .

or

Archivist: archival program incl local records, mss, and genealogical material. Continue program, reduce backlog, develop further, help w/museum operations. Req know all phases of archival work, pref photo lab bkgrnd. $18.3K–$21.4K. AFSCME union benes. Resume/ltr to . .

Textiles, eighteenth-century decorative arts and furnishings or archival work with special emphasis on photography—take your choice. These are just three examples of the diversity of focus possible in the fields of curatorial and archival work. Tremendous interest, excitement, even love of your chosen field is important as one of the principal working conditions. If you don't find your subject endlessly fascinating, it will be difficult to sustain the drive, energy and creativity needed to forge a career.

Beyond your subject area for curating or archiving, there are other areas of responsibility common to individuals in these fields, regardless of the type of institution or nature of the collection or presentation.

Administration.   There will be a variety of other staff, including custodial, managerial, research, and technical to oversee and manage. There are also policies and procedures to write and administer, and significant correspondence to originate and respond to. In addition, budget preparation is a crucial task.

Working with Volunteers.   Many historic sites, museums, galleries, installations, gardens, herbariums, zoos and historic sites employ significant numbers of skilled volunteers who require training, scheduling, observation and evaluation.

Raising Money.   Curators and archivists may not have principal charge of raising funds, but often are called upon to share in the development activities of their employer. This may mean attendance at social functions, briefing potential donors on the work of the organization, writing letters or making fund-raising telephone calls to solicit donations.

Planning/Implementing Acquisitions/Collection Changes.   Always on the lookout for an opportunity to fill a gap or trade some item for something more desirable, curators and archivists must constantly stay abreast of other collections and what items may be available for purchase or trade. This requires attendance at conferences, visits to other installations, correspondence and a significant time commitment to networking.

Researching.   To best display, maintain and educate visitors about any collection requires extensive research. As new research is uncovered, documentation likewise needs to be updated. Research is an ongoing task of the curator/archivist.

TRAINING AND QUALIFICATIONS

We hope you have found it gratifying to read many of the job announcements cited in this chapter and discover that the requisite qualification is a history degree. That, in fact, is your primary qualification. However, there are history degrees and there are history degrees! The assumption in requiring a major in history by the employer is that you know history; that you have a solid grasp of history in general and, hopefully, a more refined sense of some specific area of history (the first Japanese women scholars in America, the New England whaling industry, Mississippi river trade during the late 1880s, etc.).

There will be an expectation that you can write and speak effectively. If there is one strong message throughout this chapter, it is that these positions in curatorship and archives management are public-oriented and information brokers. You need to be comfortable interacting with diverse publics and communicating effectively in person or through scholarly articles, correspondence with members, even solicitations for development funds.

Organizational ability in managing your collection, supervising staff, and structuring time for administration and research and all of the behind-the-scenes support work of any collection is an important quality. In fact, many curators and archivists frequently cite the delicate balance between keeping themselves and the collections available to their publics for information purposes and the need to secure time for writing and research as a constant struggle to balance the two competing demands fairly.

Artifacts, prints, books, paintings, even buildings need records, identification, numbering, histories and countless other details recorded and maintained. All of this information needs to be available to meet numerous requests. How much did you spend on acquisitions this year? What was the average purchase amount? How many volunteer hours was the collection given by volunteer staff and who did the most? How many items are on loan to other institutions? You can easily see that without strong computer skills, especially data base management and spreadsheet software familiarity, your job would be an impossible task.

Serving as a volunteer or intern can help you enter museum work. The work you do will help highlight your skills and abilities and allow you to demonstrate and display those talents to others. The people you might meet during these experiences will also prove helpful as you network for job opportunities. Your direct supervisors in these intern or volunteer experiences will also be able to provide the most specific references for any future jobs in the curator/archivist role. The following internship advertisement refers directly to the qualifications listed above:

Collections Management Internship: 9 months, starting in September. Catalog 14K+ historic collections incl storage techniques, condition reports, rsrch, basic conservation, volunteer training, and touring area museums. Should have strong background in history, computers, and cataloging.

EARNINGS

Many of the job notices cited in this chapter include salary information, so you already have a sense for what you can expect to earn. Another barometer of possible earnings, although it is limited to one particular setting (art museums), is the salary survey published by The American Association of Art Museum directors. The survey is comprehensive: it includes salary information by region and percentiles within the salary range. A few of the job titles and associated salaries they include that we believe are reflective of what you as an entry-level worker can earn are:

	Lowest Salary	25th Percentile
Assistant Curator	$16,704	$25,724
Curatorial Assistant	$10,540	$18,667
Assistant Registrar	$11,594	$19,124
Assistant Conservator	$18,000	$24,255
Conservation Assistant	$13,520	$20,133

Be sure to review the salary survey for regional salary data. And, given the job notices we've seen, salaries for archivists are very similar to those shown for curatorial and other entry-level work in this employment sector.

CAREER OUTLOOK

There are well over 12,000 museums, exhibit areas, collections, libraries, nature centers and zoos in the United States today. They collect, display, and explain for the public art, science, history, natural history, and other special subjects. All these sites need workers. Thousands of people are employed either full time or part time, and tens of thousands of volunteers help them to do their job.

Archivists and curators are considered professional specialty workers, and the U.S. Department of Labor, Bureau of Labor Statistics indicates that this category of worker will increase by 37 percent through the year 2005. Increased public interest in science, history, art, and technology, along with an ever-increasing need to effectively manage information, are driving this growth. Federal government jobs are expected to grow more slowly than state and local government jobs, and also more slowly than museum, botanical and zoological garden jobs.

STRATEGY FOR FINDING THE JOBS

Directly related college coursework and work experience are essential for success in a job search for someone interested in curatorial or archival work. Your strategy must include the following: incorporating *at least one* internship into your work history, taking any related courses (museum studies, information management) offered at your college or university, finding out about issues and problems professionals are currently facing, preparing yourself to apply for and accept pre-professional technical or entry-level positions, and considering graduate study so that you can advance your career in this field.

Incorporate at Least One Internship into Your Work History

Nearly every job listing, whether it be for part-time, seasonal, or full-time work, even many internships, indicates that the position requires some level of experience. So how can you get experience if no one will hire you without it? In short, the practicum or internship. In a best-case scenario, you should plan on doing an internship in both your junior and senior year to be able to list relevant experience on your resume. *Aviso: A Monthly Dispatch from the American Association of Museums* contains internship listings, as do regional association newsletters. Be sure to contact museums you may be interested in working for to find out about their internship programs; sometimes these are not advertised. The National Archives offers ongoing internships, and *InternAmerica,* a bimonthly newsletter, often contains notices relating to curatorial/archival work. Be sure to check national publications such as *Peterson's Internships* or *The National Directory of Internships* for opportunities.

Take Museum Studies Courses If They Are Offered at Your College or University

A large group of people is attracted to the kind of work done in museum settings. And remember, you'll be competing for entry-level jobs against people who have actually majored in museum or library studies. So take advantage of any type of coursework offered at your institution that relates to this work. Also look for workshops offered by professional associations or organizations, or museums themselves. Review the last part of this chapter for association contact information to find out about these types of opportunities.

Find Out about Current Issues and Problems

Glance at a current issue of *The American Archivist,* or read through the bookstore catalogue of the American Association of Museums, and you'll realize the range of issues that these professions face today. From understanding your audience to removing barriers for people with disabilities, or improving environmental protection of collections and facility security, all are important to working professionals. Keep up on the latest concerns and trends by reading professional journals. At the end of this chapter we have listed several professional associations and publications they make available. College and university libraries and larger public libraries will carry some of these. Begin reading as many publications and journals as you have time for; it will be time well-spent as you prepare your resume and get ready to meaningfully answer tough interview questions.

Be Ready to Take Pre-Professional Entry-Level Jobs if You Don't Have a Master's Degree

Because curatorial and archival work requires a high level of specialization, the entry-level positions will be called, in some cases, internships or might have the label of "technician." Read each advertisement carefully and apply for each job that you're qualified for, no matter what it's called. This will be a building block for moving on to higher-level positions that have the title "curator" or "archivist" but that also require more expertise.

Plan on Attending Graduate School if You Want Career Advancement

There certainly are a variety of entry-level positions for history majors who have taken related coursework and who have completed an internship, but to move beyond these positions requires additional academic training and experience. If your career interests lie in curatorial or archival work, be sure to explore graduate school options. With the assistance of a career counselor or librarian, utilize resources such as *Peterson's Guides to Graduate Study* to identify appropriate graduate programs. Network with administrators of local museums to seek their advice on graduate programs that they feel qualify a worker for positions beyond those at the entry level.

POSSIBLE EMPLOYERS

As you are considering employment sites for curatorial and archival work be sure to include:

- ❏ Museums, botanical gardens and zoos

- ❏ Nonprofit organizations

- ❏ Colleges and universities

- ❏ National, state and local governments

- ❏ Corporations

Each will offer employment opportunities and your search should include investigation of each type of site.

Museums, Botanical Gardens and Zoos

Profile. There are over seven thousand museums of various types that are members of the American Association of Museums. Fourteen categories of institutions have been defined in the Association's directory, and they include (along with the number of institutions as of 1993):

- ❑ Art Museums (1,664)
- ❑ Children's Junior Museums (185)
- ❑ College & University Museums (528)
- ❑ Company Museums (27)
- ❑ Exhibit Areas (123)
- ❑ General Museums (Art & History) (885)
- ❑ History Museums (Maritime, Military & Naval) (4,597)
- ❑ Libraries with Collections Other Than Books (165)
- ❑ National & State Agencies, Councils & Commissions (124)
- ❑ Nature Centers (208)
- ❑ Park Museums & Visitor Centers (487)
- ❑ Science Museums (Zoo, Natural History & Aquarium) (1,524)
- ❑ Specialized Museums (1,523)
- ❑ Libraries with Collections of Books (80)

Those organizations classified as art museums include art associations, councils and commissions, foundations and institutes; art museums and galleries; arts and crafts museums; china, glass and silver museums; civic art and cultural centers; decorative arts museums; folk art museums; and textile museums.

History museums have also been sub-categorized: historic agencies, councils, commissions, foundations, and research institutes; historic houses and historic buildings; historic sites; historical and preservation societies; historical society museums; history museums; maritime, naval museums and historic ships; military museums; and preservation projects.

Museums falling into the science category can be any one of the following: academies, associations, institutes and foundations; aeronautics and space museums; anthropology and ethnology museums; aquariums, marine museums, and oceanariums; arboretums; archaeology museums and archaeological sites; aviaries and ornithology museums; botanical and aquatic gardens, conservatories, and horticultural societies; entomology museums; geology, mineralogy and paleontology museums; herbariums; herpetology museums; medical, dental, health, pharmacology, apothecary and psychiatry museums; natural history and natural science museums; planetariums, observatories and astronomy museums; science museums and centers; wildlife refuges and bird sanctuaries; and zoos.

As you can tell from the names, specialized museums are categorized by the specific type of collection they house. These museums specialize in: agriculture, antiques, architecture, audio-visual and film, circus, comedy, communications, costume, crime, electricity, fire-fighting, forestry, furniture, gun, hobby, horology, industry, lapidary arts, logging and lumber, maps, mining, money and numismatics, musical instruments, philately, photography, religion, scouting, sports, technology, theatre, toys and dolls, transportation, typography, village, wax, whaling, and woodcarving.

Help in Locating These Employers.   The *Official Museum Directory,* published by R.R. Bowker Publishers, and the *American Art Directory,* printed by Reed Reference, can both be used to help you locate these organizations by type of museum or by geographic location. Another valuable resource is the *Art Career Guide,* published by Watson-Guptill Publications.

Nonprofit Organizations

Profile.   Nonprofits hiring curators and/or archivists can range from conservation organizations, to religious and fraternal organizations, to professional associations. If a nonprofit organization has a prized collection, library or historical records, they'll want qualified employees to care for these resources.

Help in Locating These Employers.   Finding out about all of the potential non-profit employers will take some research on your part. Some good references to begin with include: *National Directory of Non-Profit Organizations,* published by Gale Research, VGM's *Opportunities in Non-Profit Organizations, Great Careers: The Fourth of July Guide to Careers, Internships, and Volunteer Opportunities in the Non-Profit Sector,* made available by Garrett Park Press, and *Community Jobs: The National Employment Newsletter for the Non-Profit Sector,* a publication of ACCESS, Networking in the Public Interest.

Your area's chamber of commerce may be aware of a local or regional directory of nonprofits you could utilize to locate these organizations. In addition, some regional or state-wide business journals or newspapers occasionally highlight the non-profit organizations functioning in the geographic region they cover. Check your school's career library or the local public library for copies of these types of publications.

Colleges and Universities

Profile. About one-sixth of all archivists and curators are employed by colleges and universities. Some teach or work in the institutions' libraries. Many colleges and universities also have their own museums which may house various types of collections including natural history, visual arts, anthropological or geologic specimens. These campus museums are often an integral component of the academic and cultural mission of the institution. Curators who work here usually also take on teaching duties.

Help in Locating These Employers. If you are looking for actual job listings for colleges and universities, you will want to examine *The Chronicle of Higher Education*. The *Official Museum Directory* will help those of you interested in undertaking proactive networking to determine where most of these museums are located. You could also use Peterson's *Guide to Four-Year Colleges* or *Guides to Graduate Study* to identify schools that offer a degree in museum studies; usually, they will also house a museum.

National, State and Local Governments

Profile. Federal, state and local governments continue to be the largest employers in this country, and approximately one-third of all archivists and curators work in governmental positions. In terms of federal workers, most archivists are employed by the National Archives and Records Administration or the Department of Defense. Curators work primarily for the Smithsonian Institution, in Defense Department military museums or in other museums under the direction of the Department of the Interior.

The National Archives has custody of the permanent records of the federal government, with holdings dating from 1789 to the present. The mission of this office is to arrange and describe the records, preserve them, and make them available to the public for research. In the Washington area there are various archival units, including: Textual Projects division, Textual Reference Division, Center for Legislative Archives, Special Archives Division, Center for Electronic Records, and the Records Declassification Division.

Conservators, museum curators and museum technicians are employed by the Smithsonian Institution. The Smithsonian is made up of fourteen museums and the National Zoo, and it also includes the National Gallery of Art, the Woodrow Wilson International Center for Scholars, and the John F. Kennedy Center for the Performing Arts. Generally, turnover at The Smithsonian is quite low, because the organization tries to fill higher level positions by promoting current employees. Openings tend to occur in entry-level positions vacated due to promotion. As with many government jobs, tenacity will be one of your most important job-seeking traits.

State governments also maintain historical records and run museums and libraries, and so have a need to hire archivists and curators. Other state agencies, including libraries, museums, parks and zoos, hire curators.

Help in Locating These Employers. If you are interested in exploring opportunities available with the Office of the National Archives, there are twelve regional archives, and they are listed at the end of this chapter. Contact them directly to get the latest information on hiring needs and procedures.

The Smithsonian Institution is included on a list of federal departments and agencies that employ the great majority of federal workers. Contact the Institution in Washington, DC, for current hiring information.

If you would like to review a more in-depth strategy for obtaining a federal, state or local government position, some excellent resources include: VGM's *Opportunities in State and Local Government Careers, The Complete Guide to Public Employment,* put out by Impact Publications, or *Government Job Finder,* published by Planning/Communications.

Corporations

Profile. Large corporations with record centers often employ archivists to oversee records management—certain information provides a strategic advantage to the organization and must be carefully organized, protected, and made accessible to those employees who are authorized to use it. Some organizations also house museums, including Eli Lilly and Company, Coca-Cola, Corning, Boeing, and Dupont. Research organizations also hire archivists to manage the data and information that keeps them in business.

Help in Locating These Employers. Some publications you can use to begin identifying possible employers are *The Official Museum Directory, Research Centers Directory,* and *Directory of American Research and Technology.* Work with a career counselor or librarian to identify other references that will be useful for your job search.

POSSIBLE JOB TITLES

Curator and archivist are familiar titles, but have you also considered fine arts packer or museum technician as you read through job listings and newsletters? Review the entire list shown below and consider jobs which are given these other labels. Add to the list; you'll see other titles not shown here. Don't let names fool you, read the qualifications to see if you should apply.

Archivist	Ceramic restorer
Curator	Fine arts packer
Museum curator	Museum technician
Curator of collections	Assistant director, museum
Collections manager	Site administrator
Curatorial associate	Site manager
Associate curator	Manager
Assistant curator	Associate director for historic
Artifacts conservator	resources
Art conservator	Paper Conservator
Lace and textiles restorer	

Related Occupations

Think about what curators and archivists do: they are historians, teachers, guides, explorers, and impresarios. They are thought of as artistic, enterprising and social. There are other jobs and career choices that draw on a combination of some of these, as well as other, skills and abilities. Have you also thought about these?

Arborist	Lighting designer
Art director	Marketing director
Assistant registrar	Museum registrar
Botanist	Museum sales manager
Decorator	Preparator
Folklorist	Public information director
Graphic designer	Publications editor
Information specialist	Records manager
Interior decorator	Sales representative
Librarian	Volunteer coordinator

Be sure to read up on those positions that sound interesting but that you don't know as much about. VGM's *Careers Encyclopedia,* or the *Career Information Center* can provide the additional information you might need.

Professional Associations

Because curators and archivists must, for the most part, specialize in a field of study, associations for specific types of museums and organizations are shown below. Be sure to evaluate how each association may be able to help you in your job search, and contact (or possibly join) those that offer services or products you need.

African American Museums Association
P.O. Box 548
1350 Brush Row Road
Wilberforce, OH 45384
Members/Purpose: Museums, museum professionals, and scholars concerned with preserving, restoring, collecting and exhibiting African-American history and culture.
Training: Conducts professional training workshops.
Journal/Publication: *Black Museums Calendar; Blacks in Museums; Scrip.*
Job Listings: Provides job listings for members.

American Association of Botanical Gardens and Arboreta
786 Church Road
Wayne, PA 19087
Members/Purpose: Directors and staffs of botanical gardens, arboreta, institutions maintaining or conducting horticultural courses, and others.
Journal/Publication: *AABGA-Newsletter; Public Garden;* internship directory; salary surveys.
Job Listings: Acts as a resource center for information on garden management jobs; see *AABGA-Newsletter;* internship brochure available—call for information.

American Association for Museum Volunteers
c/o American Association of Museums
1225 I Street, NW, Suite 200
Washington, DC 20005
Members/Purpose: Affiliate committee of the American Association of Museums. Serves as forum and source of information for museum volunteers.
Journal/Publication: *AAMV Newsletter; Directory of Museum Volunteer Programs; Museum Volunteer Handbook.*

American Association of Museums
1225 I Street, NW, Suite 200
Washington, DC 20005
Members/Purpose: Art, history, and science museums, art associations and centers, historic houses and societies, preservation projects, planetariums, zoos, aquariums, botanical gardens, college and university museums and others interested in the museum field.
Journal/Publication: *Aviso; Museum News; The Official Museum Directory.*
Job Listings: Maintains placement service for museum professionals; see *Aviso* for employment opportunities in museums.

American Association for State and Local History
530 Church Street, Suite 600
Nashville, TN 37219
Members/Purpose: Organization of educators, historians, writers, and other individuals; state and local historical societies; agencies and institutions interested in improving the study of state and local history in the U.S. and Canada, and assisting historical organizations in improving their public services.
Training: Conducts seminars and workshops.
Journal/Publication: *Directory of Historical Societies and Agencies in the U.S. and Canada; History News; History News Dispatch.*
Job Listings: See *History News Dispatch.*

American Federation of Arts
41 East 65th Street
New York, NY 10021
Members/Purpose: Service organization comprising not-for-profit art museums committed to fostering art appreciation in the U.S. Seeks to broaden public knowledge and appreciation of the visual arts through art, video, and film exhibits, which travel to museums, university art galleries, and other cultural and media centers.
Training: Administrates the Museum Management Institute.
Journal/Publication: *AFA Newsletter.*

American Institute for the Conservation of Historic and Artistic Works
1717 K Street, NW, Suite 301
Washington, DC 20006
Members/Purpose: Professionals, scientists, administrators, educators and others interested in the field of art conservation. Seeks to advance knowledge and improve methods of conservation needed to protect, preserve, and maintain the condition and integrity of objects or structures which because of their history, significance, rarity or workmanship have a commonly accepted value and importance for the public interest.
Training: Conducts seminars and lectures.
Journal/Publication: *AIC Newsletter; Journal; Journal of the American Institute for Conservation.*
Job Listings: See *AIC Newsletter.*

Association of Art Museum Directors
41 East 65th Street
New York, NY 10021
Members/Purpose: Chief staff officers of major art museums.
Journal/Publication: *Professional Practices in Art Museum; Museum Schools and Studio Related Programs; Art Museum Salary Survey.*

Association of College and University Museums and Galleries
The University Museum
P.O. Box 1150
Southern Illinois University-Edwardsville
Edwardsville, IL 62026
Members/Purpose: Institutions and individuals professionally involved with
college and university museums and galleries.
Journal/Publication: *ACUMG Newsletter.*

Association for Living Historical Farms and Agricultural Museums
Route 14, Box 214
Santa Fe, NM 87505
Members/Purpose: Provide a central repository of information on plants,
animals, tools, and implements used in farming in the past; assist farms
and museums in securing information; accredit living historical farms and
museums; join in publicizing the farms and museums.
Journal/Publication: Convention proceedings; *Living Historical Farms Bulletin;* membership list.

**Association of North American Museums, Libraries, Archives, Cultural
Centers, and Fraternal Organizations**
6500 South Pulaski Road
Chicago, IL 60629
Members/Purpose: North American ethnic museums, other museums, historical societies, libraries, archives, fraternal organizations, universities, university libraries, and cultural centers. Functions as vehicle for other ethnic
and non-ethnic groups to become viable art and education centers in their
communities.
Training: Sponsors seminars and exhibits.

Association of Railway Museums
P.O. Box 3311
City of Industry, CA 91744
Members/Purpose: Organizations having as their entire or partial purpose
the preservation of railway equipment.
Journal/Publication: *Report to You.*

Association of Science Museum Directors
National Museum of Natural History
Smithsonian Institution
Washington, DC 20560
Members/Purpose: Chief administrative officers of museums whose
research, education, exhibition, collection, and publication programs are
in the physical, biological, and anthropological sciences.
Journal/Publication: *Science Museum News.*

Association of Science-Technology Centers
1025 Vermont Ave., NW, #500
Washington, DC 20005
Members/Purpose: Science and technology museums. Dedicated to further-
ing public understanding and appreciation of science and technology.
Training: Conducts educational and instructional workshops to assist museum
professionals.
Journal/Publication: Annual report; update; ASTC member staff directory;
newsletter; *Traveling Exhibit Service Catalog.*
Job Listings: Job bank available to subscribers.

Association of Sports Museums and Halls of Fame
101 West Sutton Place
Wilmington, DE 19810
Members/Purpose: Seeks to improve and maintain standards of sports museums and halls of fame; enhance their operations; facilitate the exchange
of information; institute projects that may be useful to all members.
Journal/Publication: *IASMHF Newsletter;* membership directory.

Association of Systematics Collections
730 11th Street, NW, Second Floor
Washington, DC 20001
Members/Purpose: Grant researchers, educational institutions, museum
personnel, and biologists.
Training: Sponsors working council on curatorial practices.
Journal/Publication: *ASC Newsletter; The Washington Initiative.*
Job Listings: See *ASC Newsletter.*

National Foundation for Jewish Culture
330 Seventh Avenue, 21st Floor
New York, NY 10001
Members/Purpose: Jewish museums, historical societies, and nonprofit galleries united to support, encourage, and promote the development of American Jewish Museums in collecting, preserving, and interpreting Jewish art
and artifacts for public education and the advancement of scholarship.

Council of American Maritime Museums
Manitowoc Museum
75 Maritime Drive
Manitowoc, WI 54220
Members/Purpose: Museums located in the U.S. and Canada that are devoted
primarily to maritime history.
Journal/Publication: Membership list.

Intermuseum Conservation Association
Allen Art Building

83 North Main
Oberlin, OH 44074
Members/Purpose: Performs the examination and treatment of works of art, inspection and maintenance of collections, and research and education in art conservation technology.
Training: Conducts seminars for museum professionals.
Job Listings: Newsletter for members sometimes contains job listings.

National Conference of State Historic Preservation Officers
Hall of States
444 North Capitol Street, NW, Suite 342
Washington, DC 20001
Members/Purpose: Officers and deputy officers appointed by the governor in each of the states and territories. Provides an exchange of information about state and federal preservation program administration.
Training: Offers periodic training sessions.
Journals/Publication: *NCSHPO/Alert; NCSHPO/News;* directory.

National Science for Youth Foundation
130 Azaela Drive
Roswell, GA 30075
Members/Purpose: Sponsors natural science centers, junior nature museums, native animal parks, and trailside museums. Provides information service.
Training: Conducts training courses in museum and nature center management.
Journal/Publication: Conference proceedings; directory of Natural Science Centers; *Natural Science Center News; Opportunities.*
Job Listings: Maintains museum and placement service; see publication *Opportunities.*

North American Indian Museums Association
c/o George Abrams
260 Prospect Ave., No. 669
Hackensack, NJ 07601
Members/Purpose: Indian and Native American cultural centers and tribal museums, and museum professionals; affiliate members are native studies organizations, historical societies, and Indian community colleges.
Training: Sponsors national and regional workshops, internships, and museum research.
Journal/Publication: *Directory of Indian Museums;* newsletter.

Shaker Museum Foundation
Shaker Museum Road
Old Chatham, NY 12136

Members/Purpose: To preserve and interpret the arts, skills, philosophy, and economic-cultural contributions of the United Society of Believers in Christ's Second Appearing (Shakers).
Journal/Publication: *Shaker Museum and Library Report.*

Society of American Archivists
600 South Federal Street, Suite 504
Chicago, IL 60605
Members/Purpose: Professional association of individuals and institutions concerned with management of current records, archival administration, and the custody of historical manuscripts in government, business, and semi-public institutions.
Training: Conducts seminars and workshops.
Journal/Publication: *The American Archivist; SAA Newsletter;* directory of individual members.
Job Listings: See *SAA Newsletter; Employment Bulletin* (bimonthly); sponsors placement service each year at annual meeting.

Transportation Museum Association
3015 Barrett Station Road
St. Louis, MO 61322
Members/Purpose: Cultural and educational organization for museum housing a collection of more than 140 locomotives and assorted rolling stock, a city transit display representing periods from the horsecar to the motorbus, highway vehicles, and many smaller related items.
Journal/Publication: *Transport Museum-News and Views.*

U.S. Lighthouse Society
244 Kearny Street, 5th Floor
San Francisco, CA 94108
Members/Purpose: Promotes restoration and preservation of America's lighthouses.
Journal/Publication: *Bulletin; The Keeper's Log;* magazine.

NATIONAL ARCHIVES REGIONAL ARCHIVES SYSTEM

National Archives-New England Region
380 Trapelo Road
Waltham, MA 02154

National Archives-Northeast Region
Bldg. 22, Military Ocean Terminal
Bayonne, NJ 07002

National Archives-Mid Atlantic Region
9th & Market Streets, Room 1350
Philadelphia, PA 19107

National Archives-Southeast Region
1557 St. Joseph Avenue
East Point, GA 30344

National Archives-Great Lakes Region
7358 South Pulaski Road
Chicago, IL 60629

National Archives-Central Plains Region
2312 East Bannister Road
Kansas City, MO 64131

National Archives-Southwest Region
501 West Felix Street
P.O. Box 6216
Fort Worth, TX 76115

National Archives-Rocky Mountain Region
Bldg. 48, Denver Federal Center
P.O. Box 25307
Denver, CO 80225

National Archives-Pacific Southwest Region
24000 Avila Road
P.O. Box 6719
Laguna Niguel, CA 92677

National Archives-Pacific Sierra Region
1000 Commodore Drive
San Bruno, CA 94066

National Archives-Pacific Northwest Region
6125 Sand Point Way
Seattle, WA 98115

National Archives-Alaska Region
654 West 3rd Avenue
Anchorage, AK 99501

National Archives-Regional Archives System
National Archives (NAA)
7th & Pennsylvania Avenue, NW
Washington, DC 20408

CHAPTER TWELVE

PATH 3: INFORMATION SPECIALIZATION

"Information superhighway" and "information overload" are two phrases the general public is using today to illustrate and emphasize a sense of the vastness of, and sometimes the futility of trying to manage, the amazing amounts of information we encounter. Television now broadcasts twenty-four hours a day and features entire networks devoted to specialized programming, including comedy, re-runs, science fiction and, of course, news. Some of us are provided with access to over a hundred channels of television from which to choose.

Radio has joined television in specialization. All-news, all-sports and all-psychology talk shows; religion, country, and singles connections: these are but some of the formats at boutiqued stations that exist in markets all over the country. Recent technological advances in AM reception now allow us to hear commercials over AM stations even when we are passing through tunnels.

Though newspapers are undergoing consolidations and readership is down, you can receive *USA Today* over your computer at the office and scan for sections of the paper and articles that particularly interest you. Computer services offer up weather, news, and internet connections on any number of topics. Add to this the facsimile machine and the possibilities it presents for continuous receipt of information, and you begin to have a sense of the situation.

Look in your own mailbox. Sophisticated new marketing data allows us to target homeowners based on television watching patterns, grocery store purchases, credit card use and previous buying patterns. Most of us are inundated with so-called "junk mail" that has cost these marketers significant dollars to produce and to obtain the research to help them reach us, the consumers.

Technology, principally the computer and telecommunications capabilities, have accelerated not only the quantity and detail of that information, but the speed at which we can provide information to those needing it. Interactive television, facsimile machines, hand-held digital assistants, CD-ROMs and a host of other devices have us swimming, some would say drowning, in information. How do we manage it all? Can someone manage it for us? How can we select what is best and eliminate the rest? More importantly, how can we go back and retrieve something we read, saw or heard and need right now?

A library provides an excellent example of the need for information specialists. It also serves as an analogy for the work and role of the information specialist in any organization. A library, especially a large collection, is almost useless without the order imposed on it by indexing, cataloguing, shelving, and retrieval systems. The newest in on-line catalogs provide the user with a book's location and availability. Without the system created by librarians (a type of information specialist), a library would be chaotic and of very little use to us despite its potential.

But librarians do more than just order and shelve their collections. They create systems for sharing material between collections. Interlibrary loans are a good example of the information specialist's ability to provide what they don't have by establishing sharing networks with those that do. Newer consortiums of libraries often share data bases and allow us to search the catalogs of other collections for material or references we may require.

In a nutshell, the mission of the information specialist is to connect the information seeker with the desired information. Written out, it seems a simple mission. But it is far more complex a task to accomplish than it is to express and it will call upon all of the history graduate's skills to perform this job with efficiency, frequently under time and cost constraints and with the degree of specificity sought by the information requester.

Here's a recent ad that really emphasizes thoroughness, specificity and follow-through in a profit-oriented business:

Director of Information Resources. We are currently seeking an individual to manage the staff of 15+ people who build and produce the data that supports the products for sale in our catalog: You must be able to maintain product line categories that are kept up-to-date with the fast-paced computer industry. All information must be accurate and thorough. All products must have complete product descriptions which enable our on-line customers to select, with ease, the correct item the first time. Close attention must be paid to new and changing

continued

> continued
>
> product lines, upgrades, versions, and discounted products. You will
> be responsible for continually finding new and better ways to
> productively manage large amounts of information.
>
> You must be an avid reader of computer trade publications and
> stay close to industry news as it pertains to the buying and selling of
> computer products.
>
> You must be a motivated individual who has strong skills in
> directing people towards productivity issues as well as communicate
> clearly to management your process and your results.

There are a number of important skills the information specialist must master in addition to their content area. Many of these skills, however, will have been practiced and utilized in your study of history and will prove equally valuable in a career in information management. Let's identify and analyze some of these skills:

Content Mastery.   The touchstone of the information specialist is knowing their subject. If, for example, you are working in the hosiery industry, you would soon learn that hosiery is considered a "complementary" product to footwear. As the footwear market develops and changes, so must stockings. Open-toed shoes for women call for a different nylon stocking than shoes with closed toecaps. The socks worn with athletic shoes will enjoy the same market demands that the shoes do and if the entire teenage population is wearing athletic footwear and socks (or, no socks!) dress socks (and dress shoes) will be in a slump. A surge of interest by the public in more rugged hiking footwear will be accompanied by a similar demand for more substantial socks. To be a content expert in hosiery would mean having significant current information on the shoe market, as well.

Needs Assessment.   Don't expect everyone who comes requesting information resources from you to be equally articulate about what they want! One of your principal tasks will be to understand exactly what your client needs— regardless of how they express it. Skillful questioning, clarification and the ability to produce examples will help you and your client come to agreement on exactly what is needed.

Instructing/Mentoring.   An old Chinese adage often quoted states: If you give a man a fish, you feed him for a day; if you teach the man how to fish, you feed him for life. This is particularly appropriate in the retrieval of information. Your job may be to provide the information requested but there is no reason to keep your client in the dark about how that information was found and accessed. Every client you meet will benefit from your modeling and teaching your search activities to them so they can begin to understand how to mount their own search. You'll want to both help clients with their immediate needs and convey to them, at the same time, the excitement and pleasure of working on their own.

Experienced information specialists often discuss how they deal with requests that are so commonplace they could provide the answers in their sleep. Do they bark out a routine answer, their voices tinged with boredom and disdain? Absolutely not! They actually put a little "performance art" into their response and treat the clients' requests as if they were brand new. "Oh, that sounds interesting. Let's see where we might find the answer to your question. Have you tried an index to the *New York Times*? Let's see if that has something. Ah, yes, here's an article! Oh, you're welcome."

The client has his or her answer, but more importantly, they have been guided through a process they can now do on their own, freeing up the specialist for more complex and time consuming searches.

Nit-Picking.   As the ad cited above makes abundantly clear, the information specialist wants to provide *exactly* the information their clients request. "Almost" or "close" isn't good enough for the professional. If someone wants to know how many teenage girls pierce their ears, facts about ear piercing in women eighteen to twenty-five years of age isn't going to fit the bill. You'll need to dig deeper and find statistics on thirteen to nineteen year olds to satisfy this request. The information specialist is precise about facts for two reasons; clients are going to make decisions based on the information provided to them by the information resource and these decisions will ultimately have an effect on the viability of the firm and its ability to stay in business and keep you, the information specialist, employed!

Networking.   Think of the information specialist not as a "keeper" of information but as a "finder." Certainly, in any stable employment situation, the individuals charged with information resourcing will build some files of their own. But they will never be able to acquire all they need. The information specialist doesn't necessarily amass information and then distribute it as requested. He or she often may have to generate the information needed within an organization and through the combined efforts of many departments. In providing a historical analysis of window curtain treatments over the past ten years to determine trends in window dressing, you may first seek data from the sales division and then rely on your computer department for processing and printing that data. You may do some research outside the organization on competitors' sales and employ the services of a librarian or commercial data retrieval firm. You may go to a library yourself to read and view advertisements in older magazines or even view tapes of popular television shows set in homes. Very often your work is the product of cooperation among many individuals, and information specialists maintain elaborate and well-developed networks of contacts to provide them the information they need.

Juggling. You won't often have the luxury of working on one information request by itself, from initial request through to delivery. More often, you'll juggle the requests of many individuals simultaneously. Some of these requests will be complicated and involve significant research and accumulation of materials which involve time delays. Some may involve mailings and phone calls to acquire the needed answers. Because some of your work depends on others, you will find yourself working on many, many projects simultaneously.

Excellent organizational skills, time-management ability and a tolerance for stress will ease the challenges of keeping so many requests and searches going at the same time.

DEFINITION OF THE CAREER PATH

The introduction to this career path may have helped explain the need for information specialists. We have described how, in today's fast paced, information-oriented society, our need may not be for information, but for someone to extract what we need from an overwhelming oversupply. Most of us frequently have that need in our daily lives. Likewise, you can appreciate the skills and talents necessary for the information specialist to be effective in their job. But what are those jobs and what are they called? Let's look at a short list of possible job titles:

Administrative Assistant	Institutional Researcher
Assistant Editor	Intelligence Specialist
Assistant Planner	Library and Information
Biographer	Specialist
Communications Assistant	List and Segmentation
Database/Records Manager	Manager
Development Associate for	Market Researcher
Research	Media Specialist
Government Relations	Photograph Cataloger
Assistant	Registrar
Genealogist	Research Analyst
Historian	Systems Manager
Information Specialist	

The variety and confusion of working titles should indicate several important things to the job searcher: First, the field of information specialization remains largely undefined, at least in job titles. Certainly, those who employ people to act as information specialists have not yet agreed on a common terminology. The lack of a definitive job title may also indicate individual job roles vary equally as much. People working in informational services are still organizing themselves by content area and not by their more general role as information networkers. Secondly, the lack of a common job title requires you to read and carefully understand the job description for which you are applying. It is in these job duties and the delineations of responsibility that you will come to appreciate the focus and emphasis in that particular position and whether it meets not only your expectations of the job of an information specialist, but also if you have the particular skill package the employer is seeking.

Look at the variety of position descriptions shown below to begin to gain additional insight into the work of the information specialist:

Research Assistant. BA & 1–2 yrs exp req'd. Excellent communication & phone skills; good working knowledge of word processing &/or database software programs. Experience working with research data & assisting with research projects desirable. Salary $2096/mo w/benefits. Send resume to (health foundation) . . .

Assistant Planner. Perform planning duties on urban transportation studies incl. collecting/summarizing/analyzing project data. Req rel BA/BS, research skills, computer skills. Contact Personnel Office (regional planning commission) for application.

Database Network Coordinator. Managing our clinical database and supervising our 15+ user network—these are among the primary responsibilities of the organized and versatile professional our Dept of Cardiothoracic Surgery is seeking. You will oversee data entry, develop applications, and provide training, support & problem solving. Familiarity w/PC & network hardware & software, DOS, LOTUS 1-2-3 & WordPerfect essential. Send resume to (medical center) . . .

Library Reference Coordinator. MLS preferred, BA or equiv library/ research exp req'd. Slry $19,020–$24,614 + benefits. Some evenings & occasional weekends. Apply to (city library) . . .

WORKING CONDITIONS

Get ready to be popular and busy! The woman or man who can provide on-target information when it's needed is going to be a vital member of any organization. In an information specialist position, you have the opportunity to meet with co-workers from every department and level of employment within your organization. You'll be called on frequently, not just for formal requests for information but also with simple questions, such as "How many workers did we have in 1909?" or "Where exactly in the city was our first showroom?" The information resource professional is very often (and wisely) brought in early in the planning stages of most projects so they have a full understanding of the information needs of all concerned parties. This helps them to best consider how to accomplish the task.

Involvement

High-level involvement may come as a surprise to some who are unaware of the active role information specialists play, not only in providing data support to planning needs but in helping to shape strategy. Knowledge of the organization's past experiences, successes and failures and an ability to bring those experiences to bear on new efforts makes the information specialist a player, and not just a resource.

Communication

Listening, questioning, and determining needs are vital skills and to best ascertain what information is needed requires the information resource specialist to interact with people constantly. Your possession of strong interpersonal skills will help you work quicker and smarter if you can communicate successfully with various people, using an easy-to-understand vocabulary and visual aids to gain an understanding of what information people need.

Working conditions will involve lots of partnerships and cooperation with others in a variety of fields. Your networks of contacts will be vital and your day will include much telephone and computer work and probably a fair amount of written correspondence. The information specialist is far more of a communicator than a bookworm!

Quick Action

You may be surprised to hear speed mentioned in a research job. A common complaint of the information specialist is "everybody wants it yesterday." Fortunately, many requests repeat themselves with stunning regularity and the skillful resource professional will begin to build information packets to satisfy those traditional requests. But many searches are challenging and are prompted by a need to respond to some outside influence or market demand—quickly! If you begin with a clear and mutually agreed-upon definition of the materials and information requested, you have accomplished the most important element in rapid information provision. Good staff, technology, a strong memory, notetaking ability, records management and retrieval will all help you to get information-seekers what they need as quickly as possible.

Tracking and Traffic Management

Stop in at a busy information specialist's office and somewhere, on a desk, on the wall, on the computer screen, you're likely to discover a tracking chart of all the various on-going projects and their individual stages of completion. Seldom does one have the luxury of a single project; there are usually many. The atmosphere may not be exactly chaotic, but it won't remind you of the traditional image of the library. It might be closer to the newsroom of a major daily before it goes to press. The reason for this is interesting and informative about the profession. You may well ask, "Why not just work straight through on one assignment, finish it, and move on to the next?" It's a reasonable question and has an interesting answer.

Frequently, the information specialist cannot immediately acquire the materials or data she or he needs and must seek the help of another information specialist to provide that! This may involve letters, facsimile transmissions, electronic mail, or telephone calls anywhere in the world. There will be delays as these individuals have their own agenda of tasks and they, in turn, may need to seek out additional information! Keeping track of these requests and the projects they relate to can be a task in itself. There is even a name for it—traffic management!

TRAINING AND QUALIFICATIONS

Every information specialist has their own combination of skills and attributes and each brings something special to their job. Information resourcing can involve great creativity, intuition and educated guesswork. Those are hard to determine in the interview process and even harder to pin down and evaluate. There are several attributes that go into the skill package of the information specialist and though how they are prioritized might be the subject of intense debate, most would agree on the following basic list:

Organization

Every part of your job in information management cries for organization. Organizing your resources, your time, and your priorities to fulfill the information requests you receive will make constant and ever-increasing demands on your organizational ability. How frustrating and wasteful to be asked something you've done before and yet can no longer locate, necessitating an entire repeat search. In any self-assessment exercise, organization should be a strong personal quality for an information specialist.

High Level of General Information

Knowing your content area seems obvious, whether it's historical architecture or labor statistics. What may be more critical is reading the daily newspaper, watching television, and keeping up with news magazines, literature and other conduits of general information. It is in how people speak, read, and write about the facts you are dealing with that will allow you to make the necessary important connections between seemingly unrelated topics. What if your inquiry required descriptions of architecture from eighteenth-century novels or a listing of those cityscapes most often used to back the credits of situation comedies?

Listening Skills and Needs Assessment

Frequently, you'll get requests for information that you don't understand. You know that to do the best job you can, you need to be of the same mind as the information requester. That person may be unused to dealing with an information specialist and not particularly adept at expressing their informational needs. That's where your communication skills come into play. Skillful questioning, a patient manner with good eye contact and attending behavior will encourage people to express exactly what they perceive to be their request. Your questions and discussion will help clarify the request and bring your results closer to their original intention. You must be ready to do this with representatives from every department, every level of the employment hierarchy, or society in general.

Discretion

Major expansion plans for a new hospital, a new line of children's dolls based on a much-loved storybook character, the indictment of a major political figure—all these important and confidential plans share a common element. For each, the team involved in planning these activities would include an information specialist.

With top level access to executives and information in any organization, and early awareness of even tentative plans, it is essential the information specialist be trusted and valued for their confidentiality and discretion.

EARNINGS

Researcher, biographer, genealogist, database manager; the names for information specialist positions continues to grow. If you're interested in this field, which promises to continue to be an exciting and challenging one, then you probably already enjoy solving problems. Finding accurate earnings information may well be your first assignment!

To get a good handle on the possible earnings range or "spread" for an entry-level information specialist, you'll need to look at these positions (by whatever job title) across the full spectrum of possible employment sites (non-profit, business/industry, education, libraries, etc.). Government position salaries average in the low to mid-twenties for bachelor degree holders with minimum experience. College and university positions (database management, non-library science library positions) range somewhat higher to the low thirties. Research assistants in business and industry with good software skills average $26,000 in their first position.

If you bring to your first position some specific information management experience, better-than-average computer skills, and strong documentation of these abilities, you can expect your entry-level salary to more closely approximate the high end of a stated range. For stated entry-level salaries, you may be able to negotiate as much as ten percent more with exceptional experience.

CAREER OUTLOOK

The *CAM* (Career Movement and Management Facts) *Report,* a respected insider newsletter on career issues, reports Information Services is one of the "Hot Track" professions given its strong employment outlook. The irony is that the *CAM Report* and all the other specialty newsletters used by professionals in every field are just another symptom of the avalanche of information that has both spawned and fed this exponentially growing profession. The *CAM Report* cites as but one example that the *Burwell Directory of Information Brokers* has ballooned by some twenty percent a year for the past decade!

The term "information overload" has real meaning for most of us in our personal lives. We have mailboxes full of "junk" mail, newspapers and magazines, incomprehensible numbers of software packages available for our home computer, lengthy recorded messages waiting for us on our home answering machines and satellite television access to hundreds of channels. How can we possibly manage such a plethora of information? We can't, and we don't *have* to manage this personal influx of data because it is discretionary. We can choose where we put our time and energy and ignore information that doesn't interest us.

This is not the case, however, for business, medical or educational institutions, governmental agencies or any of the host of professional information receivers. The proliferation of databases, online services, print publications and internet services demands to be managed. Incoming material needs to be screened, selected and stored for easy access and retrieval. For many of these professional sites, information access can mean important advantages in the cost of doing business, in maintaining a competitive edge, or providing critical response to a consumer.

It may be a doctor seeking bone marrow transplant matching services, or a prospective college freshman asking about financial aid opportunities; the consequences resulting from either the swift provision of this needed information or the failure to provide it can be critical. In competitive business situations, it may mean the difference between who does and does not secure a valuable account.

Given all of the information needs of our society, the outlook is a positive one. However, in any growing field, this demand for specialists will engender two other demands. First, hiring criterion will become increasingly demanding, so you'll want to stay competitive. This chapter has given you the information you need to make the most of your education and experience as you seek an entry-level position. Second, the technology in this industry will continue to develop and you must stay current in this area to stay marketable. Review the next section of this chapter to enhance your job search.

STRATEGY FOR FINDING THE JOBS

Information specialists can enhance their job search by incorporating the four considerations we describe below into their efforts. Computers are becoming more important than ever in moving relevant information quickly, so it will be critical to get as much computer-related training as you can. In addition, you'll want to be sure to do some informational interviewing early on; you'll get the inside scoop on potential employers and the qualifications they are seeking. After you talk with these professionals you'll have a better sense for the kinds of information specialties that seem to match your interests and talents, and you'll want to follow that up by testing your decisions. As you do this testing in part-time employment or in internships you'll have the opportunity to begin practicing the specialized skills you'll be called upon to use regularly. Each of these efforts will prepare you to move out into the world of work.

Get As Much Computer-Related Training As You Can

The movement from the use of paper records to the use of computerized records demands that the information specialist know how to use the latest technology, both in terms of hardware (computer terminals, personal computers, printers, scanners, digitizers) and software (word processing, databases, spreadsheets, telecommunications, graphics packages). Plan on taking courses or workshops that provide you with an overview of computers and technology as well as courses that provide hands-on training on specific types of software packages. Once you learn how to use one type of database or spreadsheet, you will be able to convince a potential employer that it will be easy for you to learn the particular package they are using.

Do Some Informational Interviewing Early On in Your Job Search

Informational interviewing will help you gather more information about jobs and work environments. Library work is often thought of as being solitary, and in a very quiet setting. Talk with a professional to uncover the realities— library staff members *do* have fun, and teamwork is critical to their success. Advertising is often thought of by students as a busy, hectic and unconventional industry. Information specialists working in this industry may find themselves very busy indeed, but the work is often not as glamorous as some believe it is. No matter what type of work or work setting you are considering, find out what it's *really* like. Talk with other entry-level employees as well as seasoned veterans to get the complete picture so you can better judge for yourself whether that setting would be a "good place" to work.

Decide Which Specialization Interests You Most

In order to begin building a career as one of the types of information specialists described in this path, at a fairly early stage in your career you will have to make a decision about how you want to specialize. You will certainly be able to gain an entry-level position with a bachelor's degree, but to see career growth in an information specialty you will probably need an advanced degree. If library work interests you, for example, you would be able to obtain several types of library jobs with a bachelor's degree in history. If you hope to work as a librarian a master's in library science will be required. Let's say you are interested in organizing the information gathered by a large corporation. An advanced degree in information systems management or a more general masters in business administration would be needed to move into upper levels of management.

So how do you begin deciding what to specialize in? Part-time work, summer jobs and internships are all employment opportunities you can utilize while you're still in school to put yourself in various environments to see what they are like, to see what type of people work in these settings, and to gain a deeper understanding of the nature of the work.

One organization that offers a number of volunteer internship opportunities on an ongoing basis is the Student Conservation Association. A review of their latest *Resource Assistant Program Bulletin* included numerous opportunities that the information specialist might be interested in. One position was for a historical researcher who would conduct research and gather oral histories on construction, history and subsequent development of the Denali Highway in interior Alaska. Requirements included a major in history or a related field; self motivation, ability to work independently and with minimal supervision; and the ability to work in remote areas with adverse environmental conditions. Another position was for an assistant librarian for the Grand Canyon Park Research Library. Duties included accessioning of new library acquisitions; cataloging all incoming materials, maintaining day to day operations, and rendering assistance to staff personnel and the general public. Complete training would be provided, and the requirements included the ability to communicate successfully, both in writing and orally, and a college background in the liberal arts.

If you have already graduated, you may want to consider temporary or term employment opportunities. Recent statistics indicate that about twenty-eight percent of the new positions created in the first twenty-eight months of the current recovery were temporary positions. This situation can be useful if you want to experience several types of jobs before you make a commitment to specialize in one area or field. There are temp agencies operating in nearly every geographic location, and some of them specialize in the type of placement they make (paralegal, systems management).

Begin Acquiring and Practicing the Necessary Specialized Skills

An employer doesn't care whether you have built your skills in a classroom setting, in a part-time job or internship, or in a volunteer position. They just want to know that you'll be able to do the work they're hiring you to do. Having experience using needed skills will certainly set you apart from the group of people who simply say they *think* they can do the work. So get involved in using the computer, or learning about a subject such as market research at every available opportunity.

POSSIBLE EMPLOYERS

The information specialist will find employment opportunities lurking around every corner; your imagination may be the only factor limiting the possibilities you explore. Consider these types of employers:

- ❑ Consulting organizations
- ❑ Research centers
- ❑ Government
- ❑ Libraries
- ❑ Publishers
- ❑ Business and industry
- ❑ Non-profit organizations

Each is discussed below; be sure to add to the list as you do your own exploring.

Consulting Organizations

Profile. Consultants and consulting organizations help their clients, be they individuals or organizations, get information and solve problems. The issues can range from engineering to health care, from science and technology to pension funds. Consulting organizations with more than a few employees will have some type of information specialist on their staff. The work may involve library research, computer work, report writing, or sales presentations. Be ready to accept a job which allows you to get your foot in the door, and then will allow you to grow once you show them how effective you are.

Help in Locating These Employers. There are a variety of publications available that list this type of organization. Ask for the *Consultants & Consulting Organizations Directory* published by Gale Research, or Dun's *Consultants Directory.* There are also regional directories such as *Consultants in the Midwest,* or directories by consulting specialty, such as *Hospital Consultants Directory.* Many more are available, so check with your career counselor or librarian for additional titles.

Research Centers

Profile. If you have enjoyed your academic experience and you like the idea of working in an academic community, there are a range of research centers, often affiliated with a college or university, that provide the opportunity to work as an information specialist. Research centers might focus their work on agriculture, environmental sciences, medical issues, business, population and demography, folklore, labor and industrial relations, or nearly any other imaginable subject. Research centers hire many different types of employees, including library specialists, researchers, information systems managers, and survey managers. Identify possible employment sites by using the resources listed below, and network with managers or directors of the facilities to find out about employment opportunities.

Help in Locating These Employers. Gale Research, Inc., publishes the *Research Centers Directory;* Reed Reference publishes the *Directory of American Research and Technology* which describes corporate facilities active in commercially-applicable basic or applied research such as aerospace or urban studies. Be sure to check with colleges and universities in your area for research activities not listed in these large directories.

Government

Profile. Information specialists can find employment at many different kinds of governmental agencies, which include: state and local planning departments, intelligence operations, regulatory agencies (e.g., nuclear power), city and town libraries, environmental protection agencies, law enforcement agencies, and housing and community development agencies.

The federal government hires intelligence research specialists, program specialists, administrative assistants, historians, import specialists, management analysts, and position classification specialists, just to name a few possible titles. They work in agencies such as the National Archives, Drug Enforcement Administration, National Endowment for the Humanities, National Park Service, Smithsonian Institution, U.S. Customs Service, and the U.S. Information Agency.

State and local governments offer positions in units including administration and legislation, corrections, court systems, education, fire protection, health and human services, highway and street construction and maintenance, housing and community development, hospitals, libraries, natural resources, parks and recreation, police, sanitation, transportation, and utilities. Many entry-level positions don't have the word "information" in the job title but are, in reality, information specialist positions.

Help in Locating These Employers.   If you want your work to relate directly to your studies in history, the *Directory of Federal Historical Programs and Activities,* published by the American Historical Association, lists hundreds of federal programs and agencies and includes a program description, contacts, and a roster of current personnel for each. About 1500 public historians, archivists, and librarians in government offices are indexed. Contact people working in programs that are of interest to you to find out about employment possibilities and procedures.

If you would like to explore governmental employment possibilities that may not directly make use of your knowledge of history, there are some excellent resources you can use to begin understanding and working through what seems to be the interminable bureaucracy. These include VGM's *Opportunities in State and Local Government Careers* and *Opportunities in Federal Government Careers; Government Job Finder;* and *The Complete Guide to Public Employment.* The *Occupational Outlook Quarterly,* a publication of the U.S. Department of Labor, contains useful and informative articles if you are interested in federal employment. Be sure to contact your regional Office of Personnel Management (OPM) and review job listings such as the *Federal Jobs Digest* to get as complete a picture as you can of federal opportunities. Also talk to your state personnel office to find out how state jobs are listed. Ask for assistance in working through the application processes. Remember, there are people willing to help you cut through the mountain of red tape.

Libraries

Profile.   Libraries are often classified according to the populations they serve. These include: school libraries; college, university and research libraries; public libraries; and specialized or cooperative libraries. Each type of library has its own interests and faces its own challenges. School libraries, for example, are striving to improve their media centers, so one way to put to work your degree in history and your interest and part-time work experience in media operations is to seek employment as a media specialist in larger elementary and secondary schools.

Help in Locating These Employers.   The *American Library Directory* provides information on more than 38,000 libraries and related organizations in the U.S. and Canada. Another useful reference is the *Directory of Special Libraries and Information Centers,* published by Gale Research. Another, more specialized directory is the *Libraries, Information Centers and Databases in Science* *and Technology* made available by Reed Reference Publishing. Also watch for job listings in your local and regional newspaper, or visit your career office to review job listings such as *The Job Hunter, National Human Services Employment Biweekly,* or *Current Jobs for Graduates.*

Publishing.

Profile.   Ten years ago, if you looked on the masthead of *Time Magazine,* you would have seen research staff listed. Today, those same research positions (at *Time* or any other magazine) are more likely to be called assistant editors. You can begin a career in magazine publishing being called an assistant editor, and after a satisfying career that has seen a lot of growth, you may still be called an assistant editor. These positions, as well as many others in the industry, draw on the talents of information specialists.

Help in Locating These Employers.   There certainly is variety in the career materials available to those interested in working in publishing. Review VGM's *Opportunities in Book Publishing Careers* and *Opportunities in Magazine Publishing Careers; How to Get the Right Job in Publishing; The Publishing Job Finder; The Newspaper: Everything You Need to Know to Make it in the Newspaper Business;* and *Career Opportunities for Writers.* Each will provide its own perspective on careers in this industry and will provide information useful for your job search.

Business and Industry

Profile.   We recently saw a job advertisement for an entry-level position with a financial corporation that we would classify as an information specialist. It was called a marketing assistant, and asked for someone who is smart and energetic for a range of functions, including telephone prospecting, research, file maintenance, word processing and other support activities. They wanted a college degree with marketing exposure for a position that would provide new skills and opportunity to build a career. This calls for the information specialist! There are similar positions in advertising, information brokeraging, marketing research, pharmaceuticals, information systems and many other industries.

Help in Locating These Employers.   Don't overlook using a business career resource such as VGM's *Careers in Business,* which will orient you to the needs of the for-profit business community. You'll learn about the various industries and business functions, and the entry-level positions that they offer. Many are information specialists, in the sense that we have described here. Move on to more specific resources such as *Advertising Career Directory, Criminal Justice Careers Guidebook,* or *Opportunities in Personnel Management.* These types of books will help you focus in on skills, abilities and traits that you should highlight on your resume and during the interview process.

Nonprofit Organizations

Profile.   Whether you research donor prospects for a university, maintain a membership list for a large organization such as the American Medical Association, or coordinate volunteers for the Red Cross, you'll be using skills associated with being an information specialist. There are large, well-established nonprofit organizations that have proportionally as large a staff and run as efficiently as for-profit businesses; and smaller, grass-roots organizations that have only a few employees and have a very casual organizational culture. No matter what type of setting you prefer, these organizations must maintain information critical to their strategic advantage.

Help in Locating These Employers.   Start with a review of *Great Careers: The Fourth of July Guide to Careers, Internships, and Volunteer Opportunities in the Nonprofit Sector* to get an overview of the scope and types of organizations that exist in this sector of the economy. Then move on to other resources, including *Opportunities in Nonprofit Organizations, Careers in the Nonprofit Sector: Doing Well by Doing Good,* and *Profitable Careers in Nonprofit.* There are excellent articles as well as job listings in *Community Jobs.* If you review two or three of these resources you'll be able to determine whether the nonprofit sector is a place for you.

POSSIBLE JOB TITLES

As you look over the list of possible job titles shown below you'll begin to realize there are innumerable job titles for you to consider; there are many more titles that could be added. As you conduct your job search, add to this list based on the job descriptions you read in advertisements and in other career guidebooks.

Administrative assistant	Genealogist
Assistant editor	Government relations assistant
Assistant planner	Historian
Biographer	Historic preservation planner
Bibliographer	Historical researcher
Classifier	Information hotline specialist
Communications assistant	Information manager
Corporate historian	Information scientist
Database network coordinator	Information specialist
Database/records manager	Institutional researcher
Development associate for	Intelligence research specialist
research	Intelligence specialist

continued

continued	
Librarian	Registrar
Library and information specialist	Research analyst
Library circulation desk	Research assistant
supervisor	Research associate
Library reference coordinator	Research interviewer
Library technical assistant	Reseacher
List and segmentation manager	School librarian
Market researcher	Securities information
Media specialist	researcher
Paralegal	Software specialist
Paralegal assistant	Systems analyst
Photographic cataloger	Systems manager
Planner	Technical research assistant
Policy analyst	Travel agent

RELATED OCCUPATIONS

Think about the roles played by an information specialist: content mastery, needs assessment, instructing/mentoring, nit-picking, networking, and multiple project juggling, and you'll see there are other career choices to consider if this one doesn't seem quite right. If you're not familiar with the job descriptions that go along with the job titles shown below, be sure to find out more about them. Consider:

Actuary	Curator
Admissions officer	Customer service
Claims adjudicator	representative
Computer programmer	Employment interviewer
Counselor	Teacher

Use the *Occupational Outlook Handbook* or VGM's *Careers Encyclopedia* to read job descriptions for these titles.

PROFESSIONAL ASSOCIATIONS

In this section, we have listed a wide range of organizations that will be able to provide additional data about certain information specialties. Carefully review the members/purpose section for each organization and decide whether the organization pertains to *your* interests. Membership in one may well be worth the investment in terms of networking opportunities, job listings, or placement services. Remember, some organizations will provide limited career information at no charge, but if you want to receive publications that often include job listings, you must actually join the organization. Many do, however, have greatly reduced membership dues for full-time students.

American Association of Professional Consultants
9140 Ward Parkway
Kansas City, MO 64114
Members/Purpose: Professional consultants.
Journal/Publication: *The Consultant's Journal; The Consultant's Voice;* membership directory.

American Consultants League
1290 Palm Ave.
Sarasota, FL 34236
Members/Purpose: Full- and part-time consultants in varied fields of expertise.
Training: Offers a home study program.
Journal/Publication: Consultants directory; *Consulting Intelligence.*

American Historical Association
400 A Street, SE
Washington, DC 20003
Members/Purpose: Professional historians, educators, and others interested in promoting historical studies and collecting and preserving historical manuscripts.
Journal/Publication: *Newsletter/Employment Information; American Historical Review; Guide to Departments of History.*
Job Listings: See *Newsletter/Employment Information.*

American Library Association
50 East Huron Street
Chicago, IL 60611
Members/Purpose: Librarians, libraries, trustees, friends of libraries, and others interested in the responsibilities of libraries in the educational, social, and cultural needs of society.
Journal/Publication: ALA handbook of organization and membership directory; *ALA Washington Newsletter; American Libraries; Library Systems Newsletter; Library Technology Reports.*
Job Listings: Offers placement services; see *American Libraries* for listings.

American Society for Information Science
8720 Georgia Ave., Suite 501
Silver Spring, MD 20910

Members/Purpose: Information specialists, scientists, librarians, administrators, social scientists, and others interested in the use, organization, storage, retrieval, evaluation, and dissemination of recorded specialized information.

Training: Conducts continuing education programs and professional development workshops.

Journal/Publication: *Annual Review of Information Science and Technology;* bulletin; handbook and directory; *Jobline; Journal of the American Society for Information Science;* proceedings.

Job Listings: Maintains placement service; see *Jobline.*

American Society for Legal History
c/o Prof. M. de Landon
University of Mississippi
Dept. of History
University, MS 38677

Members/Purpose: Judges; lawyers; law educators; history, political science, and economics professors; historians, students and others.

Journal/Publication: *ASLH Newsletter; Law and History Review.*

Association of American Publishers
71 Fifth Avenue
New York, NY 10003

Members/Purpose: Trade association representing producers of hardbound and softbound general, educational, trade, reference, religious, scientific, technical, and medical books; instructional materials; classroom periodicals; maps, globes, tests, and software.

Training: Conducts seminars and workshops on various publishing topics, including rights and permission, sales, and educational publishing.

Journal/Publication: *AAP Exhibits Directory; AAP Monthly Report; Green Book of College Publishing; International Fairs Calendar.*

Association for Systems Management
1433 West Bagley Road
P.O. Box 38370
Cleveland, OH 44138

Members/Purpose: International professional organization of administrative executives and specialists in management information systems serving business, commerce, education, government, and the military, and concerned with communications, electronics, equipment, forms control, human relations, organization, procedure writing, and systems applications.

Training: Offers seminars and conferences, and courses in all phases of administrative systems and management.

Journal/Publication: *Journal of Systems Management.*

Job Listings: See *Journal of Systems Management* for occasional listings.

National Science Foundation

4201 Wilson Blvd.

Arlington, VA 22230

Members/Purpose: Independent agency in the Executive Branch concerned primarily with the support of basic and applied research and education in the sciences and engineering. Funds scientific research in many areas including social science research.

Journal/Publication: Annual report; *Antarctic Journal of the U.S.; Bulletin; Guide to Programs; Mosaic; Science Indicators.*

Job Listings: Contact the personnel office for information.

Organization of American Historians

112 North Bryan Street

Bloomington, IN 47408

Members/Purpose: Promotes historical study and research in the field of American History.

Journal/Publication: *Journal of American History; OAH Newsletter; Magazine of History.*

Job Listings: See *OAH Newsletter.*

Society for Non-Profit Organizations

6314 Odana Road, Suite 1

Madison, WI 53719

Members/Purpose: Executive directors, staff, board members, volunteers, and other professionals who serve nonprofit organizations.

Training: Sponsors seminars and workshops on nonprofit management and leadership.

Journal/Publication: *National Directory of Service and Product Providers to Non-Profit Organizations; Nonprofit World: The National Nonprofit Leadership and Management Journal;* resource center catalog.

Job Listings: Suggests job seekers review *Community Jobs.*

Special Libraries Association

1700 18th Street, NW

Washington, DC 20009

Members/Purpose: International association of information professionals who work in special libraries serving business, research, government, universities, newspapers, museums, and institutions that use or produce specialized information.

Training: Conducts continuing education courses.

Journal/Publication: *Special Libraries; Who's Who in Special Libraries.*

Job Listings: Provides employment services; see publication called *Jobline.*

CHAPTER THIRTEEN

PATH 4: BUSINESS ADMINISTRATION AND MANAGEMENT

 usiness administration and management represents, not only the broadest spectrum of employment for the history major, but also the potential for the best use of all you've learned in earning your degree. The broad scope of business allows for many possible "sites" to utilize different foci of your skill base. Business administration and management is going to demand, many, many of the skills the history major acquires in the course of his or her education. History is the record of time, animated and personalized through humanity's failures and accomplishments. The history student learns not only the sweep and panoply of human endeavor, but also to see and anticipate patterns of behavior, ingredients for conflict, signs of progress, and a host of other interpretations as they read and analyze the historical facts.

That ability to read and digest information, to collect information, to make sense of events, to draw conclusions and to perform analyses based on what you've seen and read are the very qualities all competitive enterprises need. The historical facts may be product quality failures, labor supply or demand, escalating costs, average consumer purchase trends, physician prescribing patterns, hospital operating room waiting time averages or any of the countless situations in an organization that call out for someone to go out and comprehensively review a situation, analyze the facts, draw some conclusions and then make some recommendations for change based on that analysis.

So, about now in your reading, you may be thinking, "Yes, I can do that. I just hadn't thought about my history degree and skills in that way. But now that I read about it, I see that I do have valuable skills that will work in business administration and management." That's great! The important point in understanding all of this is, just as you hadn't seen your skills in this new light, your employer will also need to be educated. Your first big job, even before you're hired, is to educate a potential employer about history majors and what they have to offer, how they can be utilized within an organization and what kinds of jobs they can be put to work doing for the betterment of the organization.

Let's take another look at those skills a history major brings to the job search:

Reading/Retention

More than many other majors, history involves copious amounts of reading and many history majors become proficient at reading and digesting large amounts of printed material. In fact, your reading skills may have been one of the reasons you decided to major in history! Business administration and management activities place just as much of a premium on reading and you may have to do as much reading, if not more, than you did as a student. Business reports, newspapers, magazines (both industrial and commercial), faxes, transcripts, trial records, and computer printouts documenting all facets of business activity all come into an organization every day. The organization itself creates correspondence, memorandums, reports, digests, fact sheets and thousands of other pieces of reading material. Read this recent ad:

> *Assistant Editor.* Copyediting/rsrch/explanatory note writing/table compilation/proofreading for statutory, admin, court rul, and judicial opinion texts. Req BA/BS/excel writ/oral comm skills, quantitative skills, desktop publishing skills. Pref know legal publishing. Send letter/resume to (legal publisher) . . .

With all this reading, it's no wonder an organization would value and esteem an individual who can read and retain what they have read. Some of this material might be culled and edited for an inter-office communications piece, or it may simply be brought out as an important and related fact of interest at a board meeting. Most importantly, you will bring the knowledge and information from your reading to bear on all your actions and decisions for the employer. The better informed the decision maker, the better the decision, is an axiom highly revered in the business community.

Data Collection

Every business enterprise creates its own history every day. Not every business is equally adept at handling the organization and holdings of the tangible records of that history, whether they are computer printouts or sample packaging materials. Very often, the organization is not aware of the importance of this material to their future. Though they frequently may bemoan the loss of some important document or piece of information, they do not and cannot relate that to their current poor practices for data collection an maintenance.

Step right in, history major, and take charge! You'll have an innate sense of what an organization needs to store, what it needs to keep at the ready in terms of data. If data collection is not providing the information a firm needs to do the job, you'll have recommendations on redesigning the data collection documents. In reading and studying your history, you've continually had to separate the relevant from the irrelevant as you follow a historical fact or event over time. The need is no different in an organization except that the process can always be improved. You can make a real difference here! Notice this next job listing where the history major could develop reports and forms to capture the information an organization truly needs:

Consultant. (Big six) public acctg/consulting firm. Admin client employee benes plans, manipulate data files, **develop reports & forms,** provide client phone support. Req BA/BS, 1–3 yrs exper incl DOS/Windows/Novell/Excel/WP, excel people skills. Resume/ltr/sal req to . . .

Research

This category speaks for itself and is probably one that you would immediately feel comfortable talking about with a prospective employer. Research is the pre-eminent skill of the student of history and it has equal value in all other areas of human endeavor. Because you've used your research talents consistently over the course of your college career, you've amassed an unusual amount of research techniques, some of which may be unconscious. Along the way, you may have enjoyed some specific library technique classes and many college programs offer seminars or workshops that further refine your skills. A professor who assigned a research paper may have had one of the library staff brief your class on library research procedures.

In addition to the training, you've had on-the-job experience with numerous papers, reports and formal research assignments. The content may have been history, but the techniques, the skills, the patience and perseverance— even the ability to seek professional research assistance is all common experience and will be directly applicable to the world of work, whether the topic is the number of women aged thirty to thirty-five who use a hair-coloring product or the relative fat content in the standard hamburger from the top five fast food restaurants. Research is research. Notice these two ads:

> *Legislative Research Assistant.* Democratic senator. Handle crime, civil rights, arts and humanities, and rules committee issues. Req BA. Send writing samples to . . .
>
> *Researcher.* (National TV news hour), research, write, check facts, clip news items, maintain research library, assist w/studio production, some driving. Resume/ltr/writ samples to . . .

Analysis

Facts are just facts until they are digested and analyzed. In any commercial enterprise, there is an on-going and insistent need for talented people who can look at data and understand what this information represents to the organization. Look at this next ad:

> *Research Specialist.* Prep policy reports & **analyses** on educ finance reform. Req excel writ skills, quantitative skills, know public policy. BA in liberal arts. Resume/ltr to (urban league) . . .

Critical Thinking

Just as so often happened in your study of history, you will begin to notice, in your review and analysis of any organization's efforts, certain trends and patterns of thinking. Some will be ingredients for success and others will be opportunities to alert the organization to patterns of thinking, behavior or goal setting that may be unproductive. Perhaps you have noticed that soon after instituting a new annual sale policy, your employer (a high quality lawn-care equipment manufacturer) began to experience severe drops in customer purchases in the months prior to the annual sale. Your analysis clearly demonstrates that the volume increase generated by the sale is only marginally better than normal annual purchases unstimulated by annual price reduction. You also have found on some customer comment cards a disturbing related fact that some customers may associate sale merchandise with less than top quality. Your presentation to management will challenge the organization with important ideas and considerations.

Writing/Communication

Just as history changes, so, too, does the way in which history is communicated. We are grateful for the great work of historians past such as Gibbon, Chabod and Toynbee. Today, our new television historians communicate by actively demonstrating and walking us through the pyramids or before cave paintings. We know and appreciate that history needs to be communicated in writing, through the spoken word, and with the help of our ever increasing armory of visual technology. Your own experience as a student has given you a sense for those writings, texts, films and other material that made the subject vivid and the issues easily understood. Your task in business will be to use the means at hand to communicate your findings. It may be anything from a simple memo to an interactive television seminar beamed across the country or the world. Notice the importance placed on communication in this ad:

> *Housing Services Coordinator.* Conduct community outreach to public/private housing agencies, fair housing officers, property owners to add to/maintain rental listings. Design and deliver seminars and workshops on housing search issues to client families. Provide information to families on housing resources. Make referrals to appropriate housing agencies. Strong presentation skills required. Qualifications: related work experience or college education; commitment to empowerment of low income people; persistence; computer literacy; reliable transportation. Salary $24–26K plus excellent benefits. Send resume & cover letter to (housing authority) . . .

Don't let your unfamiliarity with technology or the teaching role throw you. Those techniques can be learned on-the-job. What is most important to communicate to your employer is your ability to describe, explain, illustrate and demonstrate what you have to say. A simple portfolio of some of your representative work would be a helpful and practical demonstration of this.

Prescriptions for Change

There may be company historians in some very large firms, but there aren't very many. In fact, that job is more likely to be given to a very senior employee who may have no formal history training but has lived the history of the organization. The variety of skills you are offering to an organization argue for a more active, involved role in company planning and decision making.

One of the results of data analysis and the recognition of trends and recurring issues is the possibility of understanding the ingredients for success as well as avoiding the path to disaster. Your history training has taught you to be aware of events and their short- and long-term effects on ultimate causes. It's no different in the organization. When you do discover a pattern, it will be a natural thing to propose some solutions to apply to the situation.

Perhaps you are looking at customer traffic in a chain of restaurants owned by your organization. In analyzing cash register printouts and management reports, you notice a consistent drop in business in mid-afternoon and again after the dinner hour and long before closing. You have high overhead and a full staff of waitrons and cooks and you cannot afford to have them idle. You propose offering an afternoon "high tea" service with small sandwiches and pastries for patrons out shopping or business people needing a place to stop and talk and enjoy light refreshment. For the after-dinner lull, you propose a coffee bistro with espresso, fine desserts and a guitarist. None of these ideas make heavy demands on costs since the restaurant is already operating during those hours and the additional menu items are easily produced. The evening entertainment might be local college music students who will work for tips and experience.

Your research and analysis could lead to a new business strategy, increased customer traffic, improved profitability, a new dimension of services and products for your restaurant chain. History in the making!

DEFINITION OF THE CAREER PATH

We've made the case for history majors in business administration and management. They're needed, they have important skills, and there are jobs they can do. Now, you very logically ask yourself, "How do I get started finding those jobs? Where will my career start and how will it progress? What employers should I begin calling on in my job search and what will they call the jobs I qualify to do?" These are all excellent and legitimate questions. Let's take a look at some actual job listings as we begin our discussion of the career path for history majors in business administration and management positions:

> *Product Manager.* Fast growing private label importer/mfr located in picturesque waterfront town seeks energetic, detail oriented professional. Primary respon. will include: product sourcing, price negotiations, placing & tracking orders, sales & maintenance of productions status. Int'l & domestic travel reqd. Should have degree or 3–4 yrs related work exp. Send resume & sal reqrmnts to . . .

This Product Manager position is an excellent example of the kind of entry-level position for which a history major should apply because it uses so many skills you have acquired in your studies. Let's look more closely at the position.

Here's a firm that both manufacturers and imports products to be purchased and relabeled by other firms. The private label sector of the economy is a huge industry, as many excellent products and manufacturers simply do not have the name recognition nor the marketing expertise to create a strong brand name image for their organization. They find it easier to either sell their products to another organization to be relabeled or manufacture products to a large organization's specifications. Most of these firms lie outside the United States where hourly wages are lower and cost of goods is proportionately cheaper, allowing for significant mark-ups of products as they pass through the chain of distribution to the consumer.

This position requires an energetic individual. This is a personal quality that you will have assessed through your completion of the self-evaluation that opens this book. It is probably part of the job announcement because the organization is fast-paced, management may be young and very active, or there may be fewer staff filling many different roles. Pay attention to demands such as this and be honest in your response. If you're not particularly energetic and choose to misrepresent your energy level to acquire the position, soon enough both your real temperament and that of the organization will become apparent and that will be a stressful situation for both parties.

The next demand is for "detail orientation." Certainly, a student of history is not only detail-oriented but aware of the crucial importance of details; in decision making, in planning and strategy. If your contracting firm wants a product made out of one-hundred percent recycled paper, you'll know that doesn't mean seventy-five or eighty percent, and before you make some independent decision you would go back to your contracting buyer and determine how critical that product specification is.

The responsibilities of this job for sourcing products, negotiating prices, tracking orders and monitoring the status of production runs is a wonderful demonstration of the practical applications of the skills we outlined in the introduction. Reading and retention, data collection, research, analysis and critical thinking would all be skills needed every day in this exciting position.

The position also suggests travel experience, international and domestic, would be helpful. This is another personal qualification. Perhaps you have little travel experience at this point in your life. The employer for this job might be less concerned about that qualification if, during the interview, you displayed a high level of general information about world events, world politics, foreign exchange rates, and the gold standard. The demand for travel may be simply the employers belief that the individual who has traveled is going to be more aware and more culturally sensitive when conducting business over the telephone, in person, and by letter to business contacts of other cultures.

Let's look at some other actual position descriptions and see what we can learn about the jobs and your qualifications for them:

Management Trainee. (Major insurance company) will train in all aspects of life and health mgmt incl sales & marketing, operations, & tech analysis. Req BA/BS, math/quant skills/excel oral/writ comm skills. Resume/ltr/transcripts/sal requ to . . .

Business Researcher. Growing mgt consult firm. Req BA, excel analytical skills, writ/comm skills, creativity. Resume/ltr to . . .

Both these positions share a common interest in a candidate that has both strong communications skills *and* an analytical orientation. Each position seems to suggest significant research, data collection and analysis demands. One explicitly refers to the personal qualification of creativity, while the other (Management Trainee), because of its association with sales and marketing, may equally value that attribute in a candidate. Both look like excellent entry-level positions for a student of history who wants to use his or her academic preparation in the areas of business administration and management.

WORKING CONDITIONS

As you read these job announcements and contemplate a business career, you may feel both excitement and hesitation. Excitement at the idea that, yes, your skills are valuable and many employers seem to be asking for candidates with talents and attributes similar to those you have developed and perfected in your studies as a history major.

At the same time, you may only recently have begun to think of employment in a concrete way and somehow never imagined yourself in a corporation or wearing a business suit and carrying a briefcase! You may sense that businesses and even larger, more organized not-for-profit organizations have more rules about conduct, appearance, manners and hierarchy than you have been used to or would enjoy. After all, part of your decision to major in history might have been a disdain for some of the same work orientation or profit motive that prompted your classmates to major in business or computer science. Now here you are also considering the world of business administration and management and justifiably wondering, will you fit in?

Rest assured that the world of work is as diverse as the population in general and it is populated with peoples of differing interests, political persuasions, lifestyles, values and talents. There is certainly room for you, too! Your skills are valued and needed and most organizations realize that, along with your talent and education, you come with a particular philosophy and even, perhaps, a different life style.

But we'd like to suggest that some changes may have to be made. After all, a corporation is a public entity and its employees represent the organization. How they look, act and communicate while they represent the organization affects the business and, ultimately, their livelihood. Publicly traded companies with shareholders may feel this responsibility to a greater degree than the private company or family-held business. Nevertheless, a business's success rises and falls on its ability to maintain good relations with its publics.

Businesses today have become much more sophisticated about their staffs and their needs. Some offer flexible time scheduling with varying arrival and departure times for different workers. Some will allow two people to "share" a job, each splitting it in half. This kind of benefit has been helpful for parents who are interested in staying home with young children. Some larger organizations offer on-site child or elder care—a real recognition of home and scheduling problems. An increasing number of firms are offering benefits to same-sex couples and recognizing same-sex couples in social functions and invitations to those functions. Drug, alcohol and emotional issues are more out in the open and firms often offer counseling and referral services for these problems, and do so discreetly and without the stigma these problems earned employees in corporations of the past.

Many firms now offer memberships in health and fitness clubs or actually have those kinds of clubs on-site as part of their benefits program. Of course, this emphasis on exercise and diet has beneficial effects on productivity and reduced absenteeism but, even more than that, it builds self-esteem as people become prouder of how they look and feel and bring that pride into their work. It increases camaraderie and cuts across all hierarchical lines as different kinds of workers meet in the gym and weight rooms.

Many organizations have trips to the ballet, theatre, sports events and museum openings for employees and their families at greatly reduced prices. You are sure to find many, many like-minded individuals at work with equally as many opportunities to share your enthusiasms and interests in work-sponsored activities.

It might be easy to believe that because an organization is not-for-profit and may be deeply involved in doing good in the world, that many of the conditions so firmly set in a corporation would not be found in the not-for-profit. While there certainly are many non-profit organizations that have very relaxed norms for all their activities, a great many others feel that to gain the private and public dollars needed to run these organizations and inspire public trust, they need to present the same picture of organization, sophistication and determination as a corporation.

Another reasonable concern is the issue of competitiveness. Are corporate climates all that competitive or is that the stuff of myth making? Certainly as a history major you competed for grades and thought you were largely competing with yourself and past performance, you were in a sense competing with a class standard set by all members. Business is no different. While most competitive initiative is *outwardly* directed, towards other firms, there are certainly performance norms established over time by the general level of expertise in the firm. Since you are hired in large part with these norms in mind, and your resume and experience are evaluated on criterion already established for success in the organization, you will do fine. What is important is that you stay "tuned in" as an employee to performance standards and do your best to maintain your contribution.

You will participate in periodic evaluations with your direct supervisor to review your accomplishments and set appropriate goals for yourself for the next evaluation period. These evaluations will be the proper setting to discuss your understanding and appreciation of your job, your desire for additional training, or ideas for job modification.

TRAINING AND QUALIFICATIONS

Our review of some sample advertisements has made it clear that, along with your history education, computer familiarity, quantitative skills and general business knowledge would all be helpful. If your curriculum allows for it, see about adding a general business course or selected introductory courses in accounting, management, economics and operations. Don't neglect your quantitative education, either. Though your love of history may be directly in inverse proportion to your dislike of math, your analytical skills will often be applied to data involving numbers and you'll approach this part of your job with more comfort if you have kept your skills well-honed. The following recent advertisement calls for several of these skills:

> *Medical Staff Coordinator.* Full-time position for a professional, self-motivated individual who is able to work independently. Responsibilities will focus on the coordination of physician credentialing and the compilation and organization of statistical information related to physician activities. Must be detail-oriented in order to ensure compliance with all medical staff bylaws and pertinent standards. Strong interpersonal skills needed to interface with all levels of the organization. Proficiency required in Word Perfect and Lotus 1-2-3 with previous database experience. BA/BS and previous experience in medical/hospital desired. Please forward resume and salary requirements to (hospital) . . .

All of this general business education will help you to appreciate your employer's business situation, improve your communication at interviews and speed your research activities when investigating certain industries or specific companies. Some schools offer an introduction to not-for-profit organizations which would be of help to anyone interested in that employment sector.

Any kind of business internship would also assure an employer of your interest in applying your history skills in the public arena. You might look at internships in research, office administration, development, or rotating assignments where you have the opportunity to spend some time in all the departments of an organization. You'll come away from such an experience with a strong sense of what you could do for a firm and how an organization functions.

EARNINGS

Due to the breadth of this employment category, starting salaries are a function of both the general salaries in the industry you are looking at (salaries in industry will be higher than in consumer service firms) and your particular set of skills. The more specific skills (computer, math, research, etc.) you bring in addition to your degree, the higher your initial salary range. Entry-level salaries begin at about $17,000–18,000 and can rise to $27,000–$29,000 for starting pay.

CAREER OUTLOOK

The kinds of positions we have been discussing are sometimes referred to as "generalist" positions because they are not technical and the educational background required is rather loose in terms of demand. Additionally, with these generalist positions there are no firmly established criterion for entry-level positions. Much depends on the employer being approached and the particular combination of skills, talent and personality of the applicant and how that combination fits. The hiring outlook has much to do with the general trend of the economy and the size and location of the hiring organization. These types of positions often follow economic trends. If, for example, an industry and the employers within that sector are not doing well, what monies those employers have to spend on hiring new employees will probably first go towards technical expertise to improve efficiency and product quality and then to financial management staff to ensure fiscal control and solvency. The entry-level general administrator with "soft" or untried skills is not an attractive commodity at such times.

When personnel staffing monies are somewhat more available, it is easier to find and fill these positions. A corollary of this information is that these positions are also more likely to be early casualties in a downturn in the economy, through layoffs, reductions in force, enforced leaves of absence or dismissals for financial exigencies. To prevent this situation, you are encouraged to use your employed time to acquire more specific skills that would significantly alter your resume. A good example of this would be how you could self-manage for growth in an entry-level position as a Human Resource Associate for a large company. Perhaps you have been hired as an Assistant Benefits Administrator, briefing new employees on benefit program choices, and assisting in managing the smooth flow of paperwork and forms surrounding the filing and paying of claims. You could do this job in an exemplary manner for three years and yet still only be qualified for an identical job somewhere else.

Or, you could request cross-training in OSHA (Occupational Safety and Health Administration) guidelines for workers, participate in professional development programs to learn more about pay classification guidelines, volunteer to work on the team producing a new benefits brochure and pick up copywriting and graphics experience, and enroll and participate in every training opportunity provided. Ask your boss if you can sit in on contract negotiations when benefit packages are up for renewal. Soon you will discover you have built a substantial body of expertise in your field.

No longer are you a generalist with only your degree in history to recommend you, but you are now qualified as a Payroll Specialist, a Benefits Officer, an Employee Trainer or even Director of Personnel for a smaller organization.

STRATEGY FOR FINDING THE JOBS

There are many ways to prepare for the job search in business administration and management, but we have highlighted five efforts that we believe should be included in the history major's strategy. First, it is important that you realize and communicate the skill base that your study of history has brought you. Then it will be important to identify which employers need and value your skills. Use the research skills you've developed, and the tips and techniques presented in this book, to find out as much as you can about industry trends and specific employers. Then you must highlight how you can help these organizations and, finally, be proactive as well as reactive in your search.

Realize and Communicate the Skill Base That Your Study of History Has Brought You

In the introduction to the career path, we described a series of skills that the history major develops and enhances in gaining his or her degree. You are able to read volumes of information and retain it, research and collect relevant data, then analyze it and create information. You are able to identify themes, trends and patterns, write and speak about what you've observed, and make recommendations for change. All of these are valued in business, industry and commerce, and it is your job to highlight these skills for potential employers. You don't want them guessing about your potential value to the organization, so make it very clear. Be sure to review the chapter on resume and cover letters, and the one on interviewing, for specific techniques on writing and communicating these important skills.

Learn Which Types of Employers Need and Value These Skills

Your talents, skills, and abilities are valued by every type of employer we can think of, so you will have to use some other criteria to narrow down the types of jobs you will apply for. Think about hobbies and interests you may have; oftentimes there are ways to combine your interests and the work you do. If you're a handweaver, you might consider examining administrative positions available with professional associations serving the textile industry; if you have played baseball since you were a child you might consider sales positions with sports equipment manufacturers. Work with a career counselor to explore ways to tie *your* interests to the world of work. You'll probably be surprised at the connections you'll find.

Find Out about Industry Trends and Specific Employers

Once you determine a focus for beginning a job search, you'll want to educate yourself about the industry in general, and specific employers in particular. Use resources like the latest edition of the *U.S. Industrial Outlook* to get industry information, and then contact appropriate industry associations for more detailed materials. You'll also want to use references like *Hoover's Handbook of American Business* or *Ward's Business Directory* to find out about individual employers. There are many excellent resources available, so be sure to consult with your career counselor or the librarian you're working with. This background information will help you formulate a resume and speak in an informed way as you begin interviewing.

Highlight How You Can Help These Organizations

Previously we described a set of skills that your history degree helped you build. Each employment setting will place a different value on each skill, viewing some skills as more important than others. It's your job to highlight these skills in a meaningful way for each employer. You may have to revamp your resume for different types of jobs or different industries. Remember, you must identify the relevant pieces of your history that show an employer you are capable of and qualified to do the work they need done.

Be Proactive As Well As Reactive

Your job search must have two thrusts: reacting to actual job listings, and networking with potential employers to find out about hidden jobs.

Be Reactive.   Everyone knows to check the newspaper for job advertisements, and you've learned there are a series of targeted job newsletters available at most career offices and many libraries. But did you also know that most professional associations or organizations publish newsletters, available only to members, that contain job listings? A college or university library will house some of these publications, your career office may have others, and some faculty will also subscribe. Be sure to check with people in your network to determine the range of job listings available to you.

Don't Forget to be Proactive.   Use your college or university alumni career network to talk with professionals who are working in the type of job you hope to get or who are working in an industry that interests you. Be sure to contact relevant professional associations for information on job-related services that you might want to take advantage of. Just a few of these associations are listed at the end of this path. Your career counselor may have additional suggestions based on your interests. Conducting a job search can take a lot of time, so carefully choose who you will spend your time networking with.

POSSIBLE EMPLOYERS

You'll be pleasantly surprised at the range of firms which hire history degree holders. Consider the following types of companies:

- Advertising departments and agencies
- Airlines, railroads and cruiselines
- Banks, savings and loans, credit unions
- Environmentally-related firms
- Federal government
- Hospitals and other health care companies
- Hotels, motels and hospitality industry employers
- Magazines, newspapers, radio stations, cable networks, television stations
- Manufacturing firms
- Not-for-profit organizations
- Professional associations
- Public relations departments and firms
- Sports-related organizations

Decide where you'd like to begin your search and use the resources listed to help you locate that particular type of employer.

Advertising Departments and Agencies
Profile.   Every effective advertising campaign relies on the work of market researchers to answer questions such as: Should a product be made? Who will buy it? Where should it be sold? How much should be charged? Entry-level market researchers usually work on questionnaire development, coding, and data entry. They research data found in libraries and assist in project report writing.

Where You Might Fit In. If in obtaining your degree you found enjoyment in doing research, crunching numbers, reporting results, or keeping track of details, market research may be one type of advertising job you'd like to find out more about. Two major suppliers of research include Simmons Market Research Bureau and Mediamark Research Inc. Both of these firms supply secondary data on product usage and consumption. Nielson and Arbitron also provide statistics used by advertising agencies. Market researchers provide the ammunition that other advertising professionals need to promote customers' products or services.

Help in Locating These Employers. If you would like to identify the larger agencies that would typically hire this type of worker, there are several resources you can use: VGM's *Careers in Advertising,* Career Advisor Series' *Advertising Career Directory,* and Gale Research, Inc.'s *Business Rankings Annual.* Any of these books would identify employers you could consider approaching.

Airlines, Railroads, Cruiselines

Profile. Transportation, travel and tourism all hold many possibilities for the person who majored in history. In fact, you may have even specialized in transportation history or the history of a sport such as skiing. You can bring your deep understanding or specialized knowledge to your work in these industries.

Where You Might Fit In. No matter what skills you possess, the tourism, travel and transportation industries need them. If you have effective interpersonal communication skills, you may be interested in a customer service position as a travel agent, purser, or customer service representative. If you prefer to hold a less public job, positions in functional areas such as computer services or research and marketing might interest you.

Help in Locating These Employers. Quite a number of helpful resources can be found in career and public libraries. These include: *Travel and Hospitality Career Directory, How To Get a Job With a Cruise Line, Jobs for People Who Love Travel, Flying High in Travel, Exploring Careers in the Travel Industry,* and *Moody's Transportation Manual.* Check each of these and read chapters or sections that will inform your job search.

Banks, Savings and Loans, Credit Unions

Profile. The financial industry includes commercial banks, thrifts, mutual savings banks, savings and loan associations, and credit unions. Services usually include deposit and loan services, general customer service, business services, municipal services, trust services and international banking services.

Where You Might Fit In.   When you think of banking, do you also think of corporate communications, planning, legal departments, marketing, operations, personnel, public relations, purchasing or training? Large financial institutions include these departments as well. And your liberal arts degree in history will be valued in many of the positions available in any of these departments.

Help in Locating These Employers.   Several types of resources are available if you would like to learn more about this industry. Be sure to check VGM's *Opportunities in Banking Careers,* Peterson's *Job Opportunities in Business, The Banking Job Finder,* or review *Hoover's Handbook of American Business.*

Environmentally-Related Firms

Profile.   There are firms that assess the environmental impact of proposed building projects, firms that sell pollution control equipment, firms that respond to and clean up hazardous waste spills, and firms that are responsible for solid waste disposal. The state of the environment is an issue that no one can ignore, and job opportunities are increasing with growing awareness of this problem.

Where You Might Fit In.   Some of these organizations need your researching and writing skills to help prepare proposals which might bring in new business. If you are comfortable making presentations to groups, you could become part of a sales team which sells environmentally related products or services. You might have an interest in human resources and can work for the organization in helping them acquire the personnel they need to carry out specific and technical duties.

Help in Locating These Employers.   One way to begin identifying potential employers, like an international pollution control monitoring manufacturer, is to find the Standard Industrial Code (SIC) for this type of company. The *U.S. Industrial Outlook* lists these codes or provides a telephone number you can call for more information. There are many different types of pollution control monitoring manufacturers, and some of the SIC codes that are used include: 3564, 3589, 8417, 8418 and 8421. These codes can then be used to identify actual company names in resources such as *America's Corporate Families* or *Moody's Industrial Manuals.* Add to your list of potential employers by checking the Yellow Pages for company listings under Environmental, Conservation or Ecological Services. The *Environmental Industries Marketplace,* published by Gale Research, is designed to help anyone, including job seekers, gain access to the $100 billion environmental market.

Federal Government

Profile.   When you hear the number "three million," does that sound like a lot? If so, you may not have realized that is approximately the number of people who work for the federal government. These workers are employed in over a hundred governmental departments, agencies, commissions, bureaus and boards.

Where You Might Fit In.   There are several federal agencies that are specifically interested in hiring history majors, and they include: the Drug Enforcement Administration, National Endowment for the Humanities, National Park Service, Smithsonian Institution, U.S. Customs Service and the U.S. Information Agency. There are, however, a wide range of agencies that regularly hire college graduates with degrees in any of the liberal arts, including history, for positions in: environmental protection, public health, public affairs, technical information services, bond sales promotion, building management, financial administration, housing management, employee development, and examining workers' compensation claims. This list certainly is not comprehensive; your exploration of federal job opportunities will reveal many more job titles and functions.

Help in Locating These Employers.   Because federal employment is a complicated process, given the number of possible employment sites and job titles, we encourage you to take the time to *really* explore all the possibilities in federal employment. Some excellent resources include the *Occupational Outlook Quarterly's* Summer 1993 edition on Working for the U.S. in the 1990's, *Government Job Finder, The Complete Guide to Public Employment*, VGM's *Opportunities in Federal Government,* and a job newsletter such as *Federal Jobs Digest.*

Hospitals and Other Health Care Companies
Profile.   Many large hospitals are cities unto themselves, and like health care companies employ workers from janitors to doctors, billing clerks to nurses, social science researchers to employee assistance coordinators. There are many places where the graduate of history can find "a good fit."

Where You Might Fit In.   We recently saw an advertisement for a medical staff coordinator that required someone who can work independently compiling and organizing statistical information related to physician activities. The position required computer proficiency and preferred experience in a hospital, but did not require it, and also asked for a bachelor's degree. Any history major with these credentials would be qualified to apply.

Help in Locating These Employers.   *Careers in Health Care, Opportunities in Hospital Administration, Opportunities in Health and Medical Careers, Healthcare Career Directory, Job Opportunities in Health Care,* and *Encyclopedia of Medical Organizations and Agencies* are some of the resource titles available to help you identify hospitals and other health care companies that need your skills.

Hotels, Motels, and Hospitality Industry Employers

Profile.   The lodging industry is well known for moving dedicated and conscientious entry-level workers into higher level managerial positions. It is also known for its excellent training programs which provide the skills necessary to make these promotions. Large resorts and hotels have correspondingly large operations which include housekeeping, food service, convention facilities, fitness centers, laundry, purchasing, human resources and marketing departments.

Where You Might Fit In.   These larger facilities often hire convention and meeting planners. Planners are in charge of putting together a variety of events that help increase facility utilization. Whether it's planning a conference for women who work in higher education, a wedding that includes 500 guests, or a meeting of physicians studying AIDs, all have their special space utilization needs, and attention to detail is critical.

Help in Locating These Employers.   Three books which can provide useful information on working in the hospitality industry and which are worth reviewing are *Opportunities in Hotel and Motel Management, Jobs for People Who Love to Travel,* and *Travel and Hospitality Career Directory.*

Magazines, Newspapers, Radio Stations, Cable Networks, Television Stations

Profile.   If you examine the sheer volume of activity in this sector of the economy, you'll realize there are many employment possibilities for you to consider. There are over 2,500 general circulation magazines and 11,000 newspapers publishing materials; there are over 9,000 radio stations, 1,300 television stations, and 800 cable systems operating in this country. They employ writers, editors, promotion specialists, production managers, public relations specialists, researchers, librarians, and reporters. Many, many entry-level positions are filled by liberal arts majors, including history majors.

Where You Might Fit In.   Commercial and public television stations are required by the Federal Communications Commission (FCC) to provide public service announcements on air, and there are community affairs directors who coordinate these efforts at larger stations. These directors play a role in planning, writing, producing, hosting, narrating, moderating and editing announcements, programs and documentaries. The history major who writes well, has strong organizational and communications skills, and who has an interest in working in television would be an excellent candidate for entry-level positions in this type of division.

Help in Locating These Employers. There certainly is no lack of relevant reference materials when it comes to careers in publishing, radio and TV, and communications. Look at *Careers in Communications, Publishers Directory, Opportunities in Television and Video, Telecommunications Directory, Radio and Television Career Directory, Gale Directory of Publications and Broadcast Media,* and *Opportunities in Telecommunications* for direction in locating potential employers.

Manufacturing Firms

Profile. The most frequently overlooked area of employment for many liberal arts degree majors is the area of manufacturing. Pharmaceuticals, machine-tooled parts, automobiles, plastics and polymers and countless sub-contracted component parts are bought and sold around the world to specification. Whether in South America, the Pacific Rim or Eastern Europe, or at an import-export desk here at home, history majors will find they do not want to ignore manufacturing.

Where You Might Fit In. The reality is that manufacturing mimics in every manifestation every other segment of the economy. It advertises, it transports, it finances, it restructures, it repositions itself, it produces all the associated trappings of any business. What's more, it is populated and managed by skilled, educated people from a multiplicity of backgrounds, including history. Nearly all of the job titles described in other sections of this book can be found in the manufacturing sector: communications specialist, transport scheduler, controller, planner, public relations specialist, media planner, trainer, or benefits administrator, just to name a few.

Help in Locating These Employers. Manufacturing firms are listed in *Moody's Industrial Manual, America's Corporate Families, Directory of Manufacturers* (for states you are interested in), *Ward's Business Directory, Directory of Corporate Affiliations, Business Rankings Annual,* and *Hoover's Handbook of American Business.* Manufacturers may be listed by industry or by standard industrial code; if you are not familiar with these breakdowns, don't hesitate to ask the resource person on duty in your career office or library to help you with locating companies.

Not-For-Profit Organizations

Profile. The not-for-profit sector includes organizations involved in issues ranging from animal rights to homelessness, hunger to peace and disarmament, people with disabilities to women's issues. The history major could find a home in many of these organizations, but each would ask that you have a strong belief in their mission and be able to actively help them achieve their goals.

Where You Might Fit In.   Not-for-profits are creating organizational struc- tures nearly identical to those of the for-profits, so you will find positions available in the same functional areas. Look for positions in human resources, home office management, field staff direction, finance, accounting, commu- nications, publications, public relations, marketing, membership services, information systems, development, and program management.

Help in Locating These Employers.   One source which includes actual job listings is *Community Jobs.* In addition, this publication carries excellent arti- cles about working in this sector of the economy. If you would like to get a sense of the range of opportunities available, be sure to review *Great Careers: The Fourth of July Guide to Careers, Internships, and Volunteer Opportunities in the Nonprofit Sector.* Or try contacting the Society for Non-Profit Organiza- tions, located in Madison, Wisconsin.

Professional Associations
Profile.   A resource we frequently urge readers of this book to utilize in their job search is that of the professional association. They provide information on the professions, training and development, opportunities to meet col- leagues and a never-ending flow of excellent, pertinent literature. However, they are also employers and because of that, we list them in this section as well. While the individual staffs may be small, the number of organizations is huge and together that creates opportunities enough that the history major cannot and should not overlook the serious consideration of the professional association for employment.

With your degree, the association may be academic, commercial, histori- cal, educational, even partisan. Whatever the specific purpose of the group, your vested interest by virtue of your degree will guarantee that your resume gets a careful reading. Consider the professional association carefully.

Where You Might Fit In.   These organizations make available a range of printed materials (booklets, information sheets, magazines, and newspapers) which promote their cause or educate their members. If you have researching, writing, and editing skills, they will be valued. Conference planning and coordination is another area of responsibility in a non-profit organization. Membership services require excellent communications abilities and may be of interest to you.

Help in Locating These Employers.   Two publications that identify these associations are the *Encyclopedia of Associations* and *National Trade and*

Professional Associations of the United States. Both of these have several indexes to help you locate associations by geographic region, name or focus.

Public Relations Departments and Firms

Profile.   Every client, every challenge presented to a public relations department or firm requires drawing deeply on the talents, resources and expertise of the professional staff to make the best presentation of the client or product. Imagine the difficulties of representing the fur industry, cigarette manufacturers or any other controversial product, service or individual. Public relations work requires being constantly aware of and sensitive to how images and words will be interpreted or understood by the public. The history major has studied the impact of past events on current life—a perspective valued in public relations.

Where You Might Fit In.   Many of your talents will come into play as a public relations assistant in the acquisition and presentation of data and information to support company positions or strategies being communicated to outside constituencies. Look for organizations with high public visibility, including national chains in the hotel, restaurant, and hospitality industry, major manufacturers of consumer goods, including products subject to litigation (automobiles and children's toys), and, of course, advertising agencies and public relations firms.

Help in Locating These Employers.   If you're ready to use your skills in a public relations setting, be sure to review Gale's *Public Relations Career Directory,* VGM's *Opportunities in Public Relations Careers, O'Dwyer's Directory of Public Relations Firms,* or see the "Public Relations Specialists" section in the *Professional Careers Sourcebook.*

Sports-Related Organizations

Profile.   Most of you have many interests and avocations other than just your college major. You may have been a history major in college but also have a lifelong interest in sports and skiing in particular. Your degree and skiing awareness combined make you a promising candidate for many different kinds of positions in this arena.

Where You Might Fit In.   You might look for sales positions with manufacturers of ski goggles, gloves or other products which would utilize your organizational and communication skills. Or you may be interested in working on the staff of one of the many associations serving skiers: U.S. Deaf Skiers Association, Professional Snowboarders Association of North America, or National Ski Areas Association researching and analyzing industry data.

Help in Locating These Employers. *Sports Market Place,* an excellent resource for you if you're interested in combining your history degree with your sports-related knowledge or skills, will help you identify thousands of organizations. Included are trade and professional associations, multi-sport publications, TV and radio broadcasters and programmers, corporate sports sponsors, athletic management services, market data services, trade shows, and suppliers and sales agents. Each entry contains contact information such as address and telephone number, and also contains background information. Also review *Developing a Lifelong Contract in the Sports Marketplace* or *Your Career in Parks and Recreation* for additional information on the range of opportunities available to you.

Possible Job Titles

Given the range of employers, we'll provide just a few of the many job titles you will find as you do your job search exploration. Watch for these, and add to the list as you study the want ads, review resources we've listed above, and network with alumni of your institution and other professionals.

Account Representative	Market Analyst
Collaborative Projects Program Officer	Marketing Manager
	Personnel Officer
Communications Assistant	Pharmaceutical Representative
Customer Service Manager	Production Assistant
Financial Assistant	Program Director
Import/Export Coordinator/ Expediter	Program Manager
	Public Relations Officer
Income Generation Specialist	Research Assistant
Loan Officer	Salesperson
Management Consultant	Tour Director
Management Trainee	Training and Development
Manufacturer's Representative	Specialist

Professional Associations

A wide range of types of employers have been described, and a correspondingly wide range of professional associations are shown below. Examine the list to see which groups you might contact to get additional information about career choices, job opportunities, or professional development assistance. Be sure to utilize the *Encyclopedia of Associations* for the names of other organizations to contact.

American Association of Advertising Agencies
666 3rd Avenue 13th Floor
New York, NY 10017
Members/Purpose: To foster, strengthen, and improve the advertising agency business; to advance the cause of advertising as a whole; to aid its member agencies to operate more efficiently and profitably.
Journal/Publication: *Bulletin; 401(K) News; Media Newsletter; New York and Washington Newsletter;* roster.

American Bankers Association
1120 Connecticut Avenue, NW
Washington, DC 20036
Members/Purpose: Commercial banks and trust companies; combined assets of members represent approximately 95 percent of the U.S. banking industry. Seeks to enhance the role of commercial banks as pre-eminent providers of financial services through a variety of efforts.
Training: Offers educational and training programs.
Journal/Publication: *ABA Bankers Weekly; ABA Banking Journal;* many other publications.

American Hospital Association
840 North Lake Shore Drive
Chicago, IL 60611
Members/Purpose: Individuals and health care institutions including hospitals, health care systems, and pre- and post-acute health care delivery organizations.
Training: Conducts educational programs.
Journal/Publication: *AHA News; Guide to the Health Care Field; Hospital Statistics; Hospitals.*
Job Listings: Provides weekly job listing for members.

Computer and Business Equipment Manufacturers Association
1250 Eye Street, NW, Suite 200
Washington, DC 20005
Members/Purpose: Manufacturers of information processing, business, and communications products. Serves as a secretariat for information processing standards groups.
Journal/Publication: Directory; *Issues & Policies; Issue Brief.*

Hotel Sales and Marketing Association International
1300 L Street, NW, Suite 800
Washington, DC 20005

Members/Purpose: Sales executives, managers, owners, and other hotel and motor inn executives; people from allied fields; other individuals and firms.
Training: Conducts seminars, clinics, and workshops.
Journal/Publication: Directory; *Marketing Review; Update.*

Magazine Publishers of America
919 Third Avenue
New York, NY 10022
Members/Purpose: Publishers of 800 consumer and other magazines issued not less than four times a year.
Training: Sponsors seminars.
Journal/Publication: *Magazine Newsletter of Research.*

National Association of Environmental Professionals
5165 MacArthur Blvd., NW
Washington, DC 20016
Members/Purpose: Persons whose occupations are either directly or indirectly related to environmental management and assessment.
Training: Conducts professional certification program.
Journal/Publication: *Environmental Professional;* newsletter.
Job Listings: See bimonthly newsletter for placement service.

National Association of Manufacturers
1331 Pennsylvania Avenue, NW, Suite 1500 N.
Washington, DC 20004
Members/Purpose: Manufacturers. Represents industry's views on national and international problems to government.
Journal/Publication: *Briefing; Bulletin; Directory of Officers, Directors and Committees; NAM's Small Manufacturer: Issues and Information that Affect Your Business.*

National Newspaper Association
1627 K Street, NW, Suite 400
Washington, DC 20006
Members/Purpose: Representatives of weekly, semiweekly, and daily newspapers.
Journal/Publication: *National Directory of Weekly Newspapers; Publishers' Auxiliary.*

National Radio Broadcasters Association
1771 N Street, NW
Washington, DC 20036
Members/Purpose: Representatives of radio and television stations and television networks.
Journal/Publication: *Broadcast Engineering Conference Proceedings; RadioWeek; TV Today.*
Job Listings: Offers employment clearinghouse.

National Sporting Goods Association
1699 Wall Street
Mt. Prospect, IL 60056
Members/Purpose: Retailers, manufacturers, wholesalers, and importers of athletic equipment and sporting goods and supplies.
Journal/Publication: *NSGA Market; NSGA Sports Retailer; Sporting Goods Market; Sports Participation.*

Nonprofit Management Association
315 West 9th Street, Suite 1100
Los Angeles, CA 90015
Members/Purpose: Individuals who directly manage or provide management or technical assistance to nonprofit groups.
Journal/Publication: *NMA Bulletin Board; NMA Members Directory.*

Public Relations Society of America
33 Irving Place
New York, NY 10003
Members/Purpose: Professional society of public relations practitioners.
Training: Offers professional development programs.
Journal/Publication: *PRSA News;* newsletters; *Public Relations Journal; Public Relations Journal Register.*
Job Listings: Job listings contained in *Journal.* Provides job hotline telephone number.

Software Publishers Association
1730 M Street, NW, Suite 700
Washington, DC 20036
Members/Purpose: Microcomputer software companies, software manufacturers, and other firms involved in the software industry.
Journal/Publication: *International Resource Guide and Directory; SPA Membership Directory; SPA News.*

Telecommunications Industry Association
2001 Pennsylvania Avenue, NW, Suite 800
Washington, DC 20006
Members/Purpose: Companies that manufacture products for or provide services to the telecommunications industry.
Training: Sponsors seminars.
Journal/Publication: *Industry Pulse.*

Travel Industry Association of America
2 Lafayette Center
1133 21st Street, NW
Washington, DC 20036

Members/Purpose: Travel industry executives, officials of federal, state, and local governments, chamber of commerce and association executives.

Journal/Publication: Annual report; *International Travel News Directory;* newsletter; *Newsline;* directory of membership and services.

United States Telephone Association

900 19th Street, NW, Suite 800

Washington, DC 20006

Members/Purpose: Local operating telephone companies or telephone holding companies.

Training: Conducts educational and training programs.

Journal/Publication: *Phonefacts; Statistical Volumes; Teletimes.*

CHAPTER FOURTEEN

PATH 5: TEACHING

eaching is certainly an attractive and rewarding profession and perhaps the most familiar career path of those wanting to directly use their history education. It may even be that a particular teacher was the inspiration for the choice of your history major in college. To work with a body of information you love, and share that enjoyment with countless students over the years, is both challenging and enriching. It is educational for the instructor, as well as for the student. Most teachers readily admit they enjoy being students, and good teachers come to the classroom as ready to learn from their students as students arrive hoping to learn from their teachers. Good teachers maintain a regular program of professional development, continuing to learn new classroom techniques, improve their teaching methods, and add to their body of knowledge.

In any academic institution, there is a fellowship and camaraderie amongst teachers. They share anecdotes about techniques that have or have not worked in the classroom and many can also share an interest in the growth and development of particular students they have interacted with through the years. Students often come back and visit their formative teachers and that brings its own rewards.

Talk to any history teacher and they'll tell you a surprising fact about their profession. They don't teach history, they teach students! The art of teaching and the skills required in handling the dynamics of student interaction are as important as knowledge of the course content. A college history classroom is populated with considerable numbers of students majoring in history. A teacher's presentation of course material will weigh heavily in the decision process of those students considering continuing their studies in the major. But these history classrooms also have many non-majors who are taking the course as a general education requirement or for a minor. These students represent different ages, cultural backgrounds, biases, and issues, and they take their seats in the class with dramatically different degrees of interest in the subject and the teacher! With all that in the way, simply having a love of history is not enough, though that is certainly important and desirable. How could you begin to teach something you didn't truly enjoy and expect not to convey that disinterest through a mechanical approach to the subject?

Teaching something is an entirely different art than knowing something, and demands additional skills. It has very little to do with your own proficiency in the subject. The world is full of extremely skillful practitioners who, for one reason or another and quite often inexplicably, cannot teach someone how they do it! The practice of something is very different from professing it in a classroom.

For example, planning for learning outcomes is critical. Teaching history within an established curriculum means corresponding to some departmental goals and course outlines. Unless you've designed the course, there will be a written course description. To accomplish this body of learning within a set time period requires judicious planning of the material. What will be done each day? How much time to allow between assignments, readings, and labs? What materials to require and what to only recommend? Scores of decisions must be made about how material will be introduced, presented, and ultimately delivered back to you for evaluation.

Add to this the fact that students learn in different ways; some are auditory learners who enjoy listening and gain most of their information in this way. If they are required to take notes *and* listen, something may have to give and it may be difficult for them to retain the material. For others, auditory learning is less successful and they prefer a visual approach with board work, videos, handouts, their own notes, diagrams, books, and many visual materials. They retain these images and can call them up to remember the material.

Others learn best through reading in class, role plays, team projects, field trips and other activities that physically involve them. These are kinesthetic learners and they are often forgotten in planning and curriculum design. The professional teacher ensures that his or her class is satisfying the learning styles of *all* their students through judicious combinations of modalities in teaching. The professional teacher has analyzed his or her own teaching style and seeks to incorporate those other elements that come less naturally to them to ensure they reach *all* their students.

The teaching and learning that take place in a class are not static. The classroom is an emotionally charged environment for the student and instructor that may call into play questions of self-esteem and competency. People are exploring new definitions of themselves in relation to their capabilities, values, or achievement. A good teacher understands this and encourages a risk-free environment of mutual appreciation and participation. Both teacher and student are allowed to make mistakes and move on. The teacher strives to assist in establishing congruence between the self (who we know we are right now), the ideal self (who we want to be), and the learning environment being created in the classroom. Hopefully, the classroom will be a place where the student can rise up and begin to touch his or her ideal self.

Any mention of competency, self-esteem, or self-worth naturally suggests the subject of grading and the evaluations teachers provide. Grades are an expected and required part of many institutional academic settings. Establishing fair and consistent standards of evaluating your students and assigning grades is a significant challenge to many teachers who otherwise feel perfectly competent in the teaching role. Students, too, often complain about grading practices in teachers they, in every other respect, feel positively about.

The teacher of history is called upon to play other roles, too. Animating the class and inspiring attention and commitment to the material are all required in teaching. Part of this is the teacher's enthusiasm, part is teaching style, and part is effective use of ancillary materials and the ability to relate this material to a student's life. History teachers attempt to convey something of the sweep and drama of the human experience over time. More than a dry recitation of dates, places and names, the best history deals with the impact of these personalities and events on humankind. The wise history instructor can use history as an opportunity to present a variety of political and cultural diversity and expose their students to varying perspectives. History is the perfect foil by which an instructor can raise relevant questions, prompt dialogues within the class and develop within students the discipline of self-questioning and critical thinking. History teachers also clarify difficulties or obscurities in the material and draw parallels or find relationships between examples.

For a professional teacher, each class is an opportunity not only to teach the subject, history, but to teach how to learn, as well. How to question, how to record information, how to be selective, and how to retain information is an on-going lesson that takes place in every classroom to some degree.

A good teacher, be it of history or any other subject, also uses the class and the material to explain how this material reflects feelings. They will share their own agreement with or support of ideas or emotions in the material under study. Most of all, an instructor will evaluate and by example develop the student's capacity for self-evaluation through careful, caring feedback about both in- and out-of-class work. The instructor's own example of preparation, organization, personal appearance, evaluation standards, student interest and enthusiasm will remain an example long after the memory of the actual class content may have faded.

Teachers are very frequently cited as important factors in our choice of a career. Very often teachers will remember one or two of *their* teachers who were strong influences on their decision to teach. Much of that influence was a result of the teacher's presence in the classroom. They served as models of people enjoying what they were doing and doing it skillfully. They were professional and correct yet remained natural and approachable. We could watch and listen to them and think, "Maybe I could do that."

DEFINITION OF THE CAREER PATH

We'll look at two possible levels of teaching history: secondary school teaching with a bachelor's degree and college teaching, possibly with a master's degree, but more frequently requiring a doctoral degree as the essential credential.

Secondary School Teaching

Following graduation, certified teachers apply for advertised positions in public middle and high schools. Fortunately, and even in spite of stiff competition and an abundance of candidates, public school teaching positions are well advertised and all certified teacher graduates are qualified for entry-level history teaching assignments. Actually, in some situations the first-year-teacher's lack of experience can be a plus. With school budgets under terrific strain, principals, superintendents and other hiring officials may be more attracted to a relatively inexperienced teacher who will earn a lower salary than a more experienced, perhaps higher-degreed teacher who must take a larger proportion of salary funds.

The certification for history teachers is a Social Science certification and your degree will most probably be a Bachelor of Science in Social Science Education. Middle/junior and senior high schools offer a number of courses under the rubric of Social Sciences and the prospective history teacher will be called upon to have a far broader social science education than simply history. History most often predominates in the high-school social science department; however, there can be classes in geography, government, psychology and cultures. Here's a recent advertisement that calls for a combination of history and geography:

> *University/(City) Partnership:* Rare opportunity to work in a district which is being managed by a major university. Opportunity for affiliation w/(university).
> High School: Math, **History/Geography,** . . . Submit letter, resume, certification, transcripts & references to . . .

Of course, the social science education degree draws individuals interested in teaching all of these areas, as well, so in any middle-school or high-school department, teaching preferences are worked out over time and with seniority, and individuals find themselves with teaching loads that meet the curriculum demands and that they, themselves, enjoy teaching.

Is it possible to teach history at the high-school level with state certification in Social Science Education and with a Bachelor of Arts in history? Yes; in fact some public school districts that have had difficulty securing teachers, because of location or pay scales, have made provisions to grant temporary certification to non-credentialed teachers. This is, however, not very common. Some private high schools might consider a non-certified teacher, also, although with the heavy supply of and small demand for secondary history teachers, even private schools can and increasingly do require teaching preparation that equals or is very close to that which public schools require. In fact, at some private schools, it is not uncommon for a majority of the history teachers to have master's degrees, and there also exist numerous large city high schools that have attracted Ph.D.s. Read this current job advertisement for a private school job:

> *History:* U.S. History as well as Geography, World History, The Middle East, or Biography. Teaching experience required, graduate degree preferred. Dorm and two seasons of sports. Send letter, resume, transcripts, letters of reference to . . . (independent college prep boarding school)

A master's degree in history may be helpful in securing a private school teaching position at the high school level, especially if the master's degree concentration (modern world history, Asian history, etc.) corresponds to the school's needs.

Teaching with a Master's Degree

Those graduates with master's degrees and no certification at the bachelor's level may also find employment in junior and community college settings or special college programs for adult learners. These schools may welcome the teacher with a master's degree, especially if the specialty is one that corresponds to their curriculum. The following is an actual advertisement for a college-level history instructor with a master's degree:

> *History:* Instructor, tenure-track. Teach survey courses in Western Civilization and United States history and possibly the department interdisciplinary course (combining history, government and economics) or specialized courses such as the History of the African American. Master's degree in the appropriate discipline. Teaching experience is preferred. Special requirements are noted. Duties of faculty include service on departmental and college committees and other responsibilities as assigned. Salary is commensurate with experience and qualifications. Current initial instructor salary is $30,403. Community College offers a comprehensive benefit package including fully paid health, dental, and life insurance, TIAA/ CREF, and has on-site day care services. For this position, send letter of application and resume by . . .

Similar positions, even those requiring a high level of specialization, can be found in community colleges or small enrollment schools. A rewarding teaching career in history at the college level with a master's degree is possible. Two-year and community college work can provide a long and productive career within the same institution or provide the opportunity for a lateral move to a similar type of school. At the same time, however, it is important to caution you that if you are interested in moving from that type of institution to a four-year college or university, it may be difficult without an advanced degree, despite the fact that you may have years of teaching experience.

There are also some jobs teaching at the four-year college level with a master's degree in history. Nevertheless, the movement, expectation and market demand would be for the doctoral degree and it is that degree that will provide the most security of both employment and employment opportunities for a teaching career at the college and university level in history.

Teaching with a Doctoral Degree

The doctoral degree in history opens up the world of college teaching to the prospective educator. Competition here is keen, but positions are well-advertised in vehicles such as *The Chronicle of Higher Education,* a weekly newspaper reporting on higher education issues and containing the most complete listing of faculty, staff and leadership position openings for colleges and universities in the United States and some foreign countries. The following is an ad from *The Chronicle* that would be of interest to a new Ph.D. in history.

History: Assistant Professor, Department of Humanities and Social Sciences. Tenure-track position. Earned Ph.D. required. Responsible for teaching European 20th century social or urban history or in one region or country. Teaching responsibilities include a non-traditional freshman-level, one-semester world history survey, an upper level course in post-1945 world history as well as topics in European history. Secondary field in any non-European area highly desirable. Candidate should be prepared to teach in a broad interdisciplinary general education curriculum aimed at developing liberal/professional connections between the liberal arts and sciences and the professional majors. Focus is on international and intercultural perspectives in the broad areas of work, science and technology and design.

This ad is interesting for a number of reasons. First, it requires an *earned* doctorate. To apply, you must have your degree in hand. Some advertisements will encourage the application of ABD (All But Dissertation) candidates who have not yet completed their degree work but will soon. An earned doctorate will pay more than an ABD and will lead more directly and quickly to possible tenure and promotion. The ABD candidate will also have to decide how they will finish their degree (the dissertation often being the most time-consuming aspect of their academics) *and* hold down a full-time job.

The above advertisement also indicates that the successful candidate will be teaching both first-year required and general education curriculum classes. Teaching core curriculum history courses is generally part of the teaching load of new college faculty. Many of the students will be taking history classes because it is a college requirement for graduation and not because they are history majors or have chosen the course. The history or social science department performs a service to the entire college in offering this course. Generally, even senior faculty will teach at least one offering of a lower level survey of history, though as you become more senior in the faculty you can take on courses more directly related to your interests and educational background.

Applicants responding to this advertisement should be ready to document their teaching success. This could come from teaching assistantships done while working on the doctoral degree. Many students acquire this experience as graduate teaching assistants, part-time faculty, lecturers or adjunct faculty at other colleges or programs.

The advertisement also calls for social and urban history, post-1945 experience and some non-European area expertise; all could be sustained either through transcript submission showing course work in that area; published articles or papers on some aspect of those issues or recommendations from colleagues on your expertise in those areas.

The road to a doctorate is fairly long and arduous. It is hard work. Along the way, you'll meet some wonderful people, some who'll be friends and colleagues the rest of your life. Even colleagues separated by long distances have the opportunity to revisit at conferences and symposia. You'll have opportunities to write, teach, and perhaps publish—all before you finish your degree. Take advantage of these opportunities when you can. As the advertisement above suggests, some of those kinds of qualifications will be asked of you. However, it is possible to become overly involved in some of these areas to the detriment of degree progress.

How Long Does It Take to Get a Ph. D.?

There has been considerable discussion in academic circles about the number of individuals who begin doctoral programs and do not see them through to completion. In fact, Neil Rudenstine, the President of Harvard College, co-authored a book in 1992[1] describing the issue of improving and tightening

---

1. *In Pursuit of the PhD,* by Willian G. Bowen and Neil L. Rudenstine, Princeton University Press, 1992.

up the time requirements to earn a Ph.D., particularly in the humanities, where his research clearly demonstrated the longest timelines between initiating the degree and earning it, with a correspondingly high rate of mortality (drop-outs) in candidates. The median time-to-degree, as reflected in this study, for those in history Ph.D. programs was 8.3 years.

In the science areas, he found a higher completion rate and less time to degree (median: 6.1 years). This may have something to do with the more defined parameters of the fields of science, an emphasis on correct process, formula and execution. Whereas in the humanities, there seems to be less decision-making on the part of advisors, doctoral committees and other participants as to what the timeline has to be and what needs to be accomplished during that period. There were vague suggestions that a candidate needed to extend their scholarly preparation as a kind of dues-paying for the forthcoming degree. Consequently, the drop-out rate has been disappointingly high.

WORKING CONDITIONS

The working conditions for teachers of history are dramatically different according to the educational setting.

Secondary School Classrooms

The high-school history teacher has a full complement of classes, perhaps as many as five or six a day and may have study hall or lunchroom supervision duties during the week, responsibilities for some after school detention centers, or even a sports activity to supervise. The place of discipline in the secondary curriculum has a major impact in the classroom and is perhaps the single most dominant element of the working conditions for the secondary history teacher. Since the student population is not voluntary, resistance is prevalent and acting out through poor discipline and bad behavior is common.

The effective classroom teacher is one who has successfully mastered classroom management. For many young teachers, these are the most challenging lessons in teaching to accomplish and make for the most interesting stories as they grow in their profession! The balance between teaching history and classroom discipline is seldom in equilibrium and can be particularly frustrating, as when one disruptive student threatens the order of an otherwise studious class.

Most public high schools are fairly rigid systems of enforced behavior norms and the principal agents of that enforcement are the faculty. To elect high-school history education as your particular arena is to challenge your ability to maintain your poise, your focus on your subject matter and your interest in training and shaping young people, while at the same time requiring you to both enforce and administer the necessary disciplinary elements mandated by your school. These sanctions include grades, dismissal, detention, warnings, parent conferences and referrals to other helping agencies in or out of the school system.

It is a full day with fairly rigid starting and ending times and much at-home work. Some of the busiest of those at-home schedules belong to the history faculty. History curriculums in middle school and high school often emphasize content mastery, so evaluative instruments such as quizzes and examinations are frequently employed to provide feedback to both the instructor and students on their grasp of the material. Grading these exams, quizzes and essays and providing that all-important feedback is a take-home assignment night after night. Staying ahead of text and book assignments is also time-consuming, as is maintaining required records of attendance, grades, warnings, progress reports and other documentation that may be required in your school district.

High school history teachers often take on other assignments such as homeroom duty, field trips, guest speakers, chaperoning duties and advising activities for yearbooks, literary journals or clubs in the school. These also can be very time demanding and it is important that the teacher entering into secondary history teaching understand that these assignments are not so much additions but typically part of what makes up a high school teaching professional's commitment.

College Classrooms

A college teaching environment is significantly different than a middle- or high-school setting. There is less need to appease a number of outside publics. There is no school board to satisfy, no parents, no parent-teacher groups. The world of the college classroom is closed to outsiders and isn't violated by anyone outside the class. This is such an accepted convention that it is, in fact, rare to have a class interrupted by anyone outside of the room. Academic freedom protects professors in large part, allowing them to express themselves within their class material with far greater pointedness than in a high-school class.

Grading, evaluation procedures, the number of tests, and even the issue of whether to have textbooks or texts is entirely up to the faculty member, and if the rationale supports these decisions the university will seldom interfere. An added protection is the granting of tenure to established professors who have documented significant teaching histories and excellent student reviews, publications, campus committee work and outreach to the community. The granting of tenure gains teaching staff an additional degree of job security and further supports their expression of academic freedom. All of these conditions make the classroom environment and the relations of faculty and students very different than what has come before in the student's education.

The actual teaching day in a college or university setting involves fewer class hours taught per day and per week. At an institution which focuses on faculty research, the teacher would be responsible for teaching two to three courses that each meet three to four hours per week. Schools that emphasize teaching rather than research require instructors to teach three to four courses for a total of nine to twelve hours of class meetings per week. These class hours and some mandated office hours for advising class students and general advisees are the principal requirements for attendance on the faculty members part. But as the ad below makes clear, there are other expectations:

History: Qualified to teach Family and Community History, Women in the U.S. History, and Latina History or Latin American and Caribbean History and Women's Studies. ABD's will be considered with evidence of progress toward completion of the appropriate Ph.D. or other professional achievement, of commitment to undergraduate liberal education or skilled teaching and of collegiality. Responsibilities include 12–hour teaching load each semester, continued professional activity, including scholarly research and service to the department, college and community. Submit letter of application . . .

In addition to courses and advising, scholarly research is an expectation even at those colleges where tenure is not based on publication. All colleges want their faculty to contribute to the scholarly dialogue in their discipline, and this is reviewed by chairs of departments and academic deans periodically throughout the instructor's career. It may be a determining element in granting tenure or promotion to that faculty member and may influence issues such as salary negotiations, merit increases and the like.

Committee work is also important, as the faculty at most colleges are the governing and rule-making bodies who determine and vote on governance and program changes. Committee work can be issue-oriented, such as a commission on the status of women or a faculty pay equity survey. It may be programmatic, such as a committee to study the core curriculum for undergraduates or to devise a new graphic arts major; it may be related to credentials, as in a committee set up to prepare materials for an accreditation visit.

Some committees, such as those on academic standards, curriculum review, promotion and tenure, planning and administrator review committees, are permanent, though the members may change on a rotating schedule. Other groups are formed for a limited time or until completion of some task. These committees are essential and serve as a vehicle for guiding the direction of the school. Having the support of all the faculty and constantly fresh and interested members helps to ensure all voices are heard and many different opinions considered in making what are often long reaching decisions.

A college day is certainly less rigid than a high-school schedule, though it may be just as busy and as long. The difference in content is that for the high-school teacher, much of their day and commitment is enforced and required. The college teacher may certainly feel institutional and professional pressures on fulfilling certain roles, but the actual election of how to do that is up to the individual. There will be classes, office hours, meetings, and research work to do. Since college campuses are often wonderful centers of art, music and intellectual exchange there are frequently events to attend in the evening. Faculty members may act as advisors to fraternities, sororities, campus newspapers, and clubs, which may also add to their day.

TRAINING AND QUALIFICATIONS

To teach history at the secondary level requires a Bachelor of Science Degree in Social Science Education at the Secondary level and state certification for the state in which you wish to teach. These programs are well-defined options within the education curriculum or the social science department of many teacher training colleges and universities. They include a teaching practicum where you would have the opportunity to leave campus and teach actual history classes under a supervising teacher for an academic semester or quarter. Certification for the state granting the degree is usually part of the degree process and may include the requirement to participate in the National Teacher Examination (NTE). In states requiring the NTE, test preparation is usually now well incorporated into the curriculum.

Another option for the individual with a degree in history who desires to teach but lacks certification would be to enroll in a "conversion" program at a college or university. These programs offer an opportunity to add the necessary state-mandated teaching requirements to their existing degree. Depending on your undergraduate degree and whether a change of institution is involved, this could require twelve to eighteen months of academic enrollment and in some cases, a full two years.

Such conversion programs can also exist independent of a collegiate institution. Some are the product of a consortium of school districts, such as The Upper Valley Teacher Training Institute in Lebanon, New Hampshire. This unique, non-classroom teacher qualifying program takes bachelor-degreed individuals, many of whom have had other careers or significant work experience, and places them with master teachers in actual classrooms for a full year. Half the year is at one grade level and the remaining half of the year with another grade. The year includes much independent work and follows a contract established at the start of the year. There may be a requirement to participate in an associated classroom program to meet state reading certification requirements, as well.

College and university teaching requires the doctorate, or in some cases, all but the dissertation (ABD) completed. Salary and assignments may be affected by lack of an earned doctorate. In addition to the doctorate, we have seen there may be requirements for teaching experience, special depth of research or practice in a particular genre or subject area in history and some additional competencies. There is almost always the requirement of teaching basic survey classes to first and second year students.

EARNINGS

Middle and secondary school teachers of history are paid according to the same salary schedules as other teachers in their school district. Salaries across the nation vary depending on location, which affects cots of living and level of support of education as reflected in the school budget. Salary information for newly graduated teachers in the 1994 edition of *The Job Search Handbook for Educators* listed the following average teacher salaries for elementary, and secondary education by region: Northeast, $21,022; Middle Atlantic, $23,751; Southeast, $20,220; Great Lakes, $21,093; Great Plains/Midwest, $20,068; South Central, $20,401; Rocky Mountain, $19,604; Northwest, $20,196; and West, $24,447. The best source of current information on public school teacher salaries is the State Department of Education office for the state in which you hope to teach. Another source of information is the ERIC Clearinghouse on Teacher Education in Washington, DC.

The average faculty salary in 1992–93 for history positions in four-year colleges or universities for instructors (usually those people who are ABD) was $26,376 at public institutions and $30,546 at private institutions. New assistant professors earned, on average, $31,515 at public, and $31,111 at private institutions. Remember, these are average figures, and some teachers may start at a much lower level of pay.

CAREER OUTLOOK

Projected career outlooks vary greatly depending on the level of education at which you would like to teach. Be sure to review the following information very carefully and be ready to implement a job search strategy that takes the current job market into account.

Secondary School Teaching

The U.S. Department of Labor, Bureau of Labor Statistics, reported on the fastest-growing occupations requiring a bachelor's degree[2], and the market for secondary school teachers, including history and social science teachers, is expected to grow by 37 percent from 1992–2005.

Higher Education

A 1989 study of the academic job market entitled "Prospects for Faculty in the Arts & Sciences" projected a severe faculty shortage beginning in the late 1990s, especially in the humanities and social sciences. That trend has not begun yet and does not appear about to happen because so many colleges and universities have responded to shrinking student enrollments and severe budgetary cutbacks by non-reappointments of faculty and outright hiring freezes.

An article in *The Chronicle of Higher Education* (April 27, 1994) provides a current status report. It reports:

> Instead of a mushrooming demand, doctoral recipients are finding a shortage of tenure-track openings and a glut of candidates. The market has been bad for several years . . . And no one seems to have a grip on when—or if—it will improve.

Another factor to consider: 1994 marked the end of mandatory retirement for college and university faculty members, which may mean fewer openings for new teachers, or a delay in the need for them.

STRATEGY FOR FINDING THE JOBS

Depending on your level of educational attainment, the grade level you hope to teach, and the type of school where you would like to work, your strategy for finding the history teaching job will vary. We have outlined efforts to undertake if you are interested in teaching in a public school, a private school, or in an institution of higher education. Each requires its own strategy, so review the section that pertains to your interests.

2. Employment in Occupations, (1993, Fall). *Occupational Outlook Quarterly*, p. 42.

THE PUBLIC SCHOOLS

Scan Relevant Newspapers

The public school teacher candidate is advised to make a regular practice of scanning all those newspapers advertising in and around the geographic region being considered for teaching assignments. These newspapers need not be purchased, as most public libraries subscribe to a generous selection of local papers.

Check with Your Career Office

College, university and technical school career offices in your region of the state will also be on the mailing list to receive teaching vacancy announcements. Determine which schools' job postings you can view through reciprocity agreements with your own college and make these visits part of your regular job search. You will find that you become so practiced at screening newspapers and job postings that it will take very little time to quickly ascertain if any new openings have been listed.

Directly Contact School Where You'd Like to Work

Send a cover letter and resume to those schools where you would like to work. State departments of education will publish directories of all public schools in the state, indicating Superintendents, Principals and principal administrators. Names, addresses and phone numbers are regularly included in these listings. These same departments of education can provide you with similar information for the state university and technical college systems as well. This information is generally provided free of charge and requires a simple telephone call. Many libraries and college career counseling centers will have this same information on file.

POSSIBLE EMPLOYERS

Public Schools

In a 1993 report published by the U.S. Department of Education it was stated that there were approximately 2,250,000 public school teachers working in the United States in 1990. Competition for available positions was then, and is now, keen. But even when supply far exceeds demand, most teaching positions are well advertised. We often speak of the "hidden job market" in business to refer to the large number of positions that are filled without public notification. But in teaching, in an effort to secure the best pool of applicants as well as to respond to school boards and Boards of Directors, most positions are well-advertised.

Department of Defense (DOD) Schools

Since 1946 there have been schools on U.S. military bases around the world for children of military and civilian personnel assigned overseas. Just under 300 schools serve this segment of U.S. public education, and courses of study, eligibility for teachers, textbooks, and programs parallel those of the public schools in the United States. Schools in the DOD system are all accredited by the North Central Association of Colleges and Schools. Application processes are outlined in detail in the annual DOD booklet, *Overseas Employment Opportunities for Educators.*

THE PRIVATE SCHOOLS

Directly Contact Schools Where You'd Like to Work

Send a cover letter and resume to each private school you would like to work for. Private schools are equally easy to identify through sources such as Peterson's *Guide to Independent Secondary Schools* or *The Handbook of Private Schools* published by Porter Sargent Publishers of Boston. Both these reference books are standard fare for comprehensive reference sections of career centers and larger college libraries. *Independent School* is the journal of the National Association of Independent Schools. It is published three times a year and contains articles on issues of concern to private schools as well as a number of display advertisements.

Attend Job Fairs

Find out about job fairs and attend as many as you can. Job fairs for private schools, here in the U.S. and abroad, are held year-round. Many are administered by recruiting firms. These fairs serve as a major entree for many job seekers into the private school system. You register your materials with a private school placement agency, which then provides access to a private school job fair where you can meet and interact with a number of hiring officials from a regional or national base. Your college career office can put you in touch with some of these private school recruiting firms.

POSSIBLE EMPLOYERS

Private Schools in the U.S.

The U.S. Department of Education reported a total of 2.5 million teachers in the United States in 1990. Of his group, about ten percent, or 250,000, are private school teachers. Accessing the private school market is a very different process than seeking a public school situation. In general, there is not a significant amount of "crossover" between the two systems, public and private, and teachers within the private school system tend to stay within that educational environment.

Private schools list positions and send out job notices but seldom advertise in newspapers to ensure a more select pool of candidates and to maintain a lower profile than their public school counterparts. As tuition-driven institutions, they do not have the core franchise market that public schools have, and must seek students through reputation and discreet advertising.

Private Schools Abroad

Schools abroad can be researched through directories of *Schools Abroad of Interest to Americans,* also published by Porter Sargent Publishers of Boston, *The ISS Directory of Overseas Schools,* published by International Schools Services, as well as publications such as *The International Educator,* the official publication of The Overseas Schools Assistance Corporation.

Resources for Finding Both Public and Private School Openings

Educational Directories, a major publisher of educational resources, produces *Patterson's Elementary Education* and *Patterson's American Education* each year. They list public and private elementary and secondary schools, school districts and superintendents, post-secondary schools and others, including nursery schools, YMCA programs and the like. Use these directories to conduct your proactive job search activities: mailing out cover letters and resumes, networking, and conducting telephone follow-up.

Career offices often carry national job vacancy listings which include teaching positions. Some of these listings include *Current Jobs for Graduates in Education, The Job Hunter, Community Jobs,* and *Current Jobs for Graduates.*

In addition, be sure to carefully review the list of professional associations for teachers of history which follows this section. For several associations there is a line labeled "Job Listings" and any activities that the association undertakes to assist its members in finding employment are shown.

The Job Search Handbook for Educators: ASCUS Annual, an annual publication of the Association for School, College and University Staffing, Inc., presents a collection of articles related to job search issues for educators. The 1994 issue contained numerous display ads for teacher job fairs around the country, a complete listing of all state departments of education (including addresses and phone numbers) and a guide to Teacher Vacancy Listing Subscriptions around the country. This annual is distributed at little or no charge by education departments and Career Centers at colleges and universities with teacher training programs.

COLLEGE AND UNIVERSITY JOBS

Acquiring a college teaching position nearly always demands that you relocate to an institution other than where you received your degree. Higher education has limited openings at any one time, and part-time work or adjunct faculty status at one institution is no guarantee of earning a full-time spot. Most departments have budget "lines" dedicated to potentially full-time, tenured faculty. That means that faculty who are hired in those budget lines are hired with the expectation they will become a permanent part of the faculty and earn tenure and promotion when they qualify.

Consequently, though there may be schools you would enjoy teaching at or areas of the country you would prefer, the supply and demand of college professorships clearly dictate that you must follow the demand and relocate.

Go To "The Source"

The Chronicle of Higher Education is the weekly national publication listing junior college, four-year college and university teaching positions in history. Many of these advertisements are large display ads that detail in full the requirements and duties of the positions advertised. This publication is widely available on college campuses and usually many offices have individual subscriptions. Your career center, department office and college library will all have copies you can review each week.

Network with Faculty Colleagues

Another excellent source of information about college-level positions will be your own faculty colleague contacts made as you pursue your advanced degree. There is a well-established network that becomes very active when schools are seeking to fill a position and would enjoy the personal recommendation of a friend or former teaching associate to do the very best by the hiring institution. For this reason, it's important to ensure that your faculty mentors and colleagues are well aware of your teaching and research interests and geographic preferences so they can respond for you and move the process along if an opportunity presents itself.

Attend Professional Meetings

Interviews are often conducted at professional meetings where recent job openings may be announced or posted in a conspicuous place at the registration table. As a graduate student, many of these conferences are available to you at substantially reduced fees or no fee at all, and you should take advantage of them for the professional content and the opportunity to meet representatives from the departments of other higher education institutions.

Possible Employers

Some resources which can be used to identify schools if you are considering teaching history beyond high school include: *Peterson's Guide to Two Year Colleges*, *Peterson's Guide to Four Year Colleges*, *Peterson's Annual Guides to Graduate Study*, and *The College Board Index of Majors and Graduate Degrees*.

Possible Job Titles

For the professional educator, there is not a wide latitude in job title. The term "teacher" is so old and so esteemed that we use it to apply to professionals from nursery school to the most rarefied levels of post-doctoral research. All are teachers. We see variants from time to time; for example, the Resource Room Teacher in elementary school who works individually with students experiencing difficulties in particular subjects or the Skills Application Teacher on the college faculty who may have a more narrowly defined teaching role than a staff professor. To students, however, these distinctions may not loom very large and most are made to indicate bureaucratic distinctions. The teaching role remains the same.

Teacher	Professor of history
Educator	Associate professor of
Cooperating teacher	history
History teacher	Assistant professor of
Social science teacher	history
Instructor in history and	History instructor
social sciences	History lecturer

Related Occupations

Teaching skills and teacher training lend themselves to innumerable occupations and are seen as universally valuable by all other employers. The ability to explain, demonstrate, encourage, and test and spark the imagination can be transferred to countless settings in business and industry. The introduction of new products, cross training of staff, planning for change or transition, or responding to crises are all situations that call for a teacher's expertise.

Nuclear power information centers, museum programs for children, historical sites, and public relations organizations all have need of the teacher's training in presentation skills, explanation and the ability to convey meaning.

Social service programs devote much of their mission to education in the form of new programs and information for their clients that would use teachers in situations not very different from the standard classroom. The following list is a very brief and very general suggestion of the possible related careers possible for the history teacher.

Counselor	Media relations representative
Education administrator	Not-for-profit organization
Educational consultant	administrator
Employee development	Personnel specialist
specialist	Preschool worker
Employment interviewer	Public relations specialist
Environmental educator	Researcher
Hospital/community health	Sales representative
educator	Social worker
Librarian	Trainer

PROFESSIONAL ASSOCIATIONS FOR TEACHERS OF HISTORY

Finding out about and joining at least one professional association can play an important role in achieving success in your job search. There are many associations which relate to the kinds of jobs available for teachers of history. Listed below are some groups that can provide valuable information in terms of finding out about actual job listings or talking with members for networking purposes.

American Association for Adult and Continuing Education

1101 Connecticut Avenue, NW, Suite 700
Washington, DC 20036
Members/Purpose: Provides leadership in advancing education as a lifelong learning process. Serves as a central forum for a wide variety of adult and continuing education special interest groups.
Journal/Publication: *Adult Education; Adult Learning Practitioner Journal;* newsletter; membership directory.

American Association of Christian Schools

P.O. Box 2189
Independence, MO 64055
Members/Purpose: Maintains teacher/administrator certification program. Participates in school accreditation program.
Journal/Publication: Newsletter; directory; *The Builder.*
Job Listings: Teacher placement newsletter four times per year.

American Association of Community and Junior Colleges
One Dupont Circle, NW, Suite 410
Washington, DC 20036-1176
Members/Purpose: Community, technical, and junior colleges; individual associates interested in community college development; corporate, educational, foundation, and international associate members.
Training: Conducts seminars and professional training programs.
Journal/Publication: *AACJC Community, Technical and Junior College Times; Who's Who in Community, Technical, and Junior Colleges;* journal; letter; membership directory; *Statistical Yearbook of Community, Technical, and Junior Colleges.*

American Association for Higher Education
One Dupont Circle, NW, Suite 360
Washington, DC 20036
Members/Purpose: Administrators, students, trustees, faculty, public officials, and interested individuals from all segments of postsecondary education. Seeks to clarify and help resolve critical issues in postsecondary education through conferences, publications, and special projects.
Journal/Publication: Bulletin; *Change Magazine.*

American Association of State Colleges and Universities
One Dupont Circle, NW, Suite 700
Washington, DC 20036
Members/Purpose: Colleges and universities offering programs leading to a degree of bachelor, master, or doctor, that are wholly or partially state supported and controlled.
Training: Conducts national and regional workshops.
Journal/Publication: Membership list; *Memo: To The President;* proceedings; studies.

American Association of University Professors
1012 Fourteenth Street, NW, Suite 500
Washington, DC 20005
Members/Purpose: College and university teachers, research scholars, and academic librarians. Purposes are to facilitate cooperation among teachers and research scholars in universities, colleges, and professional schools, for the promotion of higher education and research, and to increase the usefulness and advance the standards, ideals, and welfare of the profession.
Journal/Publication: *Academe: Bulletin of the AAUP; Collective Bargaining Newsletter.*

American Council on Education
One Dupont Circle, NW, Suite 800
Washington, DC 20036
Members/Purpose: A council of colleges and universities, educational organizations, and affiliates.

Journal/Publication: *Educational Record; Higher Education and National Affairs; ACE/Macmillan Series on Higher Education.*
Job Listings: Job hotline.

American Federation of Teachers
555 New Jersey Avenue, NW
Washington, DC 20001
Members/Purpose: AFL-CIO. Works with teachers and other educational employees at the state and local level in organizing, collective bargaining, research, educational issues, and public relations. Conducts research in various areas.
Journal/Publication: *American Educator; American Teacher; Healthwire; On Campus; Public Service Reporter.*

American Historical Association
400 A Street, SE
Washington, DC 20003
Members/Purpose: Professional historians, educators, and others interested in promoting historical studies and collecting and preserving historical manuscripts.
Journal/Publication: *Newsletter/Employment Information; American Historical Review; Guide to Departments of History.*
Job Listings: See *Newsletter/Employment Information.*

American Society for Training and Development
1640 King Street, Box 1443
Alexandria, VA 22313
Members/Purpose: Professional association for persons engaged in the training and development of business, industry, education, and government. Undertakes special research projects and acts as clearinghouse.
Training: Maintains database of information on more than 100,000 public seminars, workshops, and conferences, and on courseware from more than 100 suppliers.
Journal/Publication: *Buyer's Guide and Consultant Directory; Info-Line; National Report on Human Resources; Training and Development Journal; Training and Development Literature Index; Who's Who in Training and Development.*
Job Listings: Check with local chapters.

Council for American Private Education
1726 M Street, NW, Suite 1102
Washington, DC 20036
Members/Purpose: Coalition of national organizations serving the interests of private schools (K–12).
Journal/Publication: *Outlook; Private Schools of the United States.*
Job Listings: List of teacher placement services.

National Association of Independent Schools

1620 L Street, NW, 11th Floor

Washington, DC 20036

Members/Purpose: Independent elementary and secondary school members; regional associations of independent schools and related associations. Provides curricular and administrative research and services.

Training: Conducts seminars.

Journal/Publication: *Independent School.*

Job Listings: They have a general teacher's packet that consists of recruitment agencies, placement firms, directories, and brochures that help with choosing the right school.

National Catholic Education Association

1077 Thirtieth Street, NW, Suite 100

Washington, DC 20007

Members/Purpose: Catholic schools and religious education centers from kindergarten through graduate school levels; individuals. Conducts research; works with voluntary groups and government agencies on educational problems.

Training: Conducts workshops and seminars.

Journal/Publication: *Current Issues in Catholic Higher Education; Forum; Momentum; Notes; Update; Parish Coordinator/Directors of Religious Education; Private Law School Digest; Seminary News.*

Job Listings: A job opportunity database: call association for application.

National Educational Association

1201 Sixteenth Street, NW

Washington, DC 20036

Members/Purpose: Professional organization and union of elementary and secondary school teachers, college and university professors, administrators, principals, counselors, and others concerned with education.

Journal/Publication: *ESP Journal; ESP Progress;* handbook; *NEA Today.*

National History Day

0121 Caroline Hall

University of Maryland

College Park, MD 20742

Members/Purpose: Encourages students in secondary schools to participate in history competitions judged by professional historians at district, state, and national levels.

Training: Conducts 3 week summer institute for secondary school teachers, which can be used to fill continuing education credit requirements.

Journal/Publication: Annual report; contest guide; *National History Day News.*

National University Continuing Education Association
One Dupont Circle, NW, Suite 615
Washington, DC 20036
Members/Purpose: Institutions of higher learning, both public and private, with active extension and continuing education programs; professional staff at member institutions.
Journal/Publication: *Continuing Higher Education Review; Guide to Independent Study Through Correspondence Instruction; NUCEA Newsletter; Guide to Certificate Programs.*

Organization of American Historians
112 N. Bryan Street
Bloomington, IN 47408
Members/Purpose: Professional historians, including college faculty members, secondary school teachers, graduate students, and other individuals in related fields; institutional subscribers are college, university, high school and public libraries, and historical agencies.
Journal/Publication: *Journal of American History;* newsletter; *OAH Magazine of History.*

Society for History Education
California State University-Long Beach
Long Beach, CA 90840
Members/Purpose: High school and college history teachers and libraries. Serves the needs of the historian who is fulfilling his or her role as a teacher at the university, college, community college, and secondary levels of education.
Journal/Publication: *The History Teacher; Network News Exchange.*

ADDITIONAL RESOURCES

ABI/Inform On Disc
UMI–Data Courier, Inc.
620 South Fifth Street
Louisville, KY 40202

Advertising Career Directory
Visible Ink Press
Gale Research, Inc.
P.O. Box 33477
Detroit, MI 48232

America's Corporate Families
Dun & Bradstreet Information Services
899 Eaton Avenue
Bethlehem, PA 18025

The American Archivist
Society of American Archivists
600 South Federal Street, Suite 504
Chicago, IL 60605

American Art Directory
American Library Directory
Reed Reference Publishing
121 Chanlon Road
New Providence, NJ 07974

Art Career Guide
Watson-Guptill Publications

Billboard Publications, Inc.
1515 Broadway
New York, NY 10036

ARTSearch
Theatre Communications Group, Inc.
355 Lexington Avenue
New York, NY 10017

AVISO: A Monthly Dispatch from the American Association of Museums
1225 Eye Street, NW, Suite 200
Washington, DC 20005

The Banking Job Finder
Mainstream Access, Inc.
Prentice-Hall, Inc.
Englewood Cliffs, NJ 07632

The Best Towns in America
Houghton Mifflin Co.
222 Berkeley Street
Boston, MA 02116

Beyond Peace
Richard M. Nixon
Random House
201 East 50th Street
New York, NY 10022

The Boston Globe
The Globe Newspaper Co.
135 Morrissey Boulevard
P.O. Box 2378
Boston, MA 02107

Business Rankings Annual
Gale Research, Inc.
P.O. Box 33477
Detroit, MI 48232

CAM Report: Career Movement and Management Facts
Priam Publications, Inc.
P.O. Box 1862
East Lansing, MI 48826

The Career Guide: Dun's Employment Opportunities Directory
Dun & Bradstreet Information Services

899 Eaton Avenue
Bethlehem, PA 18025

Career Information Center
Macmillan Publishing Group
866 Third Avenue
New York, NY 10022

Career Opportunities for Writers
by Rosemary Guiley
Facts on File
460 Park Avenue, South
New York, NY 10016

Careers Encyclopedia
VGM Career Horizons
NTC Publishing Group
4255 West Touhy Avenue
Lincolnwood, IL 60646

Careers in the Nonprofit Sector: Doing Well by Doing Good
by Terry McAdam
The Taft Group
5130 MacArthur Blvd., NW
Washington, DC 20016

Careers in State And Local Government
Garrett Park Press
Garrett Park, MD 20896

The Chronicle of Higher Education
1255 Twenty-Third Street, NW
Washington, DC 20037

College Placement Council Annuals
62 Highland Avenue
Bethlehem, PA 18017

College to Career: The Guide to Job Opportunities
by Joyce Mitchell
The College Board
P.O. Box 866
New York, NY 10101

Community Jobs:
The National Employment Newspaper for the Non-Profit Sector
ACCESS: Networking in the Public Interest

50 Beacon Street
Boston, MA 02108

Companies That Care
by Hal Morgan and Kerry Tucker
Simon & Schuster/Fireside
Simon & Schuster Building
Rockefeller Center
1230 Avenue of the Americas
New York, NY 10020

The Complete Guide to Public Employment
by Ronald Krannich and Caryl Krannich
Impact Publications
4580 Sunshine Court
Woodbridge, VA 22192

Consultants and Consulting Organizations Directory
Gale Research, Inc.
P.O. Box 33477
Detroit, MI 48232

Consultants Directory
Dun & Bradstreet Information Services
899 Eaton Avenue
Bethlehem, PA 18025

Criminal Justice Careers Guidebook
U.S. Government Printing Office
USGPO Sop SSMB
Washington, DC 20401

Current Jobs in Art
Current Jobs for Graduates
Current Jobs for Graduates in Education
Current Jobs in Writing, Editing & Communications
Plymouth Publishing, Inc.
P.O. Box 40550
5136 MacArthur Blvd., NW
Washington, DC 20016

Developing a Lifelong Contract in the Sports Marketplace
by Greg Cylkowski
Athletic Achievements
3036 Ontario Road
Little Canada, MN 55117

Dialing for Jobs: Using the Phone in the Job Search (video)
JIST Works, Inc.
720 North Park Avenue
Indianapolis, IN 46202

Dictionary of Occupational Titles
U.S. Department of Labor
Employment and Training Administration
Distributed by Associated Book Publishers, Inc.
P.O. Box 5657
Scottsdale, AZ 86261

Directory of American Research and Technology
Reed Reference Publishing
121 Chanlon Road
New Providence, NJ 07974

Directory of Corporate Affiliations
National Register Publishing
121 Chanlon Road
New Providence, NJ 07974

Directory of Federal Historical Programs and Activities
American Historical Association
400 A Street, SE
Washington, DC 20003

Directory of Manufacturers
Dun & Bradstreet Information Services
899 Eaton Avenue
Bethlehem, PA 18025

Directory of National Environmental Organizations
U.S. Environmental Directories
P.O. Box 65156
St. Paul, MN 55165

Directory of Special Libraries and Information Centers
Gale Research, Inc.
P.O. Box 33477
Detroit, MI 48232

DISCOVER
American College Testing
Educational Services Division
P.O. Box 168
Iowa City, IA 52244

Earth Work
Student Conservation Association
P.O. Box 550
Charlestown, NH 03603-0550

Effective Answers to Interview Questions (video)
JIST Works, Inc.
720 North Park Avenue
Indianapolis, IN 46202

Employer's Expectations (video)
JIST Works, Inc.
720 North Park Avenue
Indianapolis, IN 46202

Encyclopedia of Associations
Encyclopedia of Medical Organizations and Agencies
Gale Research, Inc.
P.O. Box 33477
Detroit, MI 48232

Environmental Industries Marketplace
Gale Research, Inc.
P.O. Box 33477
Detroit, MI 48232

Environmental Opportunities
Environmental Studies Department
Antioch/New England Graduate School
Keene, NH 03431

Equal Employment Opportunity Bimonthly
CRS Recruitment Publications/CASS Communications, Inc.
60 Revere Drive
Northbrook, IL 60062

Exploring Careers in the Travel Industry
Rosen Publishing Group
29 E. 21st Street
New York, NY 10010

Federal Career Opportunities
Gordon Press Publishers
P.O. Box 459
Bowling Green Station
New York, NY 10004

Federal Jobs Digest
Breakthrough Publications
P.O. Box 594
Millwood, NY 10546

Flying High in Travel
John Wiley & Sons
605 Third Ave.
New York, NY 10158

Foundation Grants to Individuals
The Foundation Center
79 Fifth Avenue
New York, NY 10003

Gale Directory of Publications and Broadcast Media
P.O. Box 33477
Detroit, MI 48232

Government Job Finder
by Daniel Lauber
Planning/Communications
7215 Oak Avenue
River Forest, IL 60305

Graduate Management Admissions Test
Graduate Management Admission Council
P.O. Box 6108
Princeton, NJ 08541

Graduate Record Exam
Graduate Record Examinations Board
Educational Testing Service
P.O. Box 6000
Princeton, NJ 08541

Great Careers: The Fourth of July Guide to Careers, Internships, and Volunteer Opportunities in the Nonprofit Sector
Garrett Park Press
P.O. Box 190B
Garrett Park, MD 20896

Guide to Accredited Camps
American Camping Association
5000 State Road 67 North
Martinsville, IN 46151-7902

Guide to the National Wildlife Refuges
by Laura and William Riley
Macmillan/Collier Books
866 3rd Avenue
New York, NY 10022

Handbook for Business and Management Careers
VGM Career Horizons
NTC Publishing Group
4255 West Touhy Avenue
Lincolnwood, IL 60646

The Handbook of Private Schools
Porter Sargent Publishers, Inc.
11 Beacon Street, Suite 1400
Boston, MA 02108

Harrington-O'Shea Career Decision Making System
American Guidance Service
4201 Woodland Road
P.O. Box 99
Circle Pines, MN 55014

Healthcare Career Directory
Visible Ink Press
Gale Research, Inc.
P.O. Box 33477
Detroit, MI 48232

Hoover's Handbook of American Business
The Reference Press
6448 Highway 290 E, Suite E-104
Austin, TX 78723

How to Get a Job With a Cruiseline
Ticket to Adventure, Inc.
P.O. Box 41005
Saint Petersburg, FL 33743

How to Write a Winning Personal Statement for Graduate and Professional School
by Richard Stelzer
Peterson's
P.O. Box 2123
Princeton, NJ 08543

Independent School
National Association of Independent Schools
1620 L Street, NW
Washington, DC 20036

Index of Majors and Graduate Degrees
College Board Publications
P.O. Box 886
New York, NY 10101

Infotrac CD-ROM Business Index
Information Access Co.
362 Lakeside Drive
Foster City, CA 94404

InternAmerica
The Internship Newsletter and News Service
105 Chestnut Street, Suite 34
Needham, MA 02192

The International Educator
Overseas Schools Assistance Corp.
P.O. Box 513
Cummaquid, MA 02637

ISS Directory of Overseas Schools
International Schools Services
P.O. Box 5910
Princeton, NJ 08543

Job Bank Series:
   Atlanta Job Bank
   Boston Job Bank
   Chicago Job Bank
   Dallas–Ft. Worth Job Bank
   Denver Job Bank
   Detroit Job Bank
   Florida Job Bank
   Houston Job Bank
   Los Angeles Job Bank
   Minneapolis Job Bank
   New York Job Bank
   Northwest Job Bank
   Ohio Job Bank
   Philadelphia Job Bank
   St. Louis Job Bank

San Francisco Job Bank
Seattle Job Bank
Washington, DC Job Bank
Bob Adams, Inc.
260 Center Street
Holbrook, MA 02343

Job Hotlines USA
Career Communications, Inc.
P.O. Box 169
Harleyville, PA 19438

The Job Hunter
The National Bi-Weekly Publication for Job Seekers
Career Planning and Placement Center
University of Missouri-Columbia
100 Noyes Building
Columbia, MO 65211

Job Opportunities in Business
Job Opportunities in Health Care
Peterson's
P.O. Box 2123
Princeton, NJ 08543

The Job Search Handbook for Educators: ASCUS Annual
Association for School, College & University Staffing
1600 Dodge Avenue, S-330
Evanston, IL 60201

Job Seekers Guide to Private and Public Companies
Gale Research, Inc.
P.O. Box 33477
Detroit, MI 48232

Jobs for People Who Love Travel
Impact Publications
9104 N. Manassas Drive
Manassas Park, VA 22111

Libraries, Information Centers and Databases in Science and Technology
Reed Reference Publishing
121 Chanlon Road
New Providence, NJ 07974

Million Dollar Directory: America's Leading Public and Private Companies
Dun & Bradstreet Information Services

899 Eaton Avenue
Bethlehem, PA 18025

Moody's manuals
Moody's Investors Service
99 Church Street
New York, NY 10007

Myers-Briggs Type Indicator
Consulting Psychologists Press, Inc.
3803 E. Bayshore Road
Palo Alto, CA 94303

National Center for Education Statistics
"America's Teachers: Profile of a Profession"
U.S. Department of Education
Office of Educational Research and Improvement
Washington, DC 20208

The National Directory of Internships
National Society for Internships and Experiential Education
3509 Haworth Drive, Suite 207
Raleigh, NC 27609

National Directory of Non-Profit Organizations
Gale Research, Inc.
P.O. Box 33477
Detroit, MI 48232

National Human Services Employment Biweekly
13137 Penndale Lane
Fairfax, VA 22033

National JobBank
Bob Adams, Inc.
260 Center Street
Holbrook, MA 02343

National Teacher Exam
Educational Testing Service
P.O. Box 6051
Princeton, NJ 08541

National Trade and Professional Associations of the United States
Columbia Books Inc.
1212 New York Avenue, NW, Suite 330
Washington, DC 20005

Non-Profit Job Finder
Planning/Communications
7215 Oak Avenue
River Forest, IL 60305

North American Horticulture: A Reference Guide
Macmillan Publishing Inc.
866 Third Avenue
New York, NY 10022

Occupational Outlook Handbook
Occupational Outlook Quarterly
U.S. Department of Labor
Bureau of Labor Statistics
Washington, DC 20212

Occupational Thesaurus
Lehigh University
Bethlehem, PA 18015

O'Dwyer's Directory of Public Relations Firms
J.R. O'Dwyer Co. Inc.
271 Madison Avenue
New York, NY 10016

The Official Museum Directory
American Association of Museums
R.R. Bowker
245 West 17th Street
New York, NY 10011

The 100 Best Companies to Sell For
by Michael Harkavy and The Philip Lief Group
John Wiley & Sons
605 Third Avenue
New York, NY 10158

The 100 Best Companies to Work for in America
by Robert Levering and Milton Moskowitz
A Currency Book published by Doubleday
Bantam Doubleday Dell Publishing Group, Inc.
666 Fifth Avenue
New York, NY 10103

Opportunities in Banking
Opportunities in Book Publishing

Opportunities in Federal Government
Opportunities in Health and Medical
Opportunities in Hospital Administration
Opportunities in Hotel and Motel
Opportunities in Human Resources Management
Opportunities in Insurance
Opportunities in Journalism
Opportunities in Magazine Publishing Careers
Opportunities in Marketing
Opportunities in Nonprofit Organizations
Opportunities in Personnel Management
Opportunities in Sports and Athletics
Opportunities in State and Local Government
Opportunities in Telecommunications
Opportunities in Television and Video
VGM Career Horizons
NTC Publishing Group
4255 West Touhy Avenue
Lincolnwood, IL 60646

Overseas Employment Opportunities for Educators
Department of Defense
Office of Dependents Schools
2461 Eisenhower Avenue
Alexandria, VA 22331

Patterson's American Education
Patterson's Elementary Education
Educational Directories Inc.
P.O. Box 199
Mount Prospect, IL 60056

Peterson's Grants for Graduate Students
Peterson's Guide to Four Year Colleges
Peterson's Guide to Independent Secondary Schools
Peterson's Guide to Two Year Colleges
Peterson's Guides to Graduate Study
Peterson's Internships
Peterson's
P.O. Box 2123
Princeton, NJ 08543

Places Rated Almanac
Prentice Hall General Reference & Travel

15 Columbus Circle
New York, NY 10023

Professional Career Series:
  Advertising
  Business
  Communications
  Computers
  Health Care
  High Tech
VGM Career Horizons
NTC Publishing Group
4255 West Touhy Avenue
Lincolnwood, IL 60646

Professional Careers Sourcebook
Gale Research, Inc.
P.O. Box 33477
Detroit, MI 48232

Professional's Job Finder
Planning/Communications
7215 Oak Avenue
River Forest, IL 60305

Profitable Careers in Nonprofit
John Wiley & Sons
605 Third Avenue
New York, NY 10158

Public Relations Career Directory
Gale Research, Inc.
P.O. Box 33477
Detroit, MI 48232

Publishers Directory
Gale Research, Inc.
P.O. Box 33477
Detroit, MI 48232

Radio and Television Career Directory
Gale Research, Inc.
P.O. Box 33477
Detroit, MI 48232

Research Centers Career Directory
Gale Research, Inc.
P.O. Box 33477
Detroit, MI 48232

Schools Abroad of Interest to Americans
Porter Sargent Publishers
11 Beacon Street, Suite 1400
Boston, MA 02108

A Short History of the Future
by Warren Wagar
University of Chicago Press
5801 Ellis Avenue
Chicago, IL 60637

SIGI PLUS
P.O. Box 6403
Rosedale Road
Princeton, NJ 08541

The Skills Search (video)
JIST Works, Inc.
720 North Park Avenue
Indianapolis, IN 46202

Social and Behavioral Sciences Jobs Handbook
Prospect Press
P.O. Box 3069, Diamond Farms Branch
Gaithersburg, MD 20878
(Out of print, but can be found in many career libraries.)

Sports Market Place
Sportsguide
P.O. Box 1417
Princeton, NJ 08542

Standard and Poor's Register of Corporations
Standard and Poor's Corp.
25 Broadway
New York, NY 10004

Strong Interest Inventory
Consulting Psychologists Press, Inc.
3803 E. Bayshore Road
Palo Alto, CA 94303

Summer Opportunities in Marine and Environmental Science
by Joy Herriott and Betty Herrin
White Pond Press
38 Litchfield Road
Londonderry, NH 03053

Telecommunications Directory
by John Krol
Gale Research, Inc.
P.O. Box 33477
Detroit, MI 48232

The Tough New Labor Market of the 1990s (video)
JIST Works, Inc.
720 North Park Avenue
Indianapolis, IN 46202

Travel and Hospitality Career Directory
Gale Research, Inc.
P.O. Box 33477
Detroit, MI 48232

Upper Valley Teacher Training Institute
106 Hanover Street, Suite 202
Lebanon, NH 03766

U.S. Industrial Outlook
Superintendent of Documents
P.O. Box 371954
Pittsburgh, PA 15250

Ward's Business Directory of Corporate Affiliations
Gale Research, Inc.
P.O. Box 33477
Detroit, MI 48232

What Can I Do with a Major in . . . ?
by Lawrence Malnig with Anita Malnig
Abbott Press
P.O. Box 433
Ridgefield, NJ 07657

Where the Jobs Are: A Comprehensive Directory of 1200 Journals Listing Career Opportunities
by S. Norman Feingold and Glenda Hansard-Winkler
Garrett Park Press

P.O. Box 190
Garrett Park, MD 20896

World Chamber of Commerce Directory
P.O. Box 1029
Loveland, CO 80539

Y National Vacancy List
YMCA of the USA
101 North Wacker Drive
Chicago, IL 60606

Zoological Parks and Aquariums in the Americas
American Association of Zoological Parks and Aquariums
Oglebay Park
Route 88
Wheeling, WV 26003

INDEX

Rodriguez